ClarisWorks 5.0
The Internet, New Media, and Paperless Documents

ClarisWorks 5.0
The Internet, New Media, and Paperless Documents

Jesse Feiler

AP PROFESSIONAL
AP PROFESSIONAL is a division of Academic Press

Boston   San Diego   New York
London   Sydney   Tokyo   Toronto

 **AP PROFESSIONAL**
An imprint of ACADEMIC PRESS
A division of HARCOURT BRACE & COMPANY

Find us on the Web! http://www.apnet.com

This book is printed on acid-free paper. ∞

Copyright © 1998 by Academic Press.

All rights reserved.
No part of this publication may be reproduced or
transmitted in any form or by any means, electronic
or mechanical, including photocopy, recording, or
any information storage and retrieval system, without
permission in writing from the publisher.

Claris and ClarisWorks are trademarks of Claris Corporation, registered in the U.S. and other countries. Mac, the Mac OS logo, and QuickTime are trademarks of Apple Computer, Inc., registered in the U.S. and other countries. Microsoft, Windows NT, Windows, and the Windows logo are registered trademarks of Microsoft Corporation.

All other brand names and product names mentioned in this book
are trademarks or registered trademarks of their respective companies.

Academic Press
525 B Street, Suite 1900, San Diego, CA 92101-4495
1300 Boylston Street, Chestnut Hill, MA 02167

United Kingdom Edition published by
ACADEMIC PRESS LIMITED
24-28 Oval Road, London NW1 7DX

Library of Congress Cataloging-in-Publication Data

Feiler, Jesse.
    ClarisWorks : the Internet, new media, and paperless documents / Jesse Feiler.
        p.   cm.
    Includes index.
    ISBN 0-12-251332-0 (alk. paper)
    1. Integrated software.   2. ClarisWorks.   I. Title.
QA76.76.I57F44 1997
005.369--dc21   97-41331
                                                                                          CIP

Printed in the United States of America
97 98 99 00 01 CP 9 8 7 6 5 4 3 2 1

Contents

Foreword	xv
Preface	xvii
Acknowledgments	xviii
"New Media"	xix
Introduction	xxi
About This Book	xxii
The Structure of the Book	xxiii
Some Interesting URLs	xxiii
What Next?	xxiv

Part I. New Concepts and Technologies — 1

Chapter 1. Your Turn — 3
    Focusing on People and Their Activities — 5
    Putting Things Together — 7
    Summary — 9

Chapter 2. Beyond Paper—More Power for Your Documents — 11
    Writing and Paper — 12
    A Brief History of Paper and Printing — 13
    Using Personal Computers for Writing and Printing — 14
        The Speed of Technological Change — 15
        The Declining Cost of Personal Computers — 17
        Managing the Increasing Complexity of Computer Software — 19
        Keeping up with Technology — 20
    The Limits of Paper — 21
    Opportunities of Interactive Media — 21
        Documents Can Be Any Size and Shape — 22
        Documents Can Move around the World at the Speed of Light (Almost) — 23
        Documents Can Easily Be Stored — 23
        Documents Can Move — 24
    Summary — 25

Chapter 3. ClarisWorks 5.0—More Power for You — 27
    ClarisWorks Assistants — 28
    Drag-and-Drop — 31
    Mouse Tracking — 32
    Modifying the Button Bar — 33
        Creating Your Own Buttons — 34
        Creating and Editing a Button Bar — 36
    Libraries — 37
        Getting Objects out of Libraries — 38
        Creating Libraries and Putting Objects into Them — 39
    Style Sheets — 41
        Creating or Modifying a Style — 41

What It Means to You	44
Equation Editing	45
Summary	45

Chapter 4. Beyond the Desktop: The Internet and Shared Information — 47

The Internet	48
Design and History of the Internet	48
Internet Layers	49
E-mail	52
World Wide Web	55
Internet, Intranets, LANs, and Shared Information	60
WANs	62
Intranets	63
Shared Information	64
Summary	66

Part II. Using ClarisWorks and the New Technologies 67

Chapter 5. Back to Paper — 69

Desktop Printers	70
Kinds of Printers	70
Features of Printers	72
Print Spooling	73
Paper	75
Preprinted Forms, Labels, and Papers	75
Handling Paper	76
Other Output Media	79
Slides	79
Overheads	81
Large-Format Printing	81
T-Shirts and Other Haberdashery	81
Summary	82

Chapter 6. Using QuickTime Movies in ClarisWorks Documents   83
   Why Use Video in Your Documents?   84
      Benefits of Video   85
      Disadvantages of Video   86
   Creating QuickTime Movies   87
      What You Need   87
      Digitizing the Video   92
      Review   99
   A Look at QuickTime   99
      Time-Dependent Media   100
      Hardware Abstraction   101
      The QuickTime Media Layer   101
   Summary   102

Chapter 7. Making Documents Interactive—Using the Links Palette   103
   ClarisWorks Links   104
   Creating and Managing Links   106
      Kinds of Links   107
      Creating Links   111
      Managing Links   116
   Designing Links   117
      Designing Links   118
      Link Considerations   119
   Summary   120

Chapter 8. Making Documents Communicate—Integrating the Internet   121
   Internet Background   122
      Why It Happened Now   122
      What This Means for the Future   124
      TCP/IP and You   125
   Internet and You   127
      Online Services   127
      ISPs   129
      Domain Names   132
   Internet and Your Computer   134
      Tips for Making Internet Connections Easier   135
   Getting to the Internet from ClarisWorks   137
   Summary   138

Chapter 9. Creating Web Pages in ClarisWorks — 139
- A ClarisWorks Web Page Example — 140
- The Basics of Web Authoring with ClarisWorks — 141
    - Two Documents with Automatic Translation — 141
    - Maintaining a Web Site with ClarisWorks — 145
- What Can You Do? — 145
    - Basic Text — 145
    - Headers — 146
    - Links — 146
    - Lists — 147
    - Graphics — 147
    - Tables — 148
    - Backgrounds — 148
    - Advanced HTML — 150
- Summary — 152

Chapter 10. Multiple Solutions to Problems with ClarisWorks — 153
- Finding the Right Document Type — 154
- The Case Study — 155
- Word Processing — 156
    - Automatic Hyphenation — 157
    - Automatic Headers and Footers — 158
    - Margin Control — 160
    - Outlining — 160
    - Pros and Cons — 160
- Spreadsheets — 162
    - Text Cells — 163
    - Titles versus Headers and Footers — 163
    - Making the Spreadsheet More Presentable — 164
    - Sorting the Spreadsheet — 166
    - Using a Hybrid Document — 167
- Databases — 170
    - Why Use a Database? — 171
    - What Does the Database Look Like? — 171
    - Creating a Database — 172
    - Modifying a Database Layout — 174
    - Entering and Editing Database Data — 179
    - Creating a New Layout with Sub-Summaries — 180
    - Using the New Layout — 187
- Summary — 190

Chapter 11. Creating an Image Map in ClarisWorks — 193

- About Image Maps — 194
- Client and Server Side Image Maps — 195
- How to Do It — 197
  - Creating the Graphic — 197
  - Locate the Hot Spots — 199
  - Modify the HTML Code — 203
- Summary — 204

Part III. ClarisWorks in the Real World — 205

Chapter 12. Creating a Newsletter — 207

- About Newsletters — 208
  - What This Chapter Covers — 210
- Assistants and Stationery — 210
  - Stationery — 211
  - Assistants — 212
- Style Sheets — 214
- Publish and Subscribe — 217
- Linked Text Frames — 226
- Summary — 231

Chapter 13. Sending the Newsletter Out — 233

- Creating the Mailing List/Contact Database — 235
  - About Databases — 235
  - Creating Your Database — 237
  - Database Niceties — 245
- Mail Merge — 250
  - Preparing the Merge — 251
  - Printing the Merged Data — 256
- Summary — 256

Chapter 14. Posting the Newsletter on the Web — 259
- Reviewing the Newsletter on Paper — 260
- Preparing the Newsletter for the Web — 262
  - File Structure and Storage — 262
  - What You Have to Modify — 263
- Adding Links and Other Web-Based Features — 269
  - Creating the Book Marks — 270
  - Creating the Links — 272
  - Other Web-Based Features — 273
- Posting the Newsletter as a Portable Digital Document — 274
  - PostScript and PDF Files — 277
  - Posting Files on the Web — 278
- Summary — 279

Chapter 15. Presenting the Newsletter in Person — 281
- About Presentations — 282
  - Presentation Formats — 282
  - Things to Watch Out For — 283
  - The Mechanics of a Presentation — 283
- Presenting a Document as a Slide Show — 284
- Creating a Presentation with an Assistant — 286
  - Modifying the Presentation — 287
  - Editing the Master Page — 288
- Creating a Presentation from Stationery — 290
- Using Image Libraries — 291
- Summary — 298

Chapter 16. Running the Small Office/Home Office with ClarisWorks — 301
- ClarisWorks Features for Business Use — 302
  - Using the Business Templates — 303
  - Other Features for SOHO Users — 308
- Keep Your Computer On — 309
  - Power — 310
  - Disk Maintenance — 312
- Backups and Archives — 313

Backups versus Archives	313
Hardware	314
Backup Strategy	314
Key Points	315
Costs	315
Networking	316
Transceivers	316
Cabling	317
Hubs	318
Routers	318
Laptops and PowerBooks	320
Summary	321

Chapter 17. ClarisWorks for Kids—for Adults — 323

The Interface	324
The Kids Interface	325
The Scripting Interface	326
Documents, Files, and Folders	327
Menus	329
Creating and Modifying Documents with ClarisWorks	331
Summary	334

What's in ClarisWorks Office — 337

JIAN BusinessBasics	338
Documentation	338
Claris Home Page Lite	338
Internet Access	339
Other Items	340

Index — 341

Foreword

A paperless world. The idea sounds at once exhilarating and intimidating. But with the exploding evolution of computers, technologies like interactive multimedia, three-dimensional imaging, electronic mail, the Internet, and World Wide Web, we are empowered to learn and communicate beyond the limits of paper. For the first time in history, we can closely mimic the mind's multidimensional capabilities.

As a leading vendor of software products for Windows and Mac OS, Claris is committed to bringing "Simply powerful software" to individuals, groups, and businesses. One of our goals is to bring the power of the new media to everyone, with tools that are easy to use, cost-effective, and versatile.

The ClarisWorks software has won numerous awards for its excellence as an integrated application, seamlessly merging the types of work users want to do most. With improved style sheets and Assistants, multimedia database fields, a links palette for creating book marks and links to documents and URLs, an editable button bar for quick access to over 100 commands, and World Wide Web publishing and access capability, ClarisWorks is a key tool for taking full advantage of the new media. Designing interactive documents and Web pages—complete with the ability to integrate jumps, movies, and sounds—is easier and faster than ever.

ClarisWorks 5.0: The Internet, New Media, and Paperless Documents reflects our commitment to giving ClarisWorks users what they need. Written with insight and clarity, this book provides beginners and experts with practical information and tips for using ClarisWorks. The need to communicate will never change, but, as Jesse notes, "the challenges of doing it effectively and lastingly transcend paper." I am confident that readers will find this book to be invaluable as they explore the power and flexibility of ClarisWorks.

BILL SUDLOW
Vice President, Product Development
Claris Corporation

Preface

This book is an overview of ClarisWorks Office (which includes ClarisWorks 5.0); it covers the new features in ClarisWorks 5.0 as well as the whole range of functionality that the ClarisWorks Office product provides. Available on both Mac OS and Windows, ClarisWorks has long been considered the premiere tool for combining sophisticated and powerful functionality with ease of use.

The book doesn't start from scratch—there is printed documentation that ships with ClarisWorks as well as on-line support. If you don't know how to save a file, there are many places to turn for help and assistance. In this book, you will find possibilities beyond the basics that allow you to create documents in a time-honored way. There is tremendous power in ClarisWorks 5.0; thanks to the incomparable interface engineering at Claris, that power is available without complexity. If you are new to ClarisWorks (or to computers), try some of the new features.

Acknowledgments

Many people have contributed to this book—not least the engineers and designers and Claris who have developed and refined ClarisWorks over the years. Also at Claris, Joan Hiraki together with Jill Holdaway and Richard Woike have been of immeasurable assistance.

At Claris Press, Ken Morton has once again provided a great environment in which to go about the very complicated process of writing a book like this. The process of getting the book onto paper (which—even in this new world of paperless documents—is still a daunting task) has been made easy by the efforts of Julie Champagne. Samantha Libby and Abby Heim have also provided much-appreciated assistance; and Mary Prescott's copy editing has once again clarified some befuddled clauses and untangled some particularly bizarre examples of syntax that seem to have sprung from nowhere.

Much help and assistance has been provided by Cindy Tipple and Peggy Alt of the Philmont Public Library's User Experience Research and Engineering Lab. Their motto ("If we can do it, anyone can") is a lesson to all.

Carole McClendon instigated this project and has provided excellent guidance along the way.

"New Media"

The phrase "new media" is often used to refer to CD-ROMs and the multimedia-rich World Wide Web. It is an imprecise term, suggesting to many more an attitude and enthusiasm for new technologies rather than any specific media. "New media" is often developed in New York City's Silicon Alley and often has an edge to it that goes beyond the illustrations in an old-fashioned CD-ROM-based encyclopedia (from the old days—like the early 1990s).

Introduction

When the now-familiar Mac OS desktop appeared in 1984, it was a very literal metaphor for a real desk. All data was contained in documents which could then be grouped into folders. These documents were acted upon by application programs (such as ClarisWorks) that were built around the document metaphor. When no longer needed, documents could be dropped into the trash.

This document metaphor was extraordinarily powerful—in large part because of its familiarity. As time marched on and people did more and more things with their computers, the document metaphor sometimes became a little stretched and frayed at the edges. Nevertheless, it was—and is—so right and useful for so much of the work that people do on their computers that its future is assured.

But there are other futures out there. Computers are still used by only a minority of people. They are too complicated for many people to use—and an awful lot of people are not interested in doing the desktop work that personal computers have addressed so well. There are opportunities that have barely been thought of in education and entertainment, in areas of business far beyond the traditional clerical and professional desktops, and in interactive communications.

With recent advances in technology (much of it reflected in ClarisWorks 5.0), the scope of activities on desktop computers has grown by leaps and bounds. It is useful to remember that the document metaphor is just that—a metaphor, not absolute reality. The world of documents implies a paper-based world, and that is the world that we are used to and that we will probably live in for many years to come—but there is much more that you can do when you start thinking of documents beyond paper.

About This Book

This book provides an introduction to the new technologies that are part of ClarisWorks 5.0. The common thread to these technologies is that they go beyond the flat two-dimensional world of paper—they are based on communications and the Internet, they do not stay still (video and telephony, for example), and they exist in more than two dimensions (three-dimensional graphics, as one case in point). There is nothing wrong with paper—ClarisWorks and this book provide many ways of working with it that are both simple and complex; it is just that there is a lot more out there than paper.

You will find some technologies that are not new in Claris-Works 5.0 in this book (the database and mail merge, for instance). These technologies also transcend paper—and they are among the ClarisWorks features that are most misunderstood.

The Structure of the Book

The first part of this book deals with the ClarisWorks, the new technologies as well as the Internet.

In the second part, you will find concrete details on how to use these new technologies—including how to create QuickTime movies, how to use ClarisWorks to create Web pages and Web graphics, and how to make link documents together with hypertext links. Also in the second part you will find comparisons of the different types of ClarisWorks documents as well as demonstrations of how to convert data from one to another—moving the same information from word processing document to spreadsheet to database.

The final part of the book covers real-life examples of the use of these technologies in ClarisWorks.

Some Interesting URLs[1]

Since this book is part of the new world that exists beyond paper, you will find references throughout the book to Internet addresses. The first one is here. It is http://www.philmontmill.com. At that address you will find updates to this book, as well as links to other sources of ClarisWorks information.

---

1. URLs—Uniform Resource Locators—are addresses on the World Wide Web part of the Internet. See "Internet, Intranets, LANs, and Shared Information" on page 60.

The second one is http://www.claris.com. That is the address of the Claris home page—the place where you can find out about new releases and upgrades of ClarisWorks itself. There are also links to useful resources and frequently asked questions (and answers) about ClarisWorks.

What Next?

Now that is a big bore. Here you are with your copy of ClarisWorks 5.0 and a book that you want to help you through the exciting new features. And now you are supposed to surf the Net? Who has time for all this? Who has the patience to learn it? Who has the software to do it? (Must be half a dozen programs, at least!)

Well, you have the software (ClarisWorks), and you do have the time. And you can understand it. In the world of computers, everything is getting cheaper; everything is getting more powerful—and it is all getting much, much simpler. This last trend has started to be noticed only in the last few years—since about 1993.

You can blame it all on the World Wide Web—a major part of the Internet. The Web made access to the vast and daunting resources of the Internet relatively easy. As tens of millions of people clicked their way through the uncharted reaches of the Internet, they started to ask why it was so hard to use desktop computers.

Meanwhile, behind the doors of software developers and managers, people started to ask why it took so long—and cost so much—to develop customized software for organizations and enterprises, particularly when it seemed as if everyone was "putting up a home page" without the benefit of a computer science degree.

All of this comes together in ClarisWorks 5.0. Unprecedented power coupled with not only the traditional ClarisWorks ease of use but also new technologies that are specifically designed to be simple makes this new world available to you.

Part I
New Concepts and Technologies

Your Turn

Computers were supposed to make people's lives easier. Go to your public library and look through the Sunday supplement magazines from newspapers in the early 1950s. The promise of the computer age was quite different from the reality that was delivered. Of course, the entire computer industry is still young, and people are still trying to define and describe what the relationship between people and their computers is and should be.

Early computers and their software (that is, computers and software from more than about 5 years ago) simply did not have the power to do what people wanted and expected. Now, however, significant advances have made possible a computer environment that at last starts to deliver on the promises made almost half a century ago.

ClarisWorks has been a leader in easy-to-use software; Claris itself and its parent company Apple Computer have long been recognized leaders in research and development efforts that continue to lead the way for the rest of the industry. While other companies have developed increasingly complex software, Claris and Apple have taken the road less traveled—they have made everything easier.

This has not been easy, and thereby hang many tales. Some people actually like complexity: the difficulty of simply connecting a printer to a computer is frustrating to many people—but it represents a livelihood for some consultants. Others think that something has to be difficult (or even obscure) to be valuable. And, of course, there are those who actually prefer working with computers and their trivia to working with people (and their own trivia).

If you like complexity or obscurity, this book—and Claris-Works—are not for you. If you want to be a programmer or computer technician, you are also in the wrong place. On the other hand, if you want to do real things—write letters, work with budgets, maintain mailing lists, or design posters for community events—this book and ClarisWorks should be right up your alley.

This part of the book gives you a high-level view of today's landscape of computing. Compared with the computer world of a decade ago, it is a world of high-powered processors, pervasive networking (not to mention the Internet), and large color monitors. All of these have come together—along with new software design methodologies—to make your life easier.

> *ClarisWorks has always been able to run on relatively modest computer configurations. You may not have a high-powered computer, a large color monitor, a network connection, or a high-speed modem. Still, today's ClarisWorks supports all of those even if you are working on an old computer with a black-and-white monitor. As the prices of computer equipment continue to fall, one day you probably will have a computer even more high powered than the fanciest machine on the market today…and your next monitor will probably be more colorful, larger, but less bulky than current devices.*

The chapters in this section explore the changes to documents that are made possible with this increase in computer power as well as the changes to software interfaces (in particular ClarisWorks) that are also made possible. It concludes with an overview of the most powerful part of today's computer environment—the Internet.

But first, this chapter summarizes the new focus in software development today. Since Claris and ClarisWorks have been pioneers in this area, experienced users may find themselves on familiar territory; if you are new to ClarisWorks—or new to computers in general—the issues merit some attention.

Focusing on People and Their Activities

You probably do not want to use a computer—few people do. You want to do things that the computer can help you to accomplish. Writing a letter, putting together a shopping list, keeping a budget, putting out a newsletter, playing a game—these are the activities that people are usually interested in. The job of the computer should be to help you do these things—and to stay in the background and out of the way as much as possible.

For the computer and its software to become as invisible as possible, many things have to fall into place. One of the most important—which is admirably demonstrated in ClarisWorks—is allowing people to do things in the way that is natural to them.

How odd it is that computers—those supposedly powerful devices—appear to be so inflexible that you have to learn to think their way before you can do your own work! Odd it is, but it is not true with ClarisWorks. Consider the part of a document shown in Figure 1-1.

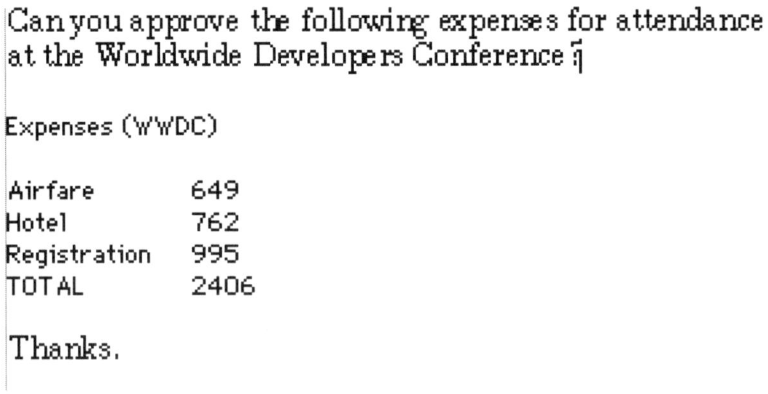

```
Can you approve the following expenses for attendance
at the Worldwide Developers Conference ?

Expenses (WWDC)

Airfare         649
Hotel           762
Registration    995
TOTAL           2406

Thanks.
```

FIGURE 1-1. Text and Table

What are you looking at in Figure 1-1? Here are your choices:

1. A word processing document with the "Expenses" section formatted using tabs and an alternative font.

2. A word processing document with a spreadsheet embedded in it.

3. A drawing document with text and a spreadsheet embedded in it.

4. A spreadsheet with a specially formatted header and footer surrounding the numbers in the "Expenses" section.

It could be any of these…because there is no one right way to do things. The computer is made flexible so that you can work the way you feel like working. There are multiple ways of doing almost everything in ClarisWorks—including getting help and assistance. The focus is on you and the things that you want to do.

Putting Things Together

And one of the things that you most often want to do is to put things together—another task at which ClarisWorks excels.

From the toddler in a playpen to the elderly person rearranging curios on a shelf, from the cubicle denizen to the free-spirited Woodstock sprite, people like to put things together. Putting things together and organizing them in various ways is perhaps the quintessential human activity. (The use of tools is more common among other animals than was thought not too long ago; however, humans may be unique in the way that they put things together.)

Putting things together may be **experimental or deliberate**—"What does it look like if I put this chair next to the window?" or "What combination of colors do I need to put together in order to get green?" The objective may be to learn something or to accomplish a particular task.

The result of this may be a **combination** in which the original components remain identifiable (as, for example, in a collection of news clippings) or the result may be a **synthesis** in which the original components have taken on a new shape (in a student's term paper based on news clippings).

The human appetite for putting things together is so strong that what would appear to be commonsense limitations of what can be combined with what else are routinely violated. People combine physical objects, ideas, and tools with impunity, forging new concepts and inventions with wild abandon.

This is called progress. It is how individuals and the species learn and develop. And it is often made incredibly difficult by computers.

ClarisWorks provides an environment in which the arbitrary barriers and distinctions foisted on you by computers can be surmounted. It provides basic document types (word processing, spreadsheets, painting, drawing, databases, and communications), but those types can be placed into other documents so that spreadsheets live equally happily in their own documents, in word processing documents, or in graphics documents. (Not all document types are combinable, but most of them are.)

The result is not just that you can work in whatever way is most natural to you, but also that your choices of tools become less critical. If you want to design a flyer for an event, you can start with the graphics, the text, or even with a spreadsheet that contains relevant information. Your choice of a convenient tool is not irreversible. As a result, the tool becomes less and less important as you focus on what you want to do.

Summary

The focus of ClarisWorks and of this book is on you and the things that you do. By making many different approaches available, ClarisWorks enables you to concentrate on your objectives, ignoring the tool. If you are someone who likes to work from the outside in, you can build gigantic outlines and then fill in the blanks—even if those blanks have graphics instead of words. Conversely, you can work from minutiae up to large structures.

From time to time, you can change the way you work—either because the mood strikes you or because you are working in concert with others who work differently. The power of ClarisWorks lies not so much in what it can do, but in the number of ways in which it can do its vast array of tasks.

2

Beyond Paper—More Power for Your Documents

Many of the new features of ClarisWorks have to do with new technologies and new media; others have to do with new ways of working with your computer and its software. In short, the power of faster processors is being harnessed to do things it was never possible to do before. This manifests itself in technologies such as QuickTime that enable you to put video and audio clips into your documents; it is also manifested in the proliferation of advanced assistants including macros and assistants that can carry out high-level tasks for you automatically.

This chapter examines some of the issues related to the new technologies—many of which share one characteristic: they cannot be represented on paper. They are intimately tied to the computer monitor and the processor behind it.

Paper is not going away, and the activities associated with it (from writing and drawing to manufacture and disposal) remain integral parts of our lives. It is just that now there is much more that can be done.

Beyond the limits of paper are new adventures, unconstrained by a limited two-dimensional world that is frozen in time. These technologies are made possible by the tremendous computer power that is now available on even entry-level computers and by sophisticated software such as ClarisWorks 5.0.

First, a warning. Do not fall into the trap of thinking that this is an either/or world. Paper is the ideal medium for many projects—from informal shopping lists to world-changing documents. (Can you imagine the Declaration of Independence in any form other than the familiar handwritten parchment? It can be rewritten and reprinted, but for two centuries the Declaration of Independence has been that single piece of parchment in the National Archives in Washington, DC.) The fact that there are new opportunities and new media does not mean that paper is finished—only that you have more choices.

Writing and Paper

Writing—most often on paper—is how people **communicate** from one to another when they do not speak aloud. Writing serves to convey ideas and information from one person to another.

It is also used by individuals to **store lists of information**—be they shopping lists, intermediate steps in mathematical proofs, or appointments to be kept.

Writing **preserves** history from one age to the next, but the words of this history are incomplete; **pictures and images**—many also preserved on paper—add to the story. Even with the addition of pictures, paper's **representation of reality may be incomplete**.

Yet all too often the **paper itself decays**; with its loss may go the loss of the words and pictures upon it.

These aspects of paper—communication among contemporaries, notes to oneself, links with the past, the power of graphics, the inability to represent completely the three-dimensional world on paper, and the fragility of paper—all have been noted throughout history.

The need to communicate and the challenges of doing it effectively and lastingly transcend paper. They are constant human needs and endeavors; paper has facilitated them for much of time. Other media have existed alongside paper (from billboards to skywriting and embroidery); in today's world electronic media based on computers are extending and advancing the role of paper.

A Brief History of Paper and Printing

Every few decades, the technology of paper has changed—from its introduction in China (105), then Japan (610), Samarkand (751), Egypt (900), and Spain (1150), to the development of papermills (Italy, 1276), the use of watermarks (1282), machines for making continuous rolls of paper (Nicolas Robert, 1798), and the use of wood pulp for making paper—rather than cloth (1860s).

Likewise, the techniques, processes, and machines used for writing and printing on paper have evolved over the centuries. Adapting implements used to scratch symbols on slate and bark, inventors developed and refined pens and pencils; printers developed movable type (pioneered in Europe by Gutenberg in the mid-1450s and in Korea some 50 years before), which, when coupled with steam-driven presses (1810), made possible the mass-produced newspapers of the nineteenth century. The typesetting machines of the late nineteenth century (such as the ones in which Mark Twain invested—and lost—a fortune) increased the speed of production (and thus lowered the cost and increased the output) of printing companies. Photographs and other images were reproduced using new techniques such as rotogravure so that it was no longer necessary to create line-drawing copies by hand. In the first half of the twentieth century, the demand for mass-market magazines kept pace with developments in color printing as fashion, travel, news, and other magazines displayed glamor on glossy pages.

By the 1980s, people's expectations with regard to the quality of printing were high. At the same time, the tools of publication (from mimeograph machines to photocopy machines to even the typewriters of the Soviet samizdat movement) became less expensive and more widespread. It is no wonder that as the personal computer began to become a common part of offices, homes, and schools, people started to demand that it be usable as a publishing and printing tool—after all, it had a keyboard and printer, and early programs made it possible to write, edit, and print text.

Using Personal Computers for Writing and Printing

Unfortunately, the early personal computers were not up to the task. Until 1984 and the advent of the Macintosh, most computer monitors displayed text as yellow, blue, or green dots formed into the shapes of generic characters against a black background. Printers could reproduce those characters with dots at a higher resolution, but still output from dot matrix printers was relatively poor (and clearly identifiable).

Low-speed letter-quality printers were developed on the basis of typewriter technology, but their relatively high cost and sensitivity with regard to paper handling exacted a high toll from their users.

When the Macintosh computer arrived, its bit-mapped graphics displayed text in various fonts and styles against a (normally) white background—much like type on paper. With thousands of pixels (bits) making up the screen images, the resolution of the text on the screen was an astonishing improvement over that on other computer monitors. The original ImageWriter printers similarly represented a step forward beyond the dot matrix printers of competitors, but the quality—although improved—was far from that expected from "real" publication processes.

In short order, Apple brought out the original LaserWriter (which brought significantly greater quality and speed to desktop printing) as well as color graphics and monitors that could display near-photographic quality images on the computer screen.

The Speed of Technological Change

The pace of change and advancement in the computer imaging industry was fast and feverish in those days. Whereas the paper-based industry had spent decades (even centuries) making improvements in the printing and publishing processes, people became accustomed to yearly (even monthly) advances. The quality of traditional publication and printing, however, continued to exceed the quality available with the new desktop publishing tools.

The schematic diagram shown in Figure 2-1 illustrates the pace of improvement in both traditional and computer-based publication. The pace of improvement in the world of computers was significantly faster than the slower pace of traditional technology, and in 1989, the paths crossed.

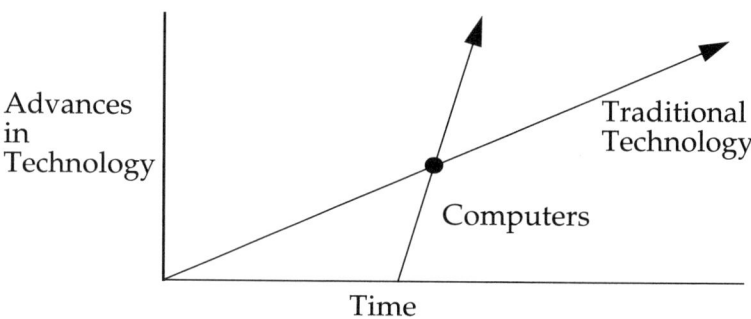

FIGURE 2-1. Pace of Improvement in Traditional and Computer-Based Publications

Publishers of newspapers, magazines, and books are constantly on the lookout for ways to improve the quality of their products, decrease the costs of production, and lessen the time it takes to turn them out. For most publishers, it was in the late 1980s and early 1990s that the balance tipped decisively in favor of computer-based technology. The quality was high enough that compromises were not necessary to achieve the savings in time and cost that the computer promised. The publishing industry—from glossy magazines, to books, to newsletters, to personal and business correspondence—embraced the personal computer as its primary tool.

Something else happened, though. The feverish pace of innovation and development continued in the computer world. The problems of the 1980s were solved—the arcane issues of spacing between lines and letters in sophisticated typesetting layouts, the myriad concerns about color matching and color printing when many inks and dyes were needed, and the differing needs of printers and computer monitors when it came to displaying images. The computer industry raced on, attacking and conquering other issues: video clips, three-dimensional images, new forms of software, automated and scripted documents that manipulate themselves, and of course the Internet.

The detritus of the old age of traditional publication—paste-up boards, matte knives, rubber cement, carbon paper, correction fluid, and mimeograph stencils—quickly fell by the wayside, replaced by computer-based tools that were faster and easier to use (as well as quieter and less objectionable with regard to smell and needs for their disposal).

The Declining Cost of Personal Computers

The new computer-based tools were expensive by today's standards. Table 2-1 shows the capabilities and costs (in 1997 dollars) of some common computer products in 1985 and in 1997.

The substantial decrease in costs (using constant dollars) is striking enough, but the phenomenal increase in power and capabilities is staggering. It is hard to pick the most remarkable of these. Perhaps it will suffice to say that the 1985 user of a personal computer would have a hard time coping with the cornucopia of processing power, storage capabilities, communication opportunities, and printing choices that are available for relatively modest costs today (that, in fact, are not even options but come as standard equipment on entry-level machines).

	1985	1997
Modem	$756 (1,200 baud)	$70 (33,600 baud)
FileMaker (database software)	299	200
External hard disk (standard size)	2,2286 10 MB	370 1,200 MB
External hard disk (large size)	5,351 45 MB	1,699 9,000 MB
Printer (high quality, high speed)	9,940 LaserWriter	2,299 LaserWriter 16/600
Printer (average quality, low speed)	910 ImageWriter	239 Color StyleWriter
Excel (spreadsheet)	576	300
Word	299	300
Computer	3,050 512 K (memory) Macintosh No hard disk — B & W monitor	2,449 16,000 KB (memory) PowerPC 7300/180 2.0 GB disk CD-ROM drive Color monitor

TABLE 2-1. Cost of Computer Products in 1985 and 1997 (Prices Adjusted for Inflation)[1]

1. Sources: *MacWorld*, August 1985, Volume 2, Number 8. MacWarehouse Catalogue Volume 72, August 1997. Department of Commerce Consumer Price Index for 1985 = 0.695 in 1997 dollars.

A concrete example of the changes over the past decade is given in the May 1989 issue of *MacWorld*. In an issue with the cover emblazoned with the headline, "MacWorld Goes DTP," the process of converting the magazine from traditional publishing to electronic desktop publishing is described. To some sophisticated computer users today who have grown up with desktop publishing, this issue is decidedly quaint. Life without laser printers, color, and scanners is unimaginable. (In fact, it is a tribute to the power and ease of use of contemporary software that some sophisticated computer users today were not even born in May 1989.)

Managing the Increasing Complexity of Computer Software

Of course, not all is happy and peaceful on this phenomenally powerful desktop. The software is much more powerful and much cheaper, but it is also harder to use. People are able to do things on personal computers that they never would have dreamed of doing in the past—and sometimes they feel that they are *required* to do them. Do you really want to deal with the intricacies of color printing and separations when you are creating a flyer for the library book sale? Is a simple spreadsheet that will help you manage your household finances really crying out for three-dimensional animated graphs?

The challenge for software designers is to harness the phenomenal powers and opportunities of new technologies and to provide them—along with the simple tools for shopping lists and personal correspondence—to people who can use them without investing an undue amount of their lives in training. This challenge has been met remarkably well over the years by the ClarisWorks team. ClarisWorks has managed to strike a balance between power and complexity; in every version, it has provided the sophisticated tools advanced users need while also providing basic tools for novices (and people who have better things to do than to spend their lives using computers).

Keeping up with Technology

If you are buying a computer today, it will come with features and capabilities that will astonish long-time computer users. If you yourself are a long-time, experienced computer user, you will find new adventures that will intrigue and excite you when you open your new computer's carton.

If your computer is not new, you and it may have seen many adventures together. As the prices of new hardware components drop and as the power of hardware and software increases, more and more people are trading up to new machines. For much of what is discussed in this book, that is hardly necessary (ClarisWorks has a well-deserved reputation for compatibility with the installed base of computers). Still, when you consider upgrading your computer, remember to look at the current prices. That computer may well have cost $5000, but its replacement now could cost half the price—and have several times the power.

One thing does need constant updating—and that is you. Everyone develops habits over the years—some are good, some are bad, some are necessary, and some are not. Remember periodically to question what you are doing. More than one person has gone in search of a printer that can handle four-part carbon-paper forms only to realize that the copies are not really necessary—and in fact that the whole form can be replaced with an e-mail message.

The Limits of Paper

Paper has a number of limits, most of which derive from its physical attributes. (Many of these limits are advantages in other contexts—for example, the fixed size and shape of sheets of paper are what make notepads and books possible.) Although paper is a relatively cheap commodity, there are significant costs associated with its production, transportation, storage, and ultimate disposal (or recycling).

Paper is also far from a permanent medium. In fact, it is remarkably fragile, subject to damage from fire, flood, and simple oxidation by everyday air.

On the other hand, paper is relatively cheap and easy to use. It is convenient, easily transported, and requires few instructions for its use.

It is not going away, and the vast opportunities for its use are outlined later in this book.

Opportunities of Interactive Media

When you create a document that is freed from the bounds of paper—a document intended to be seen only on a computer screen—many of the limitations of paper disappear. Although the computer screen is a fixed size and shape, windows with scroll bars allow people easily to manipulate images that lie far beyond the physical bounds of the monitor.

A document that exists only in an electronic form can be stored and transferred at incredibly fast speeds; many of the physical woes that can befall paper cannot affect electronic documents. Furthermore, it can move on the screen: it can contain video and sound that play by themselves, it can be manipulable so that an apparently three-dimensional object can be turned by the user, and it can contain buttons and embedded scripts and macros that carry out prepared commands. Finally, electronic documents can be assembled automatically from many sources ("**composite documents**") far more easily than can paper-based documents.

Part II of the book has details on using each of these technologies.

Documents Can Be Any Size and Shape

Freed from the physical limits of a given piece of paper, your documents can take on any size and shape that are appropriate. The notion of a part of a document (a page) undergoes a transformation when pages can vary in size and shape within a document.

The World Wide Web on the Internet is an example of the use of such documents. The Web is made up of electronic pages—they come in varying sizes and, in the best of cases, the size and shape of each page are determined not by the attributes of a piece of paper but by the size and shape appropriate to the information contained on the page. Some pages are one sentence long whereas others are the equivalent of several dozen printed pages.

Documents Can Move around the World at the Speed of Light (Almost)

Documents designed for use on a computer are stored in digital formats—formats that can be sent around the world without regard to the complications of transporting paper. As with so much of the new world, this is a mixed bag of blessings and curses. The governments of the world are still confronting the issues involved in this high-speed transportation of ideas and information. The notions of national borders, of customs, and even of copyrights are not inherently modified by the use of electronic documents, but enforcing the regulations becomes a much more complicated issue in a high-speed digital world.

The fact that a group of people around the world can collaborate almost instantaneously on the creation of a document—be it a political manifesto, a corporate policy manual, a merchandise cataglog, or a guest list for a birthday party—represents hopes, fears, opportunities, and calamities to different people with different points of views at various times.

Documents Can Easily Be Stored

Digital documents not only can fly around the globe but also can be stored easily on digital storage media (such as disks, diskettes, magneto-optical cartridges, and removable cartridge devices). The amount of space required to store digital documents is a small fraction of the space required to store paper documents; disposal of digital documents requires no recycling process or landfill—the storage space can be erased and reused with no effort. (This, of course, is also a disadvantage of digital documents—one that archivists are concerned about in preserving the history of our society.)

Documents Can Move

Documents that are not constrained by the limits of paper can incorporate motion of various sorts. This is perhaps one of the most exciting aspects of the new technologies.

Video, Sound, and Telephony

Since the end of the 1980s, it has been possible to store digitized images on computers and to play them back with high fidelity. The increased speed of processors has made it possible to view real-time video (such as broadcast or cable television or a feed from a video camera), to produce high-quality digital stereo sound, and to combine the technologies of video and sound in real time to turn the computer into a telephone system.

On the Mac OS, these technologies are incorporated into the operating system at a very basic level, without a requirement of hardware or software add-ons in most cases. If a picture is worth a thousand words, a video clip showing how to replace the toner cartridge in a photocopy machine might be worth a far more than that—particularly when a deadline looms.

Three-Dimensional Images and Virtual Reality

With Apple's QuickDraw 3D technology, the basics of displaying and manipulating three-dimensional objects are incorporated into standard system software.

Just as a video image that you place in a document incorporates all of the data needed to play itself as a live-action video, a three-dimensional object contains all of the information needed to display, rotate, and otherwise examine it in space.

While three-dimensional graphics let you manipulate an object as you view it from the outside, QuickTime VR (virtual reality) allows you to manipulate a landscape that appears to surround you in a similar way. From a vantage point selected by the developer of the image, you can look around, up, and down.

In traditional forms of presentation on paper, this could be accomplished only by providing several illustrations—"View from the East," "View from the South," etc. Instead of taking up space on the page for alternative views of the same object, one view can be placed on the page, letting the user explore and choose the vantage point that seems most appropriate.

Buttons, Scripts, and Macros

When you click on a movie or manipulate a three-dimensional image inside a document, the software supporting those objects takes over and performs operations for you (playing/rewinding a movie, rotating an object, etc.). You can also explicitly place buttons and other controls in documents. These buttons can execute preprogrammed tasks that you (or others) have prepared. These tasks may be set up as macros using the ClarisWorks programming language, or they may be hypertext links. (These technologies are described in full in Part II.)

Summary

Paper helps people carry out some of their most basic activities including communicating and remembering. Documents intended for presentation primarily on a computer can move beyond the limits of paper—unconstrained by physical limits of size and shape, able to be communicated almost instantly around the world, and full of possibilities of motion, sound, and animation, these documents put their lifeless two-dimensional antecedents to shame.

ClarisWorks has supported some of these features in the past—its database and communications documents have only the most tangential relationship to paper, and the ability to embed QuickTime movies has long provided some of the liveliness of the new technologies. In ClarisWorks 5.0, however, the possibilities are far greater than before.

ClarisWorks 5.0— More Power for You

The previous chapter covered some of the uses to which more powerful computers are put in terms of creating more sophisticated documents and using new media. The other major use to which increased computing power is put is simplifying your life. In a nutshell, the computer and its application programs such as ClarisWorks can do much more for you without appearing to make a dent in the resources available.

This chapter introduces you to some features and functions that make your use of ClarisWorks easier and more productive.

With new processors and new software such as ClarisWorks 5.0, you have new and more sophisticated tools available to you. Because ClarisWorks is backward compatible, the tools and techniques that you may have used in the past mostly still work and you may not even notice some of the new features. Here are a few examples of how your life is made easier.

Some of these are new features in ClarisWorks 5.0; others are extensions and expansions of previously implemented features. Together, they make up some of the exciting, powerful, and useful tools in ClarisWorks. For those that are new (or are new to you), this section can provide an overview. The online documentation as well as basic paper-based documentation provides further information and step-by-step instruction on the basics.

ClarisWorks Assistants

ClarisWorks Assistants automate many tasks, once again putting the computer's power at your command (rather than the reverse, which is what some applications seem determined to do!).

For example, the Table Assistant helps you insert a table into your document. Here is how it works.

First, ClarisWorks prompts you for the general shape of the table, as shown in Figure 3-1. The sample table shown in the window reflects your settings.

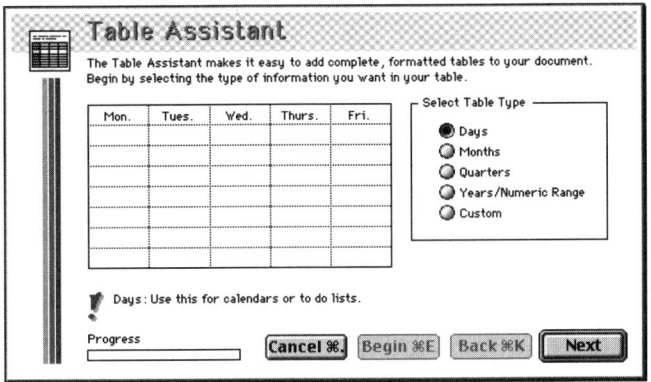

FIGURE 3-1. Table Assistant 1

In this sequence, the table shown in Figure 3-1 will be created. You don't want the days as shown in Figure 3-1, and none of the other choices appear correct. So you click the Custom button, and the display immediately changes to that shown in Figure 3-2.

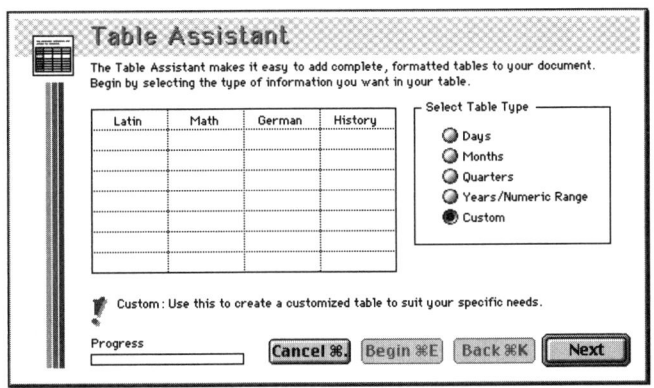

FIGURE 3-2. Table Assistant 2

You click the Next button to let the Assistant guide you through the next step, as shown in Figure 3-3.

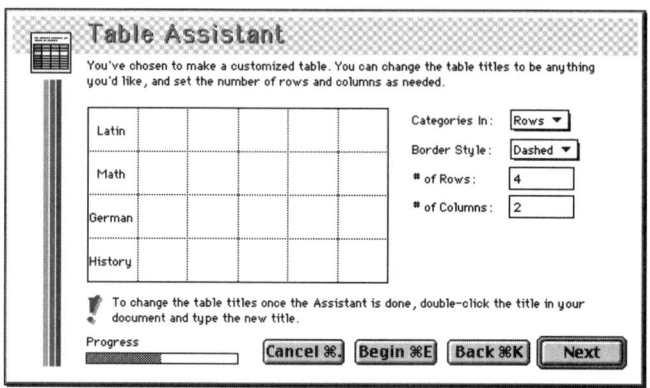

FIGURE 3-3. Table Assistant 3

As you change the pop-up menu from Columns to Rows, the table in the Assistant window changes—reflecting what you are doing before it is placed in your document. The progress bar in the lower left of the window shows how you are progressing through the sequence of windows—yet another form of feedback so that you know where you are and what you are doing. (Remember, ClarisWorks and your computer are working for you, not vice versa.)

Finally, the window shown in Figure 3-4 lets you complete the table. If you are satisfied, you click Create and Claris-Works inserts the table into your document.

Assistants like this guide you through the steps of many processes—steps that you may forget (or never have known) if you do not do the process often. There are many other ways to achieve the same purpose; ClarisWorks deliberately gives you a range of support tools that let you work with the degree of assistance that you want.

For example, if you frequently need a table in a document, you may be perfectly happy just drawing a spreadsheet frame into your document. The choice is yours.

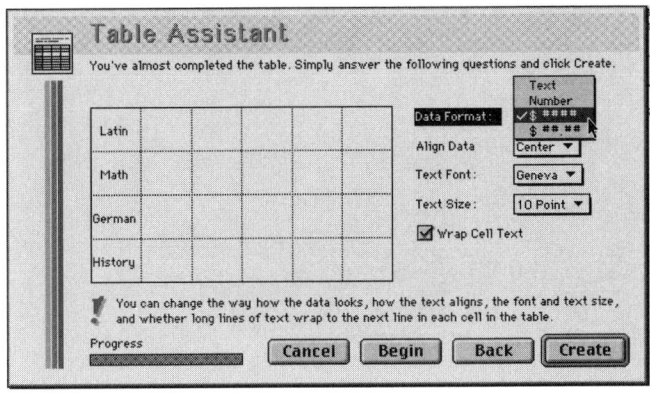

FIGURE 3-4. Table Assistant 4

Drag-and-Drop

Back in the old days of graphical user interfaces (the mid- to late 1980s), there was a persistent rhythm to the way in which you used your computer. First you selected something—a word, a paragraph, a part of a picture, or an icon on the desktop; then you did something to that selection—often by choosing a command from a menu.

For example, you selected a sentence and chose Cut from the Edit menu. That removed the sentence from the document and placed it on the clipboard. If you wanted to paste that sentence into another document or to another place in the same document, you chose the destination by clicking the mouse or selecting the text to be replaced and then chose Paste from the Edit menu.

You can still do this, but the newer drag-and-drop technology lets you make the entire operation much smoother. Instead of selecting something, choosing a menu command, and then possibly going through the routine again to complete your activity, you can simply select what you want to move and drag it to its new location—even if it is in another document or another application. More and more the increased power of computers (and the ingenuity of software developers) lets you forget even about menu commands—you just do what you want to do.

Mouse Tracking

Yet another example of the use of computer power to make your life easier is the increasing sophistication of the interface itself. As you move the mouse around, the cursor moves on the screen with almost no delay (this is called "mouse tracking" or "tracking" for short). What actually happens is that the program constantly checks to see if the mouse has moved, and if it has it redraws the cursor (or whatever tool has been selected) in the new location.

Only a few years ago, programmers figuratively cleared the decks when they had to track the mouse. Not one extraneous line of code could be allowed in the tracking routines, because every added instruction to the computer could make tracking sluggish or unresponsive. With today's faster processors, mouse tracking routines have the luxury of performing many other tasks in addition to tracking the mouse.

For example, as you move the mouse over icons in the button bar, ClarisWorks presents a brief description of each item, as shown in Figure 3-5.

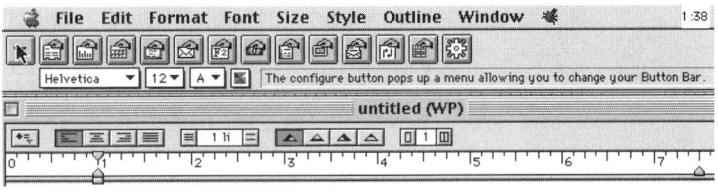

FIGURE 3-5. ClarisWorks Button Bar with Annotation

As suggested by the text in Figure 3-5, you can change your button bar to show other ClarisWorks features—such as the Assistants shown in Figure 3-6.

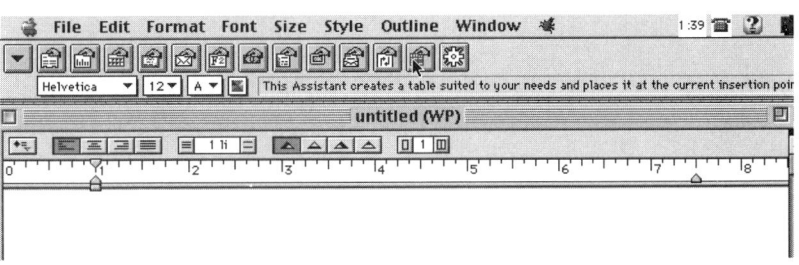

FIGURE 3-6. ClarisWorks Button Bar with Annotation and Assistants

Modifying the Button Bar

The button bar is a powerful part of ClarisWorks. Several button bars come with ClarisWorks (Default, Internet, Document, and Assistants). You can modify these, and you can create your own.

In modifying (or creating) a button bar, not only can you add and subtract buttons, but you can also create your own buttons. These can be based on common processes (such as opening a document), or they can be based on macros that you have created. (For more information on macros, see the ClarisWorks online help and basic documentation.)

Here is an example of creating a button of your own and adding it to a button bar of your own creation.

Creating Your Own Buttons

From the button bar menu, choose New Button to start, as shown in Figure 3-7.

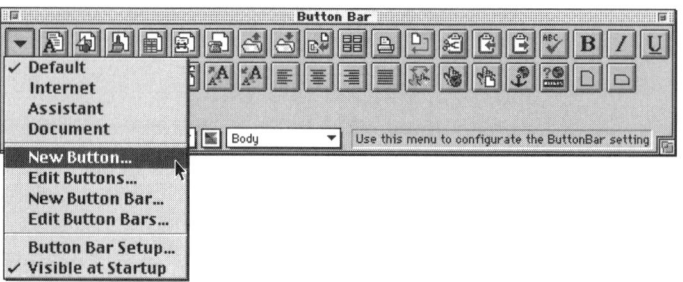

FIGURE 3-7. New Button

The window shown in Figure 3-8 immediately opens, letting you name your button. The button description that you enter will be shown in the button bar; you can choose what the button will do. In this case, it will play a macro that sets the paper orientation to portrait (vertical) mode.

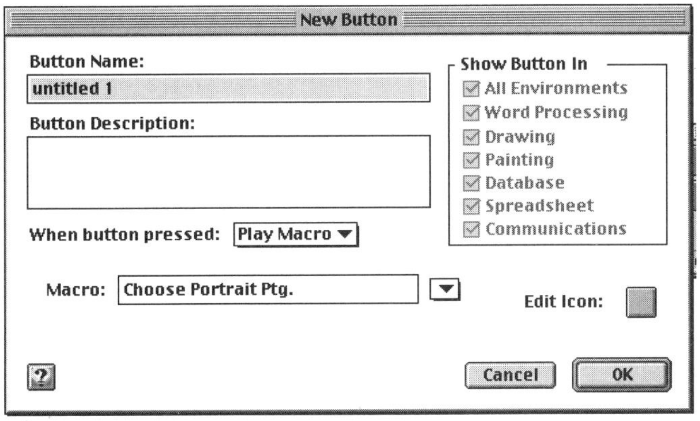

FIGURE 3-8. New Button Window

You can edit the icon by clicking the Edit Icon button in the lower right of the window. The editing window shown in Figure 3-9 will open. Draw any image that you want using any of the colors in this palette.

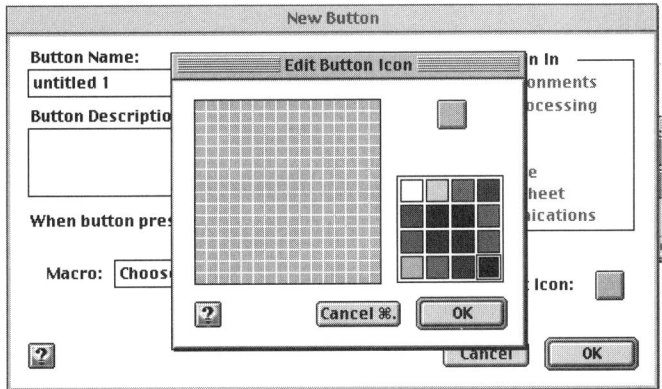

FIGURE 3-9. Edit Button Icon Window

Click OK and you are done—you have created a button bar button, named it, associated it with an action (the macro), and designed an icon for it.

Creating and Editing a Button Bar

You can create and edit button bars (your own or standard ClarisWorks button bars) from the button bars menu shown previously in Figure 3-7. For any button bar, you can choose buttons from any category and place them in the button bar by clicking on them as shown in Figure 3-10.

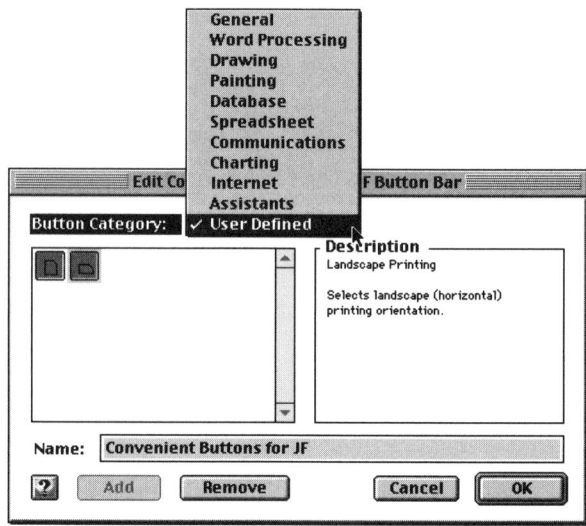

FIGURE 3-10. Editing a Button Bar

You can remove a button from a button bar by clicking on it and then clicking the Remove button at the bottom of the window.

When you have created a new button bar, it shows up in the Button Bar menu as shown in Figure 3-11. In the background of this figure, you can see the custom button bar with four buttons—the portrait and landscape orientation custom buttons, the Envelopes assistant, and the Clear button.

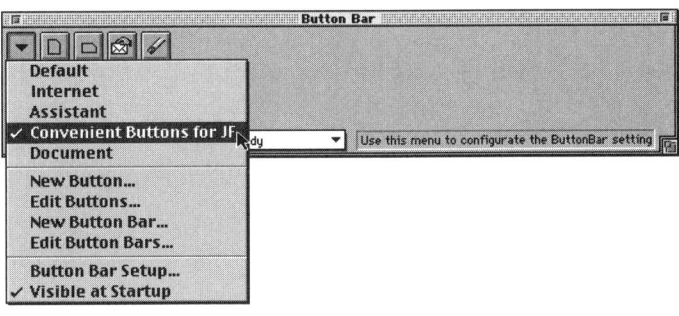

FIGURE 3-11. Your Button Bar in the Menu

Libraries

Button bars let you consolidate frequently used commands; you can use libraries to consolidate frequently used text, images, and documents. ClarisWorks comes with a number of libraries preinstalled; these libraries have a number of common graphics that you can use in all sorts of documents. You can add to these libraries (and create your own) with your own graphics (such as logos), commonly used text (copyright notices, instructions, etc.), or anything else that you want.

Libraries contain ClarisWorks objects—be they text, graphics, or spreadsheets. These objects can be as simple as a single word or paragraph—or as complex as several pages of text.

Getting Objects out of Libraries

To look at the libraries available and to get objects from them, choose the Libraries command in the File menu as shown in Figure 3-12.

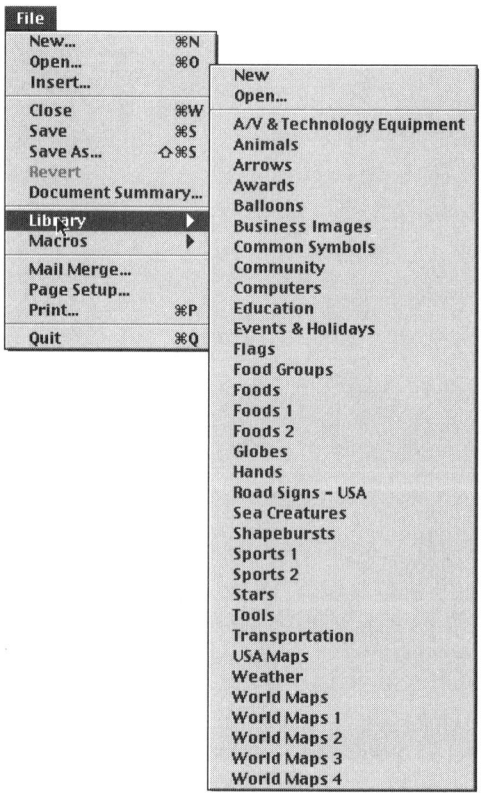

FIGURE 3-12. Library Menu

You will see the long list of libraries included with Claris-Works. At the top of the submenu, you can see that you can open any other library that you may have created—and that you can create a new library.

When you have opened a library, you can look through its objects—the Common Symbols library is shown in Figure 3-13.

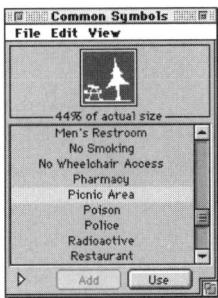

FIGURE 3-13. Common Symbols Library

You can drag an object from the library into your document or you can copy and paste it into the document.

Creating Libraries and Putting Objects into Them

You can create libraries and add objects to them; this makes it very easy to share objects among documents. For example, Figure 3-14 shows a custom library. It was created with the New Library command (shown in Figure 3-12).

Using Objects from a Library

This library contains two objects. One is a graphic object not unlike the graphics shown in the previous library; it is a corporate logo. The second object (selected in Figure 3-14) is a spreadsheet; this spreadsheet was created to list shipping charges by region and by weight. It is needed for order forms, catalogs, memos, and various other documents. By placing it in a library, you can provide that information conveniently to everyone.

Note that once the object from the library has been placed in a document, you can edit it. Thus, the shipping chart could have its fonts changed to match the document that it is placed in. These changes do not affect the library object unless you resave it into the library.

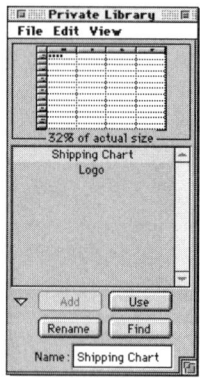

FIGURE 3-14. A Custom Library

Putting Objects into a Library

To put an object into a library, open (or create) the library that will receive it; select the object in a ClarisWorks document, and drag it into the library. It will be given a default name.

You can (and should) give it a meaningful name. To rename an object in a library, select it in the library window, type a new name at the bottom of the library window, and then click Rename. (The triangle at the bottom left of the window lets you show or hide the naming fields; if they are not visible—as is the case in Figure 3-13—click the triangle to show them as in Figure 3-14.)

Style Sheets

In ClarisWorks it is possible to create style sheets—collections of font, size, color, and style attributes that can be used together. Thus, you can create a style called "emphasis" that made selected text bold and italicized—before style sheets you had to issue two separate commands.

Creating or Modifying a Style

Selecting the attributes of a style (font, size, color, etc.) is exactly the same as selecting the attributes for text in a word processing document, a spreadsheet, a database layout, or a graphics document. The sole difference is that instead of selecting the text that you want to modify, you select the style that you want to modify.

You start by showing the Stylesheet window if it is not already shown; to do this, choose Show Stylesheets from the Window menu while any ClarisWorks document is open. Figure 3-15 shows the Stylesheet window.

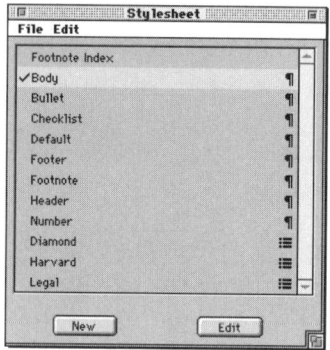

FIGURE 3-15. Stylesheet Window

If you want to create a new style, click the New button at the bottom; if you want to modify an existing style, select the style you want to modify and then click the Edit button.

If you create a new style, the New Style window shown in Figure 3-16 is shown.

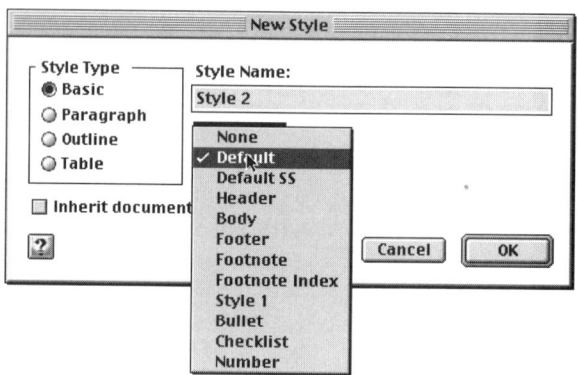

FIGURE 3-16. New Style Window

You can name the style (Emphasis, Confidential, or whatever is appropriate) and select a style on which it is based. In that way, if you want Emphasis to be the same as your basic Body style but with italics added, you do not have to repeat all the specifications for Body. Furthermore, if you change your default font in Body, that change will ripple through the Emphasis style.

You can further specify whether the style is to be basic (applicable to characters) or paragraph (applicable to paragraphs, not words or characters within them). Outline and table styles let you specify more advanced style options. (See the online help for examples.)

The Edit Style window opens next if you have created a new style; if you are editing an existing style, it opens as soon as you click the Edit button (at the bottom of Figure 3-15). The Edit Style window is shown in Figure 3-17.

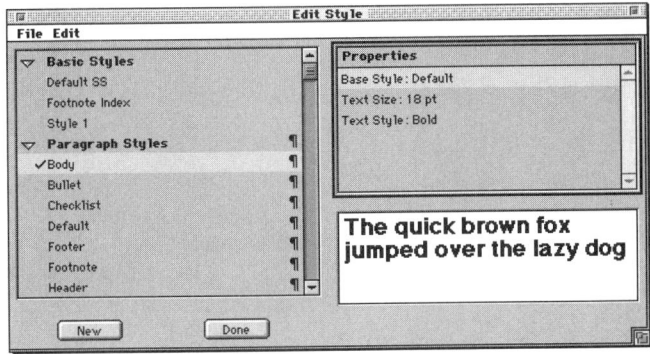

FIGURE 3-17. Edit Style Window

You use the standard editing commands in the menu or in the button bar to choose fonts, colors, etc. The sample text in the lower right of the Edit Style window reflects your current choices.

When you have finished, the style is available in the Style pop-up menu of the button bar, as shown in Figure 3-18.

Note that the Stylesheet window includes its own menus (File and Edit). You can import and export styles, copy them, and otherwise manipulate them within that window.

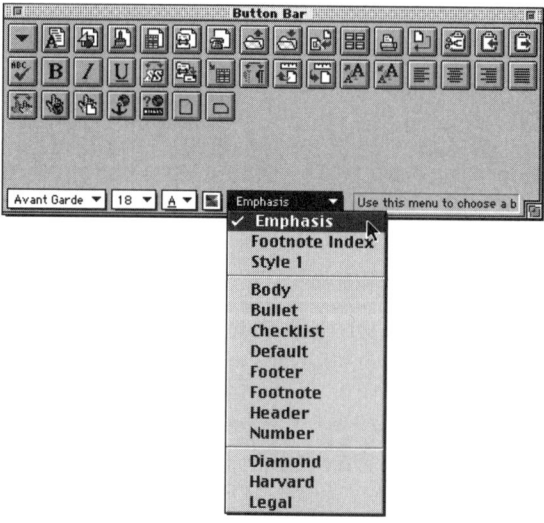

FIGURE 3-18. Styles in the Button Bar

What It Means to You

This does not just save you a few keystrokes: it allows you to think at a more sophisticated level ("emphasis" rather than "bold and italic"). Moreover, should you decide to change the representation of emphasized text (as you well might do in moving your document to the Internet, to a slide presentation, or to other media) the task is made much easier.

Increasingly, ClarisWorks lets you deal with high-level concepts rather than the nitty-gritty. To everyone who is trying to get a job done, that should be a welcome relief.

Equation Editing

Equation editing is a new feature in ClarisWorks 5.0; if you need it, you really need it, and you will jump for joy. If you don't need it, don't worry about it.

The problem it solves is that character-based typewriters and word processors have a great deal of difficulty with the mathematical symbols and special spacing of equations. With ClarisWorks 5.0, when you want to create an equation, you choose Insert Equation... from the Edit menu. ClarisWorks opens a special equation editing window that lets you construct the equation using whatever symbols and spacing you want. When you close the window, that equation is placed in your document (which can be a word processing, spreadsheet, or graphics document).

Summary

As you use ClarisWorks, you will find yourself using different tools to accomplish similar tasks. This is natural and reflects the way people normally function. Beware of people who tell you there is only one way to do something: having a multitude of options available is what lets you function in your way rather than molding yourself to the computer.

4

Beyond the Desktop: The Internet and Shared Information

With documents encompassing far more than static, two-dimensional images that can be fully realized on paper, it becomes necessary to be able to store, transmit, and view them on the computer monitors where their full capabilities can unfold. It is through networks of various sorts—ranging from shared diskettes, to infrared wireless, to local cables and the global Internet—that this can take place.

The network of networks (literally) is the Internet. This chapter is an introduction to the Internet as well as a guide to the networking that you may have in your office, home, or school.

This chapter provides an overview of the Internet and its services as well as a guide to networking on the Mac OS.

The Internet

The Internet is a network of networks; it was designed with many goals in mind, but the most important was the ability to connect disparate computers with their own specialized data communications formats so that they could communicate among themselves, regardless of how they handled data within their own networks.

The Internet has succeeded at the task. The advantage of having common ways to send and receive messages (**"protocols"**) are many and varied, and not least of these is the ability to use standard hardware and software for communications. Before the widespread adoption of the Internet, different types of networks were used to link computers together either at single sites or with private communications networks. Each network had its own idiosyncrasies that depended on the particular types of hardware involved and the software that was used to run the network.

Design and History of the Internet

In the 1960s the Defense Advanced Research Projects Agency (DARPA) funded a project whose primary objective was to allow scientists and laboratories and universities to share the very expensive computers that were installed in relatively few places in the country. (It is a sidelight to the story that these rare, expensive computers were far less powerful than what is sitting on your desk—or in your lap—today.) The mission was to allow people not just to run programs on their own computer but to run and control programs on computers that were far away. A secondary part of the mission was to allow people to transfer data between and among computers on this network. A paramount consideration in those days of the Cold War was that whatever solution was proposed had to be immune to a nuclear attack. In practical terms, this meant that the network that was developed had to be decentralized: there could be no "Internet-central" that would be vulnerable to those pesky ICBMs.

ARPANET (the Advanced Research Projects Agency Network) went online in 1969; it was replaced with the more robust Internet two decades later, and there has been no turning back. While sharing computer power has been of relatively little significance to most Internet users (since today's desktop computers are each at least as powerful as the initial four computers on ARPANET combined), the use of the Internet for communication has proved to be a major boon to most computer users.

Internet Layers

For most people, the key to the Internet is its concept of layered communication. Although today's Internet standard (TCP/IP) is only a little more than a decade old, the principle has been around from the start. The idea is that when a computer is connected to the Internet, there are programs and protocols that govern how data is transferred between that computer and the rest of the network. Those standards are independent of the data and the use to which it is put.

Packets and Multithreaded Communications

Thus, you connect your computer to the Internet and once that connection is verified, you can partake of any Internet services from e-mail to the World Wide Web to more specialized services. Furthermore, the nature of the basic connection to the Internet is such that communications are converted into small **packets** of information.

This is significant to you because since each communication between your computer and the Internet is split up into many packets that are disassembled and reassembled at each end of the connection, you can conduct a number of different operations on the Internet at any one time. You can send e-mail, browse the Web, and modify your own Web site all at the same time: each specific operation will involve its own communications and each message will be split into packets. The Internet and your computer will disassemble, assemble, and rearrange the packets into the appropriate messages as needed. In this way, your communications with the Internet are considered to be **multithreaded communications**.

Supporting Internet Protocols on the Mac OS

Because of the nature of Internet communications, you need to establish a communications link between your computer and the Internet; this link will be available to any Internet-savvy application that needs it. This is in contrast to the "olden days" when each program that needed network services created its own link. For example, in those days you could run a CompuServe program or an America Online program or a proprietary banking program to connect to the appropriate services. With the Internet, you run the basic connectivity software and each application (including modern versions of CompuServe, America Online, and proprietary banking programs) can establish its own thread.

Depending on whether you are connecting to the Internet directly or through a local network, you use different settings. For now, simply take on faith that you can establish a connection to the Internet that is available to any application that wants it. That connection is a **TCP/IP connection**. With your TCP/IP connection, you can use Internet services such as e-mail, the World Wide Web, and File Transfer Protocol (FTP).

Basic Connectivity to the Internet

For many people, access to the Internet is provided by an Internet access provider—sometimes a national organization such as AT&T's WorldNet or America Online and sometimes a local organization such as a subsidiary of a telephone or cable company or a company organized specifically to provide Internet access to a community.

Many companies and organizations have their own direct Internet access (schools, public institutions, and many commercial organizations are in this category). Regardless of how you access the Internet, your access provider will provide you with information on establishing the physical connection (i.e., the phone number if you have to dial in) as well as on the passwords and codes you need to connect.

Your Internet access provider will require you to log on with your own password and ID. You may need additional passwords to access private sites on the Internet; furthermore, if you use e-mail, you may have another password and ID for your e-mail account. (In practice, this is far less cumbersome than it appears—you usually type in your password and ID once and let the software preserve them for you.)

Internet access providers do just that—they provide people with access to the Internet. Once you are connected to the Internet, you can avail yourself of services that are available there. Internet service providers are companies that provide such services—e-mail, storing World Wide Web sites, etc. Many companies provide "one-stop shopping"—access and service with the same account. Some people find their needs are best served by using separate companies for access and for service. For this reason, it is best to differentiate between Internet access providers and Internet service providers. This distinction has been noted only in the past year or so (commercial Internet access/service being a very new industry), so you may find references to Internet service providers (the earlier term) that, strictly speaking, refer only to access providers.

E-mail

E-mail was not part of the original Internet specification, but as soon as the infrastructure of the ARPANET was in place, the scientists who had access to the network developed a way of sending messages back and forth, and the genie was out of the bottle.

People like to communicate with one another and they readily adopt technologies that facilitate that goal. The Internet is a very efficient way to communicate.

By contrast, the telephone is a very inefficient way to communicate. It requires that the parties involved be present at the same time, no matter if they are in different time zones. If the conversation involves more than two people, the difficulties of assembling the parties can be gruesome. When the topic of the conversation is a discussion of serious matters all this is worthwhile; when it concerns the date and time for a lunch date, it is bizarre.

Internet e-mail messages have four primary components:

1. The recipient's address,

2. The sender's return address,

3. The subject of the message,

4. The body of the message, and

5. (Optionally) an enclosure consisting of one or more files.

E-mail Addresses

E-mail addresses consist of an individual's mail name and the address at which that name can be found. The format is "anni@philmontmill.com" where "anni" is the mail name and "philmontmill.com" is the domain name. The domain name identifies a particular site on the Internet; these sites are divided into various categories, which are indicated by the last three characters. Thus, commercial enterprises end in .com, educational institutions end in .edu, nonprofit organizations end in .org, networks end in .net, and governmental entities end in .gov.

That is the case inside the United States. In other countries, the last two characters of the domain indicate the country (as in Canada—.ca, Australia—.au, France—.fr, etc.). Domain names are requested from the national organizations that manage the individual countries' Internet addresses (InterNIC in the United States). Once a domain has been created, the manager of that domain can assign addresses within it (such as "anni" in the example above).

If you connect to the Internet through an access provider, it will provide you with an address. For subscribers to AT&T's WorldNet service, that address might be someone@worldnet.com; to a subscriber of a local access provider such as Taconic Technology's TNet service, that address might be someone-else@taconic.net.

According to Internet standards, capitalization matters—someone@worldnet.com is a different address from SomeOne@worldnet.com. Many access providers interpret the standards loosely so that capitalization is ignored.

The structure of the Internet is such that it is not necessary to connect directly to a remote computer in order to send a message to it. The domains (such as worldnet.com) are identified throughout the network and each computer connected to the Internet is capable of forwarding messages on to other computers. The result is that you can send a message to any Internet address simply by sending it to a single Internet computer (typically your Internet connection computer). From there, the message will be passed remarkably quickly from one computer to another until it lands at the appropriate destination.

E-mail Messages

Although it is not required that each e-mail message have a subject, most e-mail software requires you to enter something in this field. This enables people to screen and prioritize their messages; it is common sense and good manners.

But the heart of e-mail is the content of the message itself. Originally, messages consisted only of text—and text typed in capital letters only. Today, such messages are rare anachronisms.

Each message can have an attachment—a computer file that can be in any format that both sender and recipient can understand. You can enclose a ClarisWorks document in an e-mail message and send it to a colleague who also has the ClarisWorks application program. In this way you can collaborate on the development of a document.

This mechanism—text for messages, any mutually agreed on format for enclosures—is quite serviceable but a little clunky. An Internet standard has been developed that allows the inclusion of certain standard data types within messages themselves. If you have e-mail software that adheres to this standard, you can send text that contains pictures, formatted text, and video. In addition to this, you can send enclosures in any format that both you and your recipient agree on.

World Wide Web

The World Wide Web was first proposed in 1990; within a few years it proved the validity of its premise—that a web of connections could quickly span the globe. The Web consists of Internet locations known variously as **sites**, **pages**, and **home pages**.

You explore the World Wide Web using a **browser**. This may be a stand-alone application (such as Netscape Navigator, Microsoft Internet Explorer, or the Cyberdog application).

World Wide Web Addresses

Each Web location has its own address, which is based on a domain name (often the same domain name as in an e-mail address). Thus, AT&T's WorldNet service has a Web address of www.worldnet.com. Internet addresses can identify different types of sites, and the full address for World Wide

Web sites is of the form http://www.worldnet.com—which is the type of address that you have probably seen on the sides of buses and in newspaper ads. The prefix (**scheme**) stands for "Hypertext Transfer Protocol" and serves to differentiate Web addresses from those used for other protocols (such as File Transfer Protocol—discussed in the next section).

When you connect to a Web site, your computer downloads a file from the remote computer, and the browsing software that you use formats that file into the pictures, graphics, and other elements that you see on a typical Web page. Figure 4-1 shows the Claris Web page—http://www.claris.com.

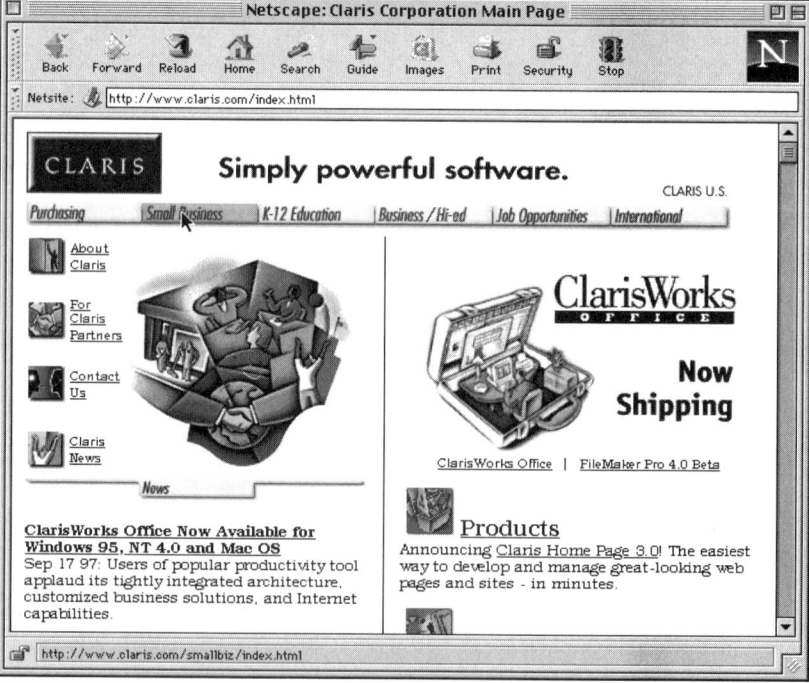

FIGURE 4-1. Claris Web Site—http://www.claris.com

> *Note that as you move the mouse over different parts of the page, they may change color; at the bottom of the browser, you may see changing text indicating the links to which you would go if you clicked in that particular location. In Figure 4-1, when the mouse is over the Small Business tab (as shown), it is highlighted; at the bottom of the browser you can see that a click at that location would take you to Claris's site for small business—http://www.claris.com/smallbiz/index.html.*

Browsing the Web

It is remarkably easy to find your way around the Web. Anything that is underlined is hot—you can click on it and go to another location that contains more or related information on that point. From there, you can click on other links to continue wandering through the Web.

At any point, if you do not like where you have gone, you can return from whence you came. In the browser, you can click on an arrow to go back one step; you also have a log of where you have been so that you can go back several steps.

Often graphics on a Web page will be hot—you can click on them as well as on underlined text. On a well-designed page, it is clear what is hot. If you are not certain, move the mouse over an area that you suspect may be hot. The Location Under Mouse text at the bottom of the browser will show you the destination that link points to. If the Location Under Mouse text is blank you know that there is no link. (And if you have to do this, you know that you have encountered a page that is not well designed.)

Sites, Pages, and Home Pages

Although many people use the terms interchangeably, there is a difference between Web sites, pages, and home pages. Strictly speaking, a Web site is a location maintained by an individual or organization. It may be http://www.claris.com (the Claris site) or http://www.apple.com (the Apple site).

When you connect to a Web site, your browser actually connects to a directory (or folder, in Mac OS, Windows 95, and Windows NT terms) on the remote computer, and it downloads a specific page that has the filename index.html. You almost never need to know this—your browser and the remote computer take care of this step. The file index.html at the Web site is the **home page** for that site—a location from which you can navigate to the other parts of the site. Each part of the site is a separate file, and each part is called a **page** (thus the home page points to other pages on the site). Each page's file has its own name, which is used to establish the link from one or more pages to that destination. You may move from index.html to another directory/anotherpage.html, but you will never know anything other than that you clicked on a link.

Unless the page is missing. Because the Web is constantly being updated, you may click on a link at a moment when its destination does not exist. Errors on the Web are reported in different ways by different computers, but none should cause fatal problems on your end. If you do get a message that says "File Not Found," just click on the back arrow and navigate to somewhere else.

This is all quite simple: do not make too much of it. The essence of the Web is organization and user control. Users do not have to enter a site through the home page—they can jump into any location for which they have the address. The best-designed sites do not insist on your visiting them in a particular order. If the Web were more authoritarian, it would never have become so popular.

Why the Web Matters

The Web is very easy to use and basically very easy to create. From a user's point of view it is a matter of looking at the screen (possibly scrolling a window up or down), clicking on links, and then clicking a back arrow if necessary.

From the point of view of the Web author, it is a matter of putting information into files and associating the appropriate links with them. While it requires judgment, experience, and skill to do this well, even relatively modest efforts at Web authoring can be successful. (The reason for this is that the user's investment of effort is so low; even if there are half a dozen extra mouse clicks en route to the desired information, that is not a catastrophe.)

Even the first step to Web publication turns out to be quite simple. All material to be put on the Web must be digitized. In this era of word processors, almost all printed materials (including illustrations) are digital at some point in their lives.

With the Web, there is a medium that can present information easily at the demand of literally millions of users. *And most important, the design of the Web is such that the users (not the content providers) retain control at all times.* That is primarily what accounts for its popularity.

Contrast the Web with the uniformly loathed voice mail systems. Both are quite similar in that you make incremental choices as you wander through a labyrinth of information.

The chief differences, however, are that with the Web you can interrupt your choices whenever you want (and resume your quest at your location), and with the Web your destination is not a live individual (who may be at lunch) but a body of information that is almost always available. The combination of user control and a much higher probability of success than with voice mail is important to remember if you consider designing your own Web site.

File Transfer Protocol (FTP)

Each Web page consists of a file (possibly several). While your browser is responsible for managing the download and interpretation of these files, the manager of a Web site is responsible not only for creating these files but also for uploading them to the appropriate computer. The **File Transfer Protocol** (FTP) is one of the original parts of the Internet specification. It allows you to look at a directory of files on a remote computer as if it were on a local hard disk. You can move files to or from the remote computer almost as easily as moving them from one directory to another on your own disk.

Internet, Intranets, LANs, and Shared Information

All networking in the contemporary world of computing adheres to a common model. It consists of layers of functionality that are as independent of one another as possible. The most basic layer—the **physical layer**—provides the mechanical and electrical connectivity. The highest layer—the **application layer**—is the layer you usually think about when you think telecommunications. It is the layer at which applications talk back and forth to one another. In between these layers are other layers (data link, network, transport, session, and presentation), each of which plays a role in sending and receiving messages.

Although this layered structure is pervasive in contemporary computing, not all computer networks adhere to it—for the simple reason that there are many networks based on older designs that are still in service. In particular, some organizations established private networks connecting computers and terminals long before this structure came into widespread use. You will find such networks—often with dumb terminals that cannot even represent graphics—in many places. The costs of these networks in terms of private leased lines, maintenance on outmoded equipment, and training for staff are very high; conversions to standard network protocols (and in particular to the Internet) typically pay for themselves in a brief period of time.

There are a usually a number of choices at each layer. For example, the physical layer may be implemented with common telephone wire (twisted pair) or with common Ethernet cables. Sometimes choices made at one layer determine choices made at another; where possible, designers of networks try to minimize these dependencies.

LANs

Local area networks (LANs) are usually located within a single office or building, LANs are used to tie together a relatively few computers and shared resources (such as printers) within a limited area. In the world of the Mac OS, LANs are much less complicated than they are in other worlds. Since 1987, all Macintosh and Mac OS computers have been shipped with networking capabilities built in. Typically, in order to create a LAN in a Mac OS world you need to buy a few cables and plug them in. (More extensive cabling is necessary when the LAN extends through walls and through floors and ceilings, but the principle remains the same.)

Whereas in the non-Mac OS world a lot of LAN software must be bought, in the Mac OS world the LAN software is part of the operating system. The Chooser allows you to select a printer on the network to use for your print jobs; the File Sharing control panel lets you control whether or not people can connect to your computer over the network; the Users & Groups control panel lets you narrow that control to specific individuals or groups. This is "network administration" on the Mac OS.

For LANs larger than a few machines, one computer may be designated to control the network. Instead of allowing individual users to connect to other individual machines as needed, one computer can be designated a server; shared files are placed on the server and the control of the network—through the server's Users & Groups as well as through the Apple Share application—can be placed in the centralized hands of a network administrator.

Two types of LANs are commonly encountered today in the Mac OS: those based on the original AppleTalk network and those based on the industry-standard Ethernet.

WANs

When a LAN must extend beyond the bounds of a single office or building—when telephone lines linking sites must be used, it can be called a WAN (wide area network). WANs are intrinsically more complicated than LANs, and they are losing popularity for that reason. WANs are being replaced by intranets and the Internet.

Intranets

The standard protocols of the Internet are so well supported by hardware and software that organizations find they can save enormous amounts of money and effort by standardizing on the Internet standards. It is possible to use the Internet standards on a private network as well as on the public Internet; such a network is called an **intranet**.

The point of an intranet is that it uses the common standards but it is not accessible by the general public. In the most extreme case, an intranet can have no connection whatsoever to the public Internet—there is no physical way that messages of any sort could come in or go out. Such intranets are relatively rare. Most commonly, the links between the private intranet and the public Internet are managed by special hardware and software called **firewalls**. Firewalls can be configured to allow only certain types of messages in and out.

With the improvement of security and firewalls, organizations are finding that they can satisfy their security requirements with passwords, encryption, and authentication mechanisms. Thus, they can create private areas on the public Internet. The distinction between a private area on the public Internet and a totally private intranet is small for all practical purposes.

Shared Information

The specifics of configuring your computer for networks are provided in Part II of this book. At the conceptual level, however, what matters are the implications of sharing information. A document is a snapshot of a specific combination of information at a given point in time. With hypertext links to URLs, a document can contain links to other documents, it can contain links to FTP directories that have files being added and removed from them, and it can have remote Web pages shown in them. Two people viewing the document at two different moments—or on two different computers—are likely to see very different things. The metaphor of the static piece of paper is replaced by the reality of ever-changing experience.

Some people throw up their hands and deal with the issue by refusing to use any dynamic links; their documents contain only unchanging content that cannot be affected by the vagaries of networks and the Internet. In some cases this is an absolutely correct approach—who would want an invoice that did not stay constant during the billing and paying process?

Managing shared information is not terribly difficult if you start from the premise that everything changes and that you must adapt to the constant of change. Any other strategy is like putting your finger in a dike—the next leak is just a moment away.

Recognizing that information can change constantly requires that you look at your documents and their constituent parts and determine what can change and what cannot; of the things that can change, identify those over which you have control and those which you do not. Then plot your course accordingly.

For example, if you are in charge of a human relations department, it may be your lot to provide employees with information on completing a W-4 form to provide information on withholding exemptions for payroll taxes. Whether you provide this information on a Web page, in an e-mail message to new employees, or in a document on a shared file server, it probably contains the following information:

- What a W-4 form is, why it is needed, and when it needs to be completed. (This can be considered as unchanging information over which you have no control.)

- Tax tables for computing tax liability. (This is changing information over which you have no control—it is determined by the Internal Revenue Service.)

- What the form looks like. (Again, this is changing information you do not control.)

- Where to obtain completed forms and where to turn them in. (This is changing information that you do control—it varies from organization to organization, and in most organizations a certain degree of internal office movement is constant.)

Based on this analysis, it is not hard to see that the document you construct should have some explanatory information, a link to the IRS Web site where tax tables and the current form are available, and a link to an easily modifiable file that tells employees where to obtain and submit forms.

Planning for a shared environment really means little more than planning ahead. If you provided a reproduction of the tax tables or the W-4 form itself in your document (rather than providing links to the IRS), you would have to modify your document each year. Similarly, keeping the corporate information about where to obtain and submit the forms in a separate file means that that information can be updated quickly and easily without any chance of inadvertently damaging the rest of the information.

Summary

If any message should emerge here it is that this new world is lively and exciting—and ultimately simple in each of its components. The complexity of a document that combines e-mail, video, and the World Wide Web cannot be denied, but each component is simple, and that is what makes these new technologies so powerful.

Remember the Web mantra—look at it, click if it is underlined, and go back when you are done. And look at who is surfing the Web—schoolchildren, grandparents, office workers, and artists. They are not doing it for show. If you have not joined the Internet revolution yet, ClarisWorks can be your gateway. And if you have, you can use ClarisWorks to integrate this technology more productively with the rest of your activities.

Part II
Using ClarisWorks and the New Technologies

Back to Paper

Notwithstanding the virtues and advantages of digital and electronic media, there are times when you need to produce paper output. While printing from a computer is a fairly old and basic technology, there are some new wrinkles (color, for one) that are worth thinking about.

Most important of all is deciding how you want to format your document:

- Is it to be produced primarily on paper?

- Is it to be an electronic document with a secondary version on paper?

- Is it necessary that it be equally usable on a computer screen and on paper?

If the document is to be equally at home on paper and on the computer screen (or if it is to be used primarily on paper), you seriously need to reconsider whether video and three-dimensional images belong in it. (Color, in fact, may be problematic.)

Whatever your output medium, ClarisWorks can help you get the most out of it. Here are a few tips.[1]

Desktop Printers

The most common output device for hard copy is a desktop printer. Here is an overview of the kinds of printers in use today and some of their features.

Kinds of Printers

Desktop printers come in several varieties these days:

- **Laser printers** are generally the fastest and most heavy-duty printers; they are also the most expensive. They produce output by fusing small granules of dust-like toner onto paper; this process requires high heat for the imaging to occur. Fortunately, the heat is limited to a very small part of the laser printer; laser printers do not give off much more heat than photo-

---

1. This chapter has benefited from major contributions by Joseph Roberts, Chair, Department of Communications Design, Pratt Institute.

copy machines (which use a very similar process). Laser printers produce the sharpest type; picture quality is often not quite so good as that of color ink jet printers.

- **Ink jet printers** spray tiny bubbles of ink onto paper to produce their images. Heat is not involved. Ink jet printers are slower and less expensive than laser printers; their quality can be very high, although high-end laser printers are usually of higher quality than high-end ink jet printers for text.

- Dot matrix printers rely on the same mechanical process as typewriters: an impression is made on an inked ribbon, and the places where the ribbon has been hit transfer ink to the paper. Dot matrix printers produce the poorest quality; they are not often used today except for special purposes. Because they rely on a mechanical impression, they can produce multi-part forms (such as bills). In addition, because the paper is often fed through the printer using a tractor feed (those little perforated holes on each side of "computer paper"), dot matrix printers can handle heavier paper than other printers. They are not suitable for pictures.

- **Thermal wax printers** are similar to ink jet printers, but they use hot wax (rather than liquid ink) to transfer color to the paper.

- **Dye sublimation printers** use special paper and produce high-quality photographic images.

Choose your printer based on the type of work that you normally do; service bureaus can print special jobs for you. If you are not in an area where a service bureau is available, check the ads in the back of a computer magazine; a number of reliable service bureaus will process output quickly for you if you send it to them via overnight courier service.

Features of Printers

Printers may have microprocessors, memory, and disk drives of their own. With these devices, they can store fonts and output for processing. If a printer has memory (or disk), you can send a print command to it and it will store the data until it is ready to print. This can significantly speed up your work, because the transfer of data to the printer is much faster than its actually processing of the print job.

Networked Printers

If a printer has a microprocessor, it can be attached to a network rather than being attached to an individual computer. In such cases, the printer can be used by a number of people. Laser printers often are sharable in this way. Low-end laser printers cannot be networked on their own—they must be attached to a computer. (These printers often have the word "Personal" in their name.)

Non-Networked Printers

Printers that are attached to individual computers may be able to be networked and shared with other people on the network, but they use the processing and networking capabilities of the computer to which they are attached. As a result, if someone prints to a printer that is attached directly to your computer, you may suddenly notice a lack of responsiveness as the computer handles the printing request.

Print Spooling

Because print jobs can be sent to a printer in a fraction of the time that it will take the printer to actually process the job, spooling of printing is implemented in printers and in operating systems. When ClarisWorks (or any other program) prints something, it creates a print job and sends it to be printed. Either (or both) of two spooling mechanisms then comes into play:

1. The operating system may queue up the print job for the designated printer. Once the job has been accepted, the program believes that it has been printed. It is up to the operating system to do the work.

2. The operating system then sends each job in turn to the printer. If the printer has its own storage, it, too, may implement spooling. Once the printer has accepted the entire print job, the operating system (and its spooling software) believes that the job has been printed.

On Mac OS, print spooling is implemented with the menu shown in Figure 5-1 and the window shown in Figure 5-2. The Printing menu is added to the menu bar whenever you select a desktop printer (a printer icon on the desktop that is created automatically by the system when you choose to use a printer).

FIGURE 5-1. Printing Menu (Mac OS)

If something is going wrong with your printer, the best thing to do is to stop the print queue. Do this by clicking once on the desktop printer icon and then choose Stop Print Queue from the Printing menu. This will give you a chance to troubleshoot and solve the problems. Note that while the print queue is stopped, you (and others) can still send print jobs to it: they will be queued up until the print queue is started again.

When you stop a print queue, the printer does not stop immediately. Since it may have one or more pages in its memory, it will continue processing until its current work is done.

Figure 5-2 shows the Print Spooling Window on Mac OS (it is similar on Windows).

FIGURE 5-2. Print Spooling Window (Mac OS)

You can select print jobs by clicking on them; you can then use the four icons at the top left of the window to hold them, print them, set a time or priority for printing them, or remove them from the print queue.

By stopping the print queue and manipulating the jobs in the queue, you can control what happens—and avoid reprinting jobs that may be innocent bystanders to problems.

Paper

Your printer's instruction manual provides details on the kinds of paper that it can handle. For special purposes, office supply stores stock papers designed particularly for ink jet or laser printers. For most purposes, though, common photocopy paper provides satisfactory results.

Preprinted Forms, Labels, and Papers

You will find an ever-increasing variety of forms, labels, and papers designed for use with computers. Even if you have only a black-and-white printer, you can find paper with colored backgrounds (solids or patterns) that you can combine with text and black-and-white images to create your own letterhead. Matching paper for postcards, business cards, and envelopes is also available.

Standard peel-off labels for mailing, labeling of folders, and "Hi, my name is…" are also available. If you have an office supply superstore near you, you can browse to your heart's content; if you do not, most stationery stores have catalogs that you can examine in the store. Common sizes of stationery and labels are supported in ClarisWorks.

Note that ClarisWorks has two Assistants that can help you with mailings: one Assistant prints an envelope; another prints business reply envelopes. In either case, you can use plain white envelopes or envelopes partially printed with colored backgrounds and graphics.

Handling Paper

Paper is identified by size, color, weight, and brightness. Size is the simplest measurement of all—it is the actual dimensions of the page (as opposed to other commodities such as lumber, which are "milled" to sizes other than their purported ones).

Color is—as always—a subjective perception. Although there are common colors of paper (white, gray, goldenrod, blue, etc.), one man's goldenrod is another man's canary.

Paper Weights

When you are buying paper for use with your computer, it is often satisfactory to buy the least expensive paper at a stationery or office supply store. However, if you have a special project or just want to understand what the label on a package of paper means, here is a summary.

Paper comes in offset text, bond, and cover weights. The weight is sometimes referred to as basis or substance (or some combination thereof). Essentially, paper weight can be thought of as thickness.

Cover papers are the heaviest; many of them will not go through a printer. If they do, they may jam or even cause damage to the rollers by pushing them out of calibration.

Before you use heavy cover stock, consult your printer's manual. (Sometimes cover stock can be used on your printer's manual feed setting if it cannot be fed automatically.)

Bond paper has a smooth finish as opposed to the slightly rougher finish of offset text paper.

The weights of different kinds of paper are not the same. For bond paper, 24 pound (24#) bond is thicker than 16 pound (16#) bond. However, 60 pound offset text is approximately the same as 24 pound bond.

Since you are often paying more for heavier weight paper, remember this in comparing prices.

Preserving Paper

Paper is a surprisingly fragile medium: it fades and oxidizes. If you need to produce archival quality output (that is, paper output that must last for a long period of time), you should look for acid-free or archival paper. Technically, archival paper has a neutral pH balance, both acid and alkaline free. This means that it neither oxidizes nor deteriorates.

Paper today is made from a combination of fabric (often cotton, sometimes linen), wood pulp, various forms of recycled waste, and filler. The highest quality paper is considered to have a high cotton content; this paper also is the longest lasting. (100% cotton paper is preferred for handwritten social notes.) Most computer printers work best with lower quality paper: the fabric content of high-quality paper absorbs ink quickly and may not give a crisp result. Do not waste expensive social stationery trying to run it through your computer printer: it is a waste of time, ink, and paper.

> *"A long period of time" in the previous paragraph does not mean centuries. The quality of paper can deteriorate very rapidly. As an experiment, leave a newspaper on a windowsill for a day or two and then compare the color and texture of the paper with those of a new newspaper from the same publisher. You will be astounded at the difference.*

Humidity

Paper absorbs water and is highly susceptible to changes in humidity. Within the vast middle range of temperature and humidity, paper, ink, and printers function without problems. You may encounter difficulties at extremes of humidity.

When the humidity is very low (as, for example, it can be in the winter in northern North America), laser toner may not adhere properly to the paper. You may find that the images look good at first, but after handling the paper, you may notice that some of the toner comes off (on the back of other pages or on your hands). If you notice this happening, increase the humidity in the area near the printer. (For most people, this is also beneficial to their sinus membranes.)

With high humidity (as, for example, in North America during the summer), paper can absorb some of the water vapor and become harder to handle. It becomes heavier because of the added water; in addition, as it goes through the high-heat area of a laser printer, the water vapor can evaporate suddenly, curling the paper and jamming the printer. If you encounter printer jams during the summer, try to reduce the moisture in the air.

You can air-condition the area near the printer, but that may not be feasible. Another approach is to keep the paper in an airtight container (such as are made for food storage by Rubbermaid and Tupperware). Start with paper that is as dry as possible, seal it in the container, and take out only as much as you need for each batch of printing. Depending on your environment, you may have no problem, you may need to take out only enough paper for a day's work—or (in a jungle) you may need to take out only enough paper for a few minutes' work.

To dry out paper, take a package of paper to a cool, dry location—such as a movie theater for an hour or two. Far-fetched though it may seem, this does work, provided that you then place the paper in an airtight container. It is also likely that your boss has never heard this particular reason for taking time off and going to the movies.

Other Output Media

In addition to paper, you may have occasion to produce output for other static media. Here are a few tips for using slides, overheads, large formats, and haberdashery.

Slides

Although ClarisWorks provides the ability to present any document as a slide show, that requires you to have a computer and a monitor (usually a projection monitor) available for your presentation. If those resources are not available (or as a backup), you may want to output a document to 35-mm slides for use in a standard slide projector.

Output devices that produce slides directly as if you were printing to paper are called film recorders. If you have such a device, select it as your printer and print as you normally would.

Most people do not have such output devices; if you need to produce slide output, you need to use a service bureau or printing company. You normally provide them with a file that they can print onto slides. You have two routes to take:

1. If they have ClarisWorks, you can give them the ClarisWorks document together with any nonstandard fonts that are used in the document; they can then output the document onto slides. (To be safe, you can provide copies of all of the fonts used in the document, subject to copyright restrictions.) You normally copy the document and the fonts to a removable data cartridge—such as a Zip, Jaz, or Syquest cartridge. Before proceeding, check with them to see what data format they want and what fonts they already have.

2. Alternatively, you can produce a PostScript file, which can be printed on any output device.

In either case, make certain to use Page Setup to select a horizontal layout and a size that is appropriate for slides.

If you are using a service bureau to prepare slides or other forms of output that you normally do not deal with, you may be thrown off by some of the jargon. In particular, you may wonder why they want to rip your output. In the first scenario above—where the output is printed from the ClarisWorks document by actually running ClarisWorks—what happens is that the service bureau selects their high-quality printer or film recorder as an output device and prints to it (just as you would print to your own printer). These high-quality printers have a front-end processor called a rasterized image processor (RIP); the process is called ripping, even though it includes the subsequent step of printing or producing slides.

Overheads

Overhead transparencies can be produced both on ink jet printers and on laser printers; you must purchase overheads that are specially prepared for each type of printer. There is nothing that you need to do other than follow the instructions on the package of the transparencies (they usually need to be fed manually into the printer).

Large-Format Printing

Today, billboards and signs on the sides of trucks and other large objects are usually prepared using large printers that produce multicolor output on special papers. However, the documents that are printed on those large printers can be ClarisWorks documents: all you need is a service bureau that can accept your ClarisWorks document or a PostScript file. The procedures are the same as you use in creating slides (see the previous section).

T-Shirts and Other Haberdashery

There are service bureaus that will print your file on special material and transfer it to T-shirts for you. Many service bureaus will do this—or can arrange to have it done fairly quickly. Who would have thought that you could go into the fashion business with ClarisWorks!

In preparing a graphic for use on T-shirts, remember that you are dealing with a medium that is less responsive to detail than paper: fine lines don't cut the mustard.

Summary

There is a long distance from the original computer printers that used ALL UPPERCASE LETTERS to today's sophisticated printers that use the latest technologies to produce high-quality images on all sorts of materials. Once you have prepared your documents in ClarisWorks, it is easy to print them—on paper, slides, T-shirts, or billboards.

6

Using QuickTime Movies in ClarisWorks Documents

It is very easy to add video to ClarisWorks documents: you just choose Insert... from the file menu, choose a QuickTime movie, and there it is in your document. So simple! So easy!

But why? "Making your documents come alive" is a nice advertising slogan, but is there more to it than that? There are times when video significantly improves your ability to communicate—as well as times when it is inappropriate.

Where do QuickTime movies come from? What are they? This chapter provides a step-by-step guide to getting movies onto your hard disk from devices such as VCRs and camcorders: just follow these steps and it will work. If you want to use video on occasion in your documents, this guide will be sufficient to help you do so.

Finally, you will find a section about QuickTime. If you want to understand what it is all about and some of the things beyond the basics that you can do with QuickTime, this section is for you.

Why Use Video in Your Documents?

There is a convergence of the digital media—which is just a fancy way of saying that once anything is converted to a digital format it can be manipulated just as any other digital document. A disk file that contains a QuickTime movie can be moved, copied, and renamed exactly the same way that a disk file containing a word processing document can.

Software like ClarisWorks can read the digital contents of these different types of files and display them appropriately on the screen or (to a limited extent) on paper. The attractiveness of this digital world is obvious to anyone who has suffered with the incompatible formats of film, slides, and video. In the digital world, still images from movies can be copied to documents, entire sections of video can be embedded in documents, and everything just works.

Most of the time.

The experience is certainly easier for the viewer of the document than for its author. As you look at Web sites you probably encounter sound, video, and many still images. In most cases you rarely notice the fact that you are moving from medium to medium as you click through a Web site.

As an author, however, you still must be quite aware of the distinctions among the media. Preparing graphics—

whether by using draw or paint documents from ClarisWorks or by scanning prepared graphics—is a different process from creating digitized video.

In general, ClarisWorks is the wrong product to use to create a QuickTime movie complete with special effects, crossfades, and so on (although there is no limit to what a determined person can do). ClarisWorks, however, is an excellent product to use to incorporate QuickTime movies into other documents.

Benefits of Video

Adding video to your documents provides a number of benefits:

- Even more than still images, video can identify and clarify objects that you are talking about.

- When a process occurs over time or involves a number of steps, video can make it clearer (for example, the process of changing a toner cartridge in a printer).

- If you are attempting to describe something in which timing or energy matters, video can be invaluable (for example, it is very easy to demonstrate the speed with which an exercise should be done or the relative amount of pressure you should have to exert to open the printer's toner cartridge door).

- Video is unbeatable at showing a person or event that matters (for example, a video clip showing Queen Elizabeth II launching the Royal Web Site).

The last point is quite broad—a person or event "that matters" could be your 2-week-old child (in the proper context) or it could be yourself singing "O Sole Mio" (in the proper context—whatever that might be).

Just as with any other medium—pictures, print, and speech, for example—it is wise to make certain that your audience cares to hear what you want to say.

A variation on this point is when the audience is yourself. You can store QuickTime movies in a ClarisWorks database arranged by any keys of retrieval you choose. There is nothing wrong with collecting things that only you find interesting, as long as you do not inflict them on others.

Disadvantages of Video

The idea of storing all sorts of video clips brings up the most significant problem with video: it tends to require substantial amounts of disk space. A picture may be worth a thousand words, but it may well take up a million words' worth of disk space (somewhat upsetting the equation). Storage space is cheap and getting cheaper over time; even when you are sending video and documents containing video through e-mail and over the Internet, the size of these documents becomes less and less urgent over time. Still, when you consider that a 2-minute video clip can easily approach 30 MB of disk space, the size of movies can be daunting.

Largely for this reason, that is why you often see small video frames with short clips in them—the small frames require significantly less storage space than larger frames or full-screen video, and storage space is also directly related to the length of the video clip. Notwithstanding this, even small frames with short clips can be very effective in adding to your ClarisWorks documents.

QuickTime itself provides built-in compression mechanisms to reduce the size of movies (often quite substantially). The following section describes the process of creating a QuickTime movie and shows you how to experiment with compression.

The other disadvantage of video is precisely the same as its advantages: does it add to your document or distract from it? Whether your document is serious work, frivolous play, or some combination, make certain that video adds to it.

Creating QuickTime Movies

This really is not that hard. Perhaps the most reassuring thought is that you can create a QuickTime movie from a tape on your VCR without having to fix the clock that is blinking 12:00. In fact, on most VCRs, it is easier to create a QuickTime movie than to fix the clock.

What You Need

In order to play movies on your computer you need the QuickTime extension, which is part of the Mac OS and is widely available for Windows as well. In order to create movies on your computer, you need more equipment. Specifically you need:

1. A video source to record from—a television set, a camcorder, or a VCR

2. A digitizing card inside your computer to convert the video image to a digital format that can be stored on disk

3. Digitizing software for the card (this almost always comes with the digitizing card)

4. A dubbing cable to connect the video source to the digitizing card.

Some computers come with digitizing capabilities built into them. Apple's Power Macintosh 8600 model and its predecessors (the 8500 and the AV Power Macintosh and Quadra models) have video digitizing built into them.

The Video Source

You almost always record your video first to tape and then digitize the tape. Nothing prevents you from digitizing directly from a live television broadcast or directly from a camcorder; however, if anything goes wrong with the computer (you run out of disk space, for example), you have lost your input. You will quickly discover that videotape is much cheaper than the disk space required to store a digital version of the video.

Your video source must have output connections for your dubbing cable. The most common connections in the consumer electronics market are composite video (also known as RCA plugs). These come in sets of two or three and are color coded (the colors are fairly consistent across the industry):

- A yellow plug is for the video signal.

- A white plug is for one stereo sound channel.

- A red plug is for the other stereo sound channel.

Devices that have only monaural sound have only a yellow and a white plug (most camcorders fall into this category).

Higher end devices use S-Video connections for the video signal; white and red RCA plugs provide the audio connection. Look at your video source (and consult its instruction manual) to find out the kind of video output that your device has. (Remember that what is input to the computer is output from the video source!)

Not every television set has video output that you can feed into your computer. Just about every VCR and camcorder does have such output.

The Digitizing Card

This card fits into your computer (or has already been installed there); it allows you to digitize video from a video source. Most digitizing cards also work in the other direction—you can send output from your computer through them to standard video devices. For example, you can use a projection television to display a large image of your computer's screen during a presentation.

The digitizing card has two sets of plugs: one is marked In and one is marked Out. The In plugs are where you plug a video source in; the Out plugs are where you would plug a projection television. (And, just as with a video source, if you are using a projection television, the output from your computer is plugged into the projection television's input plug.)

Each set of plugs has an identical set of connections:

- A yellow composite video (RCA plug) connection

- A white RCA plug for one stereo channel
- A red RCA plug for the other stereo channel
- An S-Video connection for S-Video

Not all digitizing cards have both the S-Video and yellow composite video plugs. It is important to check the output on your video device with the input on your digitizing card (particularly if you are buying one or the other). Make certain that they agree on a video connection.

Digitizing Software

This is provided with the digitizing card (or with your computer if the video capabilities are built in). Apple Video Player is a simple product distributed with Apple computers; Strata VideoShop is a more sophisticated product that lets you edit video.

Dubbing Cables

You can probably rely on the fact that the cables do not come with anything. Because it is not clear what other device is being connected to your computer, camcorder, VCR, etc., each vendor lets you choose and buy the appropriate cable. This is one of those "gotchas" that show up on Christmas morning: make sure you have the cables you need.

For the video, you will need either an S-Video cable or a yellow coded cable with an RCA plug, depending on the equipment you have (given a choice, the S-Video produces a higher quality image). The audio connection is made with the appropriate cables. Note that if your camcorder is monaural (many are), you will need a special cable that combines both channels into one for connection to your digitizing card (which is almost always stereo).

When you buy cables, buy the longest ones you can (12 feet is good). Shorter cables are great for permanent installations where you do not want clutter, but if you are using video only on certain occasions, you will be packing up and putting away this whole collection of cables, camcorder/VCR, etc.—and the last thing that you need is the further complication of not having cables that are long enough.

You may find packages of cables that combine some of these features. For example, a single package may have a three-ply white/yellow/red RCA plug set, another package may have a three-to-two set that goes from a stereo device (white/yellow/red) to a monaural device (white/yellow), and yet another may have the audio cables (yellow and red) packaged together. Expect to pay $10 to $15 for your cables—more if you buy individual cables rather than a package. The cables are widely available at consumer electronics stores.

Using a Tripod

Depending on what you are videotaping, a tripod may be helpful or even essential. If you are creating a video of an object or of an operation (such as changing a toner cartridge) or if you are taping an individual speaking directly to the camera, a tripod can make everything much simpler.

The tripod should have a leveling device so that the camera is not only held steady but held parallel with the floor. A satisfactory tripod should be able to be found for $30 to $50 in a camera store. Tripods costing significantly more are also available, but you should be able to do very well with one in this price range. You are concerned primarily with its stability, the ability to adjust it in any direction, and the presence of a level (not all tripods have a level).

> *An additional benefit of a tripod for many people is that you can set it up, turn the camera on, and tape yourself. You can experiment over and over with the process without fraying anyone's temper. Tape, view, digitize, and repeat the process until you feel that you are comfortable with it. Some people learn well in a public, cooperative environment; other learn best by themselves.*

Videotape or Cartridges

If you are digitizing directly from live video input (either broadcast television or directly from a video camera), you do not need any videotape or cartridges. As noted previously, however, most people prefer to record to videotape and to digitize that in a second step.

Accordingly, make certain that you have plenty of tape around. videotape is cheaper than the disk space needed to store its digitized version. Many people find that they digitize and keep only a very small portion of the footage that they tape. (This is common throughout the film and video industries: the ratio of file or tape shot to that used is remarkably high.)

Digitizing the Video

Assuming that you have taped something that you want to digitize, here are the steps you go through to do so.

The basic steps are:

1. Connect the appropriate cables as described in the last section.

2. Using your digitizing software, start to record the movie.

3. Start the playback from the camcorder or VCR.

4. When done, stop recording, stop the playback, and save the movie you have produced.

Connecting the Cables

As noted before, connect all the cables. If you are using RCA composite video plugs, connect the color-coded cables to like color plugs on the camera or VCR and the computer. If you are using S-Video, connect the single S-Video port on the camera or VCR to the single S-Video port on your computer.

Using Your Digitizing Software, Start to Record

This step and the following one should be done in rapid sequence: you want to start recording to the computer and start playing back from the camera or VCR as close to the same moment as possible. If you start to record before you start to play back, you will have a short section of black, silent movie before the playback starts; this is probably safer than missing the first few moments as you would do if you started to play back before you started to record.

Here are examples of the use of two kinds of digitizing software; both ship with Power Macintosh video-ready computers (such as the Power Macintosh 8500 and 8600 lines). You will see that they are quite similar.

APPLE VIDEO PLAYER This software from Apple comes with many Macintosh computers; it is simple to use and will handle many of your routine needs for viewing and recording video.

The application has two windows, which are shown in Figure 6-1. (If the Controls window is not shown, you can open it by choosing the Show Controls Window commands from the Windows menu.) As you see in the illustration, Balloon Help is provided for all of the controls.

Select the appropriate video source—a TV tuner built into your computer, composite video, or S-Video (not all may be available to you). You can adjust brightness, hue, color, etc. if necessary—usually these adjustments need to be made only to your VCR or camera if they need to be made at all. If you click on the video capture button (the camera at the top left of the controls window), you will see the Record button; click it to start recording. Click Stop when you are done.

FIGURE 6-1. Apple Video Player Window

In Figure 6-2 you see the Preferences available to you in the Apple Video Player.

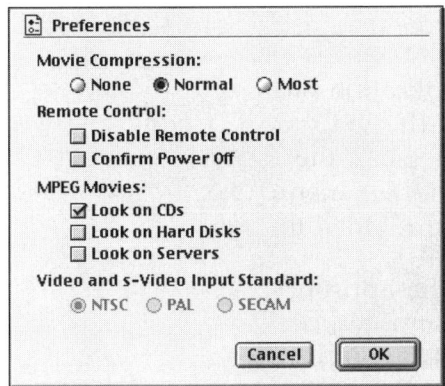

FIGURE 6-2. Apple Video Player Preferences

For your purposes, all that you are concerned about here is the degree of compression that you want. Normally, the more compression, the more the chance of degrading the playback image. It is a simple trade-off of quality against disk space. This is one of the reasons for experimenting with digitizing and redigitizing a tape: you can find out the degree of compression that is right for you.

STRATA VIDEOSHOP This product ships with the digitizing cards built into the Apple Power Macintosh 8600 line of computers. It does much more than the Apple Video Player, but you will see that the controls are quite similar.

You open the Recording window from the Windows menu, as shown in Figure 6-3.

Click the Rec button to start recording; when done, click the same button (the name of which will have changed to Stop). As in the Apple Video Player, you can watch the video in the window as you digitize it. At the top of the window is a small folder icon: you click it to set and reset the folder in which you want to store the digitized movie (in the Apple Video Player you are asked to supply a specific filename when you save the file on completion of digitizing).

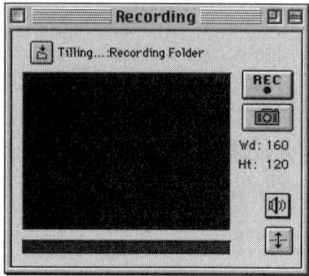

FIGURE 6-3. Strata VideoShop Recording Window

From the menu bar, you can access many more controls for VideoShop in the Recording menu as shown in Figure 6-4. If you choose to look at the Video Settings…, for example, you will find many more compression options than the three simple ones provided in Apple Video Player.

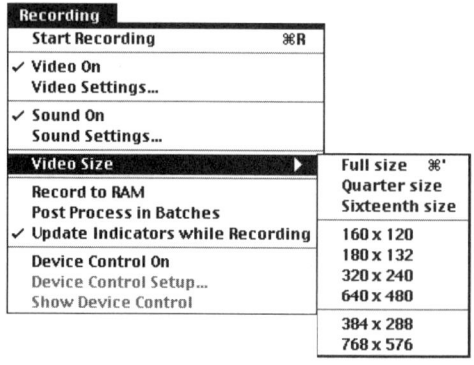

FIGURE 6-4. VideoShop Controls

As you can see, the process is quite straightforward no matter what software you are using.

MANAGING SOUND You may need to adjust the sound controls on your computer using the Monitors & Sound control panel as shown in Figure 6-5.

(Note that on some versions of the Macintosh prior to 7.6 this control panel had a different look to it and was called the Sound control panel.)

What matters here is that the sound input should be shown as coming from the AV Connector rather than from a CD or from the microphone. Even if AV Connector is not one of the choices, make certain that you do not choose microphone or CD—the other alternative will be correct.

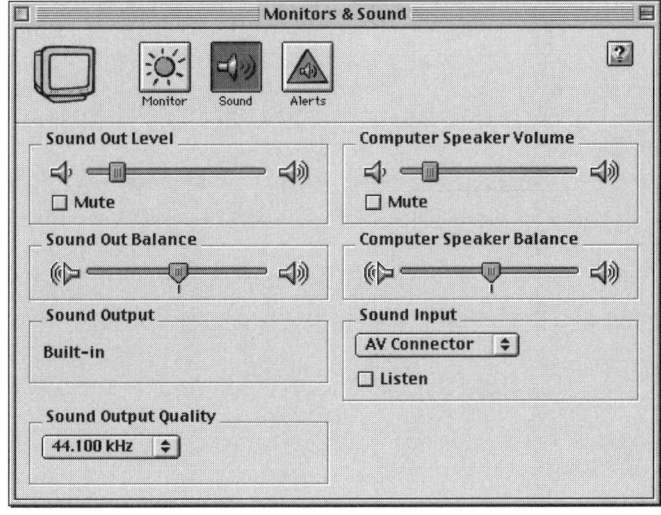

FIGURE 6-5. Monitors & Sound Control Panel

Start the Playback

Next, push the Play button on your VCR or camcorder to play back the tape. What you play back will be digitized. If you are using a live video feed, instead of pushing the Play button, just turn the camera (or television set) on: the sound and images will flow through to be digitized.

Finish Up

When you are done, click the Stop button on the digitizing software or the Stop button on the VCR or camcorder (or just turn them off). Your digitized file will be saved on disk.

Try the process a few times: unless you want to get involved in video editing (which really is not very hard), you will most likely digitize only a small section of your videotape. You will then be able to use that section in a document.

Preparing Movie Files for the Internet

When you save a QuickTime movie, you may want to save it as a cross-platform movie: one that can be played on any of the platforms that support QuickTime. If you do so, you can post the movie on the Internet. The option to save a movie as a cross-platform movie may be in the options or preferences of your digitizing software; if in doubt, consult the manual or online documentation.

If you are working on Mac OS, make certain to prepare the file for Internet use by running it through the Internet Movie Tool. You can get the Internet Movie Tool for free from the Internet at http://quicktime.apple.com. It is a small application (6K) and is downloaded quickly. Once you have prepared your movie, simply drag it onto the Internet Movie Tool application and the file will be modified for Internet use. Alternatively, you can double-click the Internet Movie Tool; from the File menu, use the Open command to Open the QuickTime movie. In a few seconds it will be modified.

If you must know what is happening, Internet Movie Tool removes the resource fork of the Mac OS QuickTime file and consolidates all movie information into the data fork of the movie file.

Review

That is all there is to it. This section has been quite detailed because although the process is quite simple, it involves lots of equipment and enough cables to trip you up (literally). Once you have been through it a few times, you will find that it is really not a problem to create simple digitized video for your documents.

A Look at QuickTime

QuickTime is a very powerful cross-platform software architecture for creating, editing, and publishing digital media. For all practical purposes, two major features stand out (because they affect you):

1. QuickTime specializes in working with time-dependent media—that is, movies (and sound files) that need to be played back at specific speeds.

2. QuickTime provides a layer of abstraction from underlying hardware in a component-oriented way.

Although this is fairly technical, its implications are quite simple.

Time-Dependent Media

QuickTime deals primarily with media that require playback at given speeds without distortion. Because a computer's processor may suddenly be devoted to other tasks while a QuickTime movie is playing, QuickTime assumes that this may occur and contains code that adjusts for that situation. It skips individual frames or groups of frames within a movie so that it gets to the right spot at the right time. Playing a QuickTime movie on a computer that is very busy may produce a jerky playback as it jumps through the movie; however, you will not get the distortions of sound or video that you would get on a tape recorder or other device as power fluctuates.

Because it is capable of keeping track of time, QuickTime easily handles multiple tracks within a given movie. Typically, a movie has two tracks: the video and audio tracks. (Stereo sound is a single audio track, not two.) However, a movie can have any number of tracks that are played back simultaneously. One common track that is often added to audio and video is a text track that displays subtitles. Because QuickTime synchronizes tracks, you can easily control the moments when given text is displayed.

All of this is done in QuickTime editing application programs; examples are Adobe After Effects and Premiere as well as Strata's VideoShop, which was shown previously.

Hardware Abstraction

QuickTime is designed to run on abstract representations of hardware rather than to work directly with specific digitizers and other devices. The practical result of this for you is that movies and other QuickTime features work the same on different types of hardware. In addition, QuickTime does not care too much whether certain functionalities are implemented in hardware or software. QuickTime movies require significant amounts of disk and processor resources; in the old days (a year or two ago), it was necessary to have hardware accelerators to provide really high-powered performance of movies. Now, in a world with faster (and multiple) processors, software can accomplish the same feats—and more.

Because QuickTime does not deal directly with the hardware but only with its abstractions of the hardware, such changes are seamless to the user. From your point of view, it means only that video will be faster, cheaper, and even easier to use tomorrow than it is today.

The QuickTime Media Layer

QuickTime is a part (the main part) of Apple's QuickTime Media Layer—a set of cross-platform, interactive, multimedia technologies. Major other components of the QuickTime Media Layer are QuickDraw 3D, which allows you to create and manipulate three-dimensional images, and QuickTime VR, which allows you to create and manipulate virtual reality landscapes and movies.

The technologies of the QuickTime Media Layer interact with one another: you can create three-dimensional objects using QuickDraw 3D and place them in QuickTime VR landscapes.

Currently, ClarisWorks supports only the QuickTime and QuickTime VR components of the QuickTime Media Layer. But stay tuned....

Summary

ClarisWorks can display QuickTime movies in its various documents and the database. You can use the third-party tools described in this chapter to produce your own QuickTime movies for inclusion in these documents.

Adding movies to documents can make them more persuasive, more understandable, and more entertaining—depending on what your objective may be. If you take an afternoon to experiment with a camcorder, you will quickly master the basic techniques. And you can do an awful lot with those basic techniques!

The addition of video (or sound, for that matter) to a document is a very significant step. It moves that document beyond paper: the full meaning of the document can be found only on the computer monitor. It truly moves you into the twenty-first century.

In the next chapter, ClarisWorks links show you how to extend the flexibility of your documents even further.

7

Making Documents Interactive— Using the Links Palette

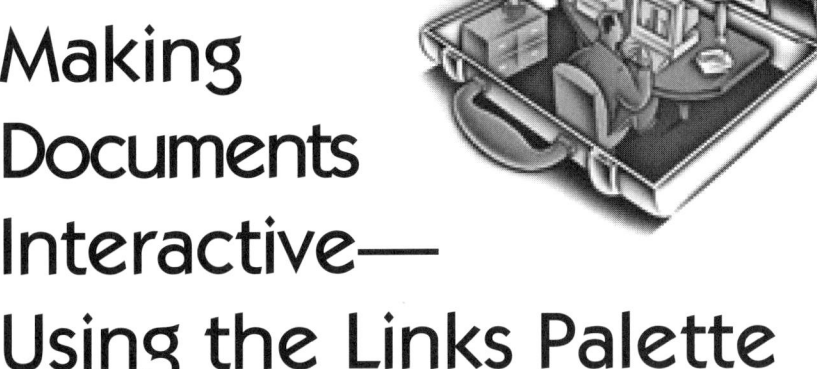

In the previous chapter, you saw how to add video to documents. This can improve the documents by adding to their information, making them more persuasive and interesting, and providing additional tools with which you can communicate to your readers and viewers.

However, as noted in the first part of this book, movies in documents immediately bring you into the world of paperless documents. A document with a movie in it can never be satisfactorily printed on a piece of paper. With video, only a computer screen can provide the full range of information that you have placed in your document.

Links in documents defy paper even more: in some cases, they are barely visible on paper. Whereas you can always print a key frame of a video to provide some indication of what lies beyond the printed page, you cannot always provide even a thumbnail sketch for a link—it may go to a dynamic location.

Far from being hindrances, these are the opportunities that links provide. When you are freed from the tyranny of the fixed-size two-dimensional world of paper, you can start to work in exciting new ways.

This chapter describes the links that are available in ClarisWorks (starting with version 5); it shows you how to create and use them and then ends with a discussion of link design.

ClarisWorks Links

The word hypertext was first used in 1981 to describe the system whereby a user could click on a word or phrase and get further information about it. A footnote, for example, no longer needed to be banished to the bottom of a page or the end of a chapter: a phrase that merited a footnote could be marked in some distinctive way so that the user could know that further information would be available with the click of a mouse.

Clearly this is a computer-based process since clicking on a piece of paper is a rather pointless endeavor. The success of the World Wide Web is due in large measure to this technology: it is a Web because words and phrases within each of its pages are linked to other locations on the Internet. People have grown used to this technology very quickly, and, because it is easy to learn and to describe, it has been adopted rapidly around the world.

Hypertext has been expanded beyond its original implementation so that now people are used to clicking on images and other nontextual objects in order to jump to links elsewhere.

In ClarisWorks 5, you can create links in ClarisWorks documents; these links can jump to other locations within the same document, to locations within other ClarisWorks documents, and to URLs (Uniform Resource Locators—Internet addresses).

Links based from words or phrases look very much like links on Web pages—they are underlined (in blue, if you have a color monitor). Figure 7-1 shows a ClarisWorks document with two links.

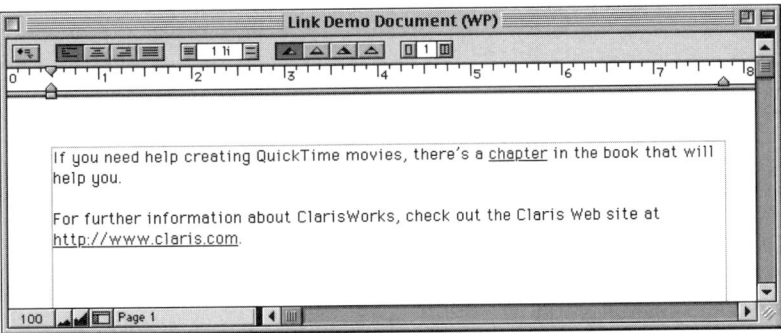

FIGURE 7-1. Link Demo Document

The first link ("chapter") will send you to another text file if you click on it. The second link ("http://www.claris.com") will send you to the Claris home page on the Internet. Note that the second link happens to have the same textual representation as its URL; nothing prevents you from rephrasing that sentence:

```
                  For further information about Claris, check out the
                  Claris Web site.
```

In this formulation (which actually is better), the link from "Web site" to "http://www.claris.com" is set up without burdening the user with actually having to see the address. After all, the point of hypertext links is to make these transitions easier for users.

Creating and Managing Links

You create and manage links in ClarisWorks using the Links palette which is opened from the Windows menu. The Links palette is shown in Figure 7-2.

FIGURE 7-2. Links

Kinds of Links

You can manage three kinds of links with the Links palette. The pop-up menu shown in Figure 7-2 lets you choose which type of link you want to work with:

Book Marks

Book marks are markers of specific places within documents. (In the world of HTML, they would be called anchors.) A book mark can be associated with anything that you can select within a ClarisWorks document: a word, a paragraph, a graphic, a movie, etc. If you can select it, you can bookmark it. Each book mark has a name (which you choose).

Document Links

Document links are links that you create from a word, phrase, or graphic to another location in a document. You create a document link by selecting the object that will respond to a mouse click (the "hot object"), creating a document link, and then choosing the destination of that link—where the mouse click will take the user. The destination can be either a ClarisWorks document as a whole or a book mark within a ClarisWorks document. A document link can point to a book mark within the same document as the hot object.

URL Links

URL links are links to locations on the Internet. You use the same process to create a URL link as you would a document link: you select the object that will be hot, create a new link, name it, and provide the destination. In the case of the URL link, you type in its address.

ABOUT URLs URLs provide a simple way to locate individual files on specific computers on the Internet. They take advantage of the fact that all computer files on all computer systems are arranged in a hierarchical structure of directories and subdirectories (folders and subfolders on Mac OS). As long as each computer has a unique name, its managers can assign names for directories without fear of duplicating other directories elsewhere.

This is analogous to the way in which telephone numbers are provided. A local telephone company is in charge of a specific exchange within an area code (in the United States, area codes are three digits long and so are local exchanges). Thus, for area code 518 and local exchange 392, all telephone numbers are assigned by a single company. If the number 0000 is assigned to that area code and exchange, it becomes the phone number (518)392-0000, which is totally different from (212)392-0000 and from (518)828-0000.

Since a URL consists of a series of names (for computer, directory, subdirectory, and file), there needs to be something to separate the parts of the URL: the / is used for this. By convention, a URL that identifies a file starts with two // symbols; each part of the URL is then separated by another /.

For example, to identify a file called index.html on the Claris Web site, you could construct the following URL:

```
//www.claris.com/index.html
```

The URL starts with the double //; www.claris.com is the identifier of the computer; and index.html is the identifier of the file. If there were a directory in which that file were located, the URL might become

```
//www.claris.com/customers/index.html
```

In this case, index.html is located within the directory called customers.

The computer name (www.claris.com) is based on a unique domain name assigned to organizations by Internet management (Internic, in the United States—http://www.internic.net). The domain name is claris.com and is guaranteed to be unique on the Internet. The owner of the domain can then subdivide that domain as it sees fit: here, Claris has provided a computer named www.claris.com.

SCHEMES A URL contains a prefix called a **scheme,** which is one of the standard Internet protocols. This tells you (and your software) how to attempt to read the file. Typical schemes are:

- http (hypertext transfer protocol)—used for Web pages

- ftp (file transfer protocol)—used for files that will be transferred from one computer to another

- telnet (terminal emulation protocol)—used to connect to computer programs over the Internet using "old-fashioned" nongraphical interfaces

The scheme is part of the URL, which is why you normally see Web addresses presented in the format

```
http://www.claris.com
```

Many browsers recognize that most of the time people are browsing Web page; they supply the http:// at the beginning of addresses that you type in. The fact that you do not type http:// does not mean it is not there. Even though you type in only www.claris.com, the actual address is http://www.claris.com.

Furthermore, many browsers allow you to take a further shortcut: they append .com to an address that you type in. They may prepend not only http:// but also http://www. As a result, you may be able to type in

```
claris
```

and have your browser modify it to

```
http://www.claris.com
```

The assumption made here is that if you do not want to go to an address ending in .com (commercial sites) or that if you do not want to go to a Web page (http://) you will supply that information. Even if someone's business card or advertisement leaves off the http:// at the beginning of a Web address, remember that it should be there.

URLS FOR FILES URLs identify files on a given computer as noted previously. There is a shortcut that may come in handy for you that allows you to use URL links to open non-Claris-Works files on your own computer. If the computer name is blank, it is assumed to be the computer that you are working on.

Thus, it is perfectly valid to have a URL that identifies a file on your computer that should be opened as a file (that is, using the file scheme). Such a URL looks like

```
file:///myharddisk/mysubdirectory/myfile
```

After the // that starts the URL, there is no name for a computer and your computer is assumed; a / follows immediately, indicating the end of the (nonpresent) computer name. You can then identify any file using disk names and path names. In this way, you can create links from ClarisWorks documents to any document on your hard disk.

Creating Links

Links have two ends: the hot spot, which you click on to take you to the link destination. From the Links palette pop-up menu you choose which type of link you want to work with—book mark (to define a destination), document, or URL.

For each type of link, the menus are similar. The first item provides a brief description; the others let you create, edit, delete, or test book marks. Figure 7-3 show the Links menu of the Links palette.

Creating a Book Mark

Remember that a book mark is the destination of a link: it is a place to which you (or others) will want to jump. Open the document that contains the destination and select it—whether it is text, a picture, a movie, a cell in a spreadsheet, etc.

112 • Chapter 7: Making Documents Interactive—Using the Links Palette

FIGURE 7-3. Links Palette Links Menu

From the Links palette (see Figure 7-2), select Book Marks from the pop-up menu and New Book Mark from the Links menu (see Figure 7-3). The dialog shown in Figure 7-4 will open; name the link with a meaningful name so that you (and others) will be able to identify it when you need it in the future.

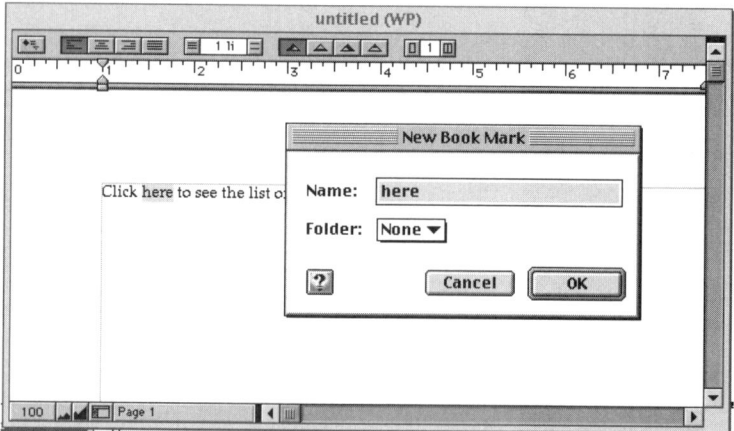

FIGURE 7-4. Book Mark Dialog

You can group links into folders so that links within a document are easier to find. There is more information on this topic in "Managing Links" on page 116.

Creating a Document Link

Start from the document containing the hot object—the source of your link. Select whatever you want people to click on in order to jump to the link (it can be text, a graphic, a cell in a spreadsheet, etc.).

Then, from the Links palette, choose Document Links from the pop-up menu and choose New Document Link from the Links menu. The dialog shown in Figure 7-5 will open.

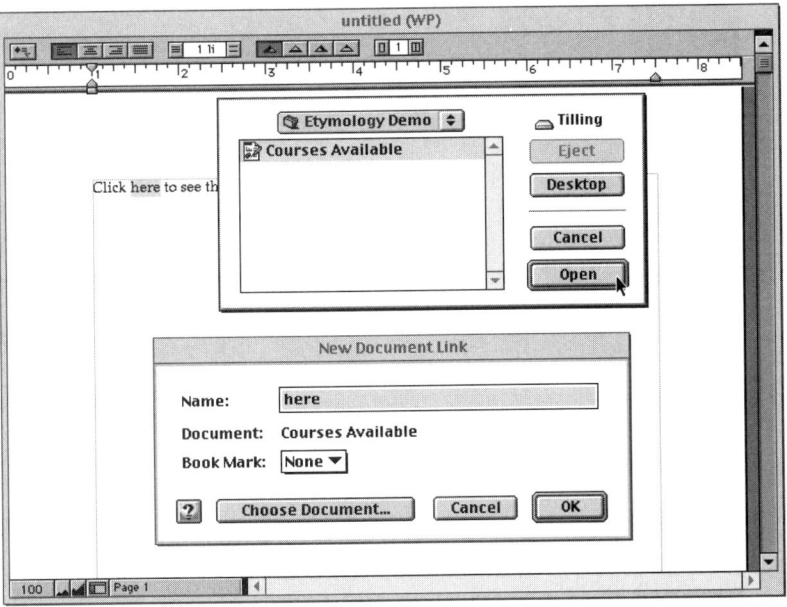

FIGURE 7-5. New Document Link Dialog

In the New Document Link dialog, you can choose the document to which you want to link by clicking Choose Document.... The standard file opening dialog shown above the New Document Link dialog in Figure 7-5 opens; once you have found the document to which you want to link, you click Open, and the file opening dialog closes.

Then, you can use the pop-up menu in the New Document Link dialog to choose which (if any) of its book marks you want to target for the link. If you do not choose a specific target, the link will just go to the beginning of the document.

Creating a URL Link

To create a URL link, you follow exactly the same steps, but you choose URL Links from the Links palette pop-up menu. In other words, you select the text, graphic, or other element of your ClarisWorks element that will be hot (the source of the link), you choose New URL Link from the Links menu of the Links palette, and you type in the full URL to which you want to go in the dialog box shown in Figure 7-6.

Note that the name of the link (be it a book mark, document, or URL link) initially is set to the text that you have highlighted as the hot spot. As shown in Figure 7-6, you can replace that default link name with any other name that you like.

Remember the preceding discussion of URLs—particularly the point about your browser being able to fill in parts of the URL that you do not supply. For a Web page, the URL will always start with http://. If you type in something less, your browser is completing the address. Other people may not use the same browser as you do, and the URL that works on your computer may not work on theirs.

When testing Internet links, always test the link on a machine other than your own before being certain that it is correct. Often links fail when you try them in another environment (another computer, another browser, etc.). In fact, this caution goes for everything that you do concerning the Web. It is very easy to create a Web site on your computer, upload it to the Internet, and have it fail when others attempt to access it. The underlying problem—default files and values that work on a single computer—is the same as with links that rely on a particular browser's operation.

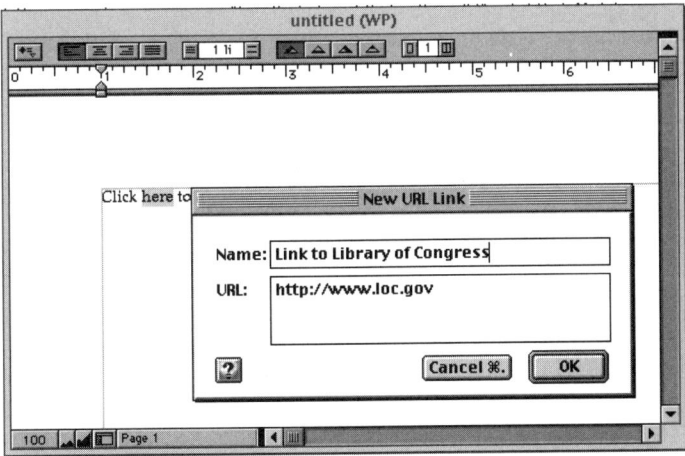

FIGURE 7-6. New URL Link Dialog

Managing Links

The Special menu in the Links palette lets you create folders into which you can group links: Figure 7-7 shows links arranged within a folder.

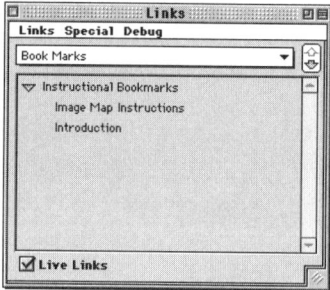

FIGURE 7-7. Links Folders

Maintaining Links

To edit, delete, or test links, you must have selected a link in the Links palette; a selected link is shown in the background of Figure 7-8.

You can use the Special menu to sort and resort the links that are shown in the Links palette (only links of one type are shown at a time).

FIGURE 7-8. Links Palette Special Menu

Designing Links

The possibility of using links can make your ClarisWorks documents very different. The most significant feature of links is that you can avoid repeating information over and over in various documents: the constant information can live in its own document and you can link to it from any document that needs it.

Of course, this is the same principle as that of Web pages (not surprisingly, as the Web is also based on links). You could create Web pages—either stand-alone Web pages or pages on the Internet or your own corporate intranet. In cases in which outsiders are using the information, that is a very practical way of doing things. In other cases, though, creating Claris-Works documents that themselves contain links to other documents or to the Web is more suitable. Even with modern graphical HTML editors, it is much easier to create Claris-Works documents than to create Web pages. Furthermore, ClarisWorks is more powerful (yet also more compact) than most Web browsers.

Designing Links

There are two common situations in which you use links:

1. You may have a number of existing ClarisWorks documents on your computer or network; if they contain information relevant to new documents that you create, you can link to them to avoid repeating the information. You also can link to Web pages via URL links. Links of this sort let you not worry about updating changing information (provided that the target of each link is properly updated).

2. You may be creating a body of information; by deciding to split the information into various documents, you can update each piece appropriately; furthermore, people can link to each document (or book mark within a document) as they need to.

If you are designing a system of links and documents, you may find it productive to design the whole structure in only the most general terms. Then, as you actually create the documents, build in the smallest links. As you accumulate these small links in various documents, you and your users will discover that linking from one document to another reveals the host of links that the second document contains—without your having to worry about a grand scheme of links. As the World Wide Web has amply demonstrated, this bottom-up concatenation of links is the most productive and efficient way of producing a network of data. If you wait to design the grand architecture, you may wait a long time.

Link Considerations

Here are a few points to consider in dealing with links:

Distractions

Links should not distract from the primary purpose of a document. By now, people have gotten used to blue text with underlining as a link; nevertheless, it is definitely a distraction to the casual reader.

Do not show off how many links you can put in a paragraph. It may be less intrusive to have a book mark at the end of your document with many links contained within it. You can place "for more information" links at appropriate places within a document (usually a screen's worth of data) and let the user go to the centralized link section.

Missing Links

Few things are worse than missing links—links that end in dead air. Particularly if you are linking to documents or Web sites that you do not control, you may have to check routinely that all links are valid in your documents. You can easily do this by opening the Links palette, highlighting each link in turn, and choosing the Go To Link command from the Links menu.

If your document is to be used over a network, test its links on a computer other than the one on which it was created: links that work on one machine may not work when the document is moved.

Summary

Links truly break down the boundaries of paper: your document becomes only a part of an interactive, networked system of information, persuasion, or fun (depending on what you are doing). Since links allow you to take advantage of work that you or others have done in other contexts, you can focus on the part of your work that is unique and new. Similarly, others can concentrate on their specific contributions and integrate your efforts into their work.

Links are most familiar to people today from the World Wide Web. Most people today still do not use the Internet; even those who do generally use only a small fraction of its features and a minuscule portion of its content. The next chapter provides a practical overview of the Internet today—including how it affects you and how you can make the most of it.

8

Making Documents Communicate— Integrating the Internet

By now it is clear that the Internet is not just hype. In the history of computers, some technologies and features have been supported more by vendors than by end users and consumers. In the case of the Internet, it is clear that its popularity is broad based and that real people actually derive a benefit from its use. It has caught the imaginations of people as diverse as politicians, technologists, teachers, purveyors of junk e-mail and dubious investment schemes, anarchists, artists, and titans of industry. It must be doing something right.

This chapter provides a summary of the Internet as it is today as well as a guide to getting online and integrating it into your life with ClarisWorks.

Internet Background

The Internet grew out of the need to share scarce and expensive computer resources in the 1960s. Until the 1980s, the Internet was limited to government, scientific, and engineering users. Commercial activities were prohibited. The bar to commercial activities was dropped at the same time that people were acquiring personal computers that were starting to be powerful enough to be useful and challenging. In the early 1990s, Internet use among ordinary people began to take off.

Although most people think of the evolution of computers as a process of providing increasing computational capabilities, in fact the biggest benefit of the proliferation of computers has been in the area of telecommunications. Productivity is enhanced far more by being able to collaborate on projects with team members who are far-flung geographically than by having a nifty word processor. Furthermore, because communication and collaboration are basic activities, anything that assists in these ends is inherently attractive to people.

Why It Happened Now

Although the Internet has been in place for several decades, its greatest boost came with the development of the World Wide Web (which was first proposed in 1989). The Web—which for many people is synonymous with the Internet—is a way of linking information all over the Internet by using hypertext links. (The ClarisWorks links discussed in the last chapter are a small-scale case study.)

Although implementations of the World Wide Web exist that use only text, the Web is associated in most people's minds with multimedia and graphics-rich content. This helps to explain the rapid rise in interest in the Web during the early 1990s.

A new generation of computers came onto the market at that time: they were powered by new chips (PowerPC and Pentium) that were significantly more powerful than their predecessors. These chips were capable of handling the demands of multimedia, and the ability to play movies on personal computers became pervasive.

At the same time, prices of monitors were coming down, and color became a standard on personal computers. People who may have bought their computers only for word processing discovered that they had the ability to use multimedia, but they did not have too much of it lying around in those old documents.

And just to complete the picture, dial-up modems were getting faster and cheaper. In 1997, the standard modem speed is 28.8 kilobaud. It is not important to worry about what the units are; what does matter is that only a few years ago the standard was 0.300 kilobaud (300 baud). The increased speed of modems means that far more information can be transmitted within a given time span (the bandwidth of the communication).

The Web—with its graphics, multimedia, and tremendous power—thrived in this environment. More and more people had the computing power and monitors to process and display the graphics on the Web, and the faster and faster modems meant that getting all of that information into the computer from a distant source was faster all the time.

What This Means for the Future

The theme is repeated over and over—faster, cheaper, and more powerful. Ten years ago, a major bank implemented a system using "smart terminals"—what today would be fairly pitiful personal computers but what at that time far exceeded the power of personal computers. Their telecommunications needs were served by dedicated telephone lines monitored by sophisticated equipment to support their high-speed communications: 9.600 kilobaud. Today, when 28.8 kilobaud is standard over ordinary phone lines, the tale seems nothing but quaint.

But it is an important tale. There is no reason to think that the change in the next 10 years will be any less dramatic. The improvements in every part of the computing world—processors, storage, monitors, and modems—have been consistent. The top-of-the-line computer installation that you see at the latest trade show is worth a photo: a few years from now you can pass it around and laugh with your friends at how antiquated it is.

Some people believe that this pace cannot continue. The electronics on computer chips are linked by very high speed connections, and the electrons that flow along these connections cannot move faster than the speed of light. Some very real physical limits are being approached.

But innovators can work around such limits. The speed of light cannot be changed, but more and more computers built around multiple processors are coming onto the market. New technologies in monitors and telecommunications promise to open new avenues where old ones are blocked by limits of any sort.

For you, this means that you periodically have to recalibrate your expectations when it comes to computers. Just as the modems of yesteryear were measured in baud rates (300 baud, 9600 baud, etc.) and the new ones are measured in kilobauds (0.300 kilobaud, 9.6 kilobaud, etc.), you periodically need to reconsider what is feasible. If you are an experienced computer user, you may have an inbred fear of sending large documents across telecommunications links; you may worry about incorporating video into any document. People who were used to struggling with machines with limited memory or disk space habitually take steps that are no longer required to minimize their demands on memory or disk. Relax and use the new technologies.

TCP/IP and You

The Internet itself is a network of computer networks. It is tied together physically by a series of backbone links among Internet participants. Messages travel quickly over the Internet, finding their way from senders to recipients in a very simple and efficient manner.

You can find many details of the Internet's implementation elsewhere, but in fact only one technical matter is of practical significance for most people. All messages on the Internet are sent using a standard called TCP/IP. You do not deal directly with TCP/IP and it rarely becomes visible, but its implications do matter to you.

At its heart, TCP/IP is a way for telecommunications software to break a message up into small sections (packets), each of which is addressed and sent separately.

It is very much like the problem you would face if you were to send the contents of a file cabinet to someone through the mail. If you placed the contents of the file cabinet in a single container, it would have to be a very strong and large box. It would be too large to be sent by the post office; you would have to send it using a freight carrier. However, you could take the contents of the file cabinet and pack them up in a series of separate boxes that would be small enough to send through the mail. You would address each one and indicate which box was which ("1 of 12," "2 of 12," etc.). Even if the boxes were delivered over a period of 2 or 3 days and even if they were delivered out of sequence, your recipient could easily place them in a file cabinet at the destination.

Your messages on the Internet—whether e-mail messages, Web pages you download, or anything else—are automatically split into packets and routed through the Internet. The packets may in fact arrive out of sequence: the TCP/IP software reconstitutes them properly.

What this means is that multiple messages can be moving over your network connection at the same time. Each message's packets are disassembled and reassembled independently of other messages' transmissions. This is the underlying technology that allows you to check your e-mail while you are downloading a Web page.

It also means that your Internet applications are normally geared to handle several things at the same time. Internally, they are structured differently from older types of software; this type of structure is becoming increasingly common in software development.

Once again, the increased power of today's computers comes into play; people expect to be able to do several things at once. ClarisWorks provides quick access to the Internet from its button bar as well as from the URL links that you can add to documents. With a single mouse click you go from a ClarisWorks document onto the Internet and then perhaps back to yet another type of ClarisWorks document.

Internet and You

The Internet is becoming an increasingly important part of the computing environment. Companies large and small have discovered that the cost of technical support delivered via the Internet is a fraction of the cost of telephone support. The benefits of worldwide 24-hour-a-day communication are evident. And computer users are certainly less likely to be afraid of the Internet than users of other devices (such as blenders or chain saws).

For most people, there is a choice of two ways to connect to the Internet: you can use an Internet service provider (ISP) or an online service such as America Online.

There is a third option available to you if you are part of a large organization such as a corporation or school. Such organizations often have their own networks which themselves are connected to the Internet. In such a case, that network and its organization are like an Internet service provider. From a technical point of view, the issues are those that are discussed in this section; from a practical point of view, you should consult whoever manages your network for further information.

Online Services

Online services such as America Online and CompuServe provide many people with their Internet access. You dial into the service and from there can do what you want on the Internet.

These services evolved from their early incarnations, which had nothing to do with the Internet. Originally, each service was a world unto itself. You could send e-mail to other members of the service but rarely could you send e-mail to members of other services. Information was provided on the services: each had its stock quotes, some online newspapers, and bulletin boards where people could leave messages for one another.

With the advent of the Internet, people began to ask for access to Internet services through their online services. Gradually, the online services evolved to the current hybrid in which each service provides certain proprietary information available only to its members as well as access to public Internet sites.

The online services generally provide their own software for e-mail and the Web. In addition to proprietary information, they often provide additional services related to the Internet—screening of certain types of sites, for example.

If you decide to use an online service, you should determine which one to use based on several factors:

- Remember that your computer will be dialing in frequently as you use the Internet. Make certain that the phone number you dial is a local call or as inexpensive as possible. (Some services provide toll-free numbers, but they may add a surcharge to your bill.)

- If you are interested in particular information (chat areas, etc.), join the online service that has those areas. However, remember that you can send e-mail to any member of any service via the Internet and you can get to Internet news groups from any service (subject to possible screening as noted previously).

ISPs

Internet service providers (ISPs—also sometimes called Internet access providers) provide direct access to the Internet for many people. You make a telephone connection from your computer's modem to a modem at your ISP. Once your computer is connected to their computer, you can send messages through their computer to any Internet address that you want (and receive information back).

Connecting to an ISP

There is no cost to send messages half way around the world on the Internet; however, there very well may be a cost for you to dial into an ISP over a regular telephone line. (The telephone cost is the cost of the telephone call as billed by your telephone company; your ISP bills you separately.)

Many people use simple dial-up access to an ISP using a modem and a telephone line. If you are a heavy user of the Internet, you may want to explore other options.

A number of technologies are being made available for telecommunications. The nature of data calls is very different from that of voice calls, and equipment and technologies are evolving to serve the increasing and specialized needs in both areas. Here are some of them.

ISDN ISDN is an advanced telephone technology that uses digital rather than analog communications. In brief, the voice telephone system was designed for analog data (sound, in this case). The digital information for data transmission is converted to standard sounds that are transmitted over the voice network (it is those beeps and squeals that you hear if you pick up a telephone that is being used for data or fax transmission).

All of this translation of data to and from the analog format takes time and can incur errors. (A modem in fact is a device used to modulate and demodulate the data stream.) ISDN transmits digital data: it can do so at rates that are much higher than those achieved for analog data. ISDN can be used both for speech and for data; as you might expect, in the case of ISDN it is the analog data (speech) that needs to be converted for transmission over the digital circuit.

ISDN can offer significant benefits if you are transmitting large amounts of data to or from your Internet service provider. ISDN is not a panacea; its pricing is inconsistent from area to area—sometimes it is prohibitively expensive. Furthermore, you need equipment to replace your modem, and your ISP must support ISDN.

You should evaluate ISDN on a case-by-case basis: it may be cost effective for someone in one town and not cost effective for someone a few miles away. Because of these and other factors, you are best off if you can find someone close to you who is actually using ISDN with the ISP that you are going to use: offer to take them to lunch and pick their brain.

Furthermore, ISDN is not universally available, and its rates vary significantly from one area to another. If you find yourself in an area with available, relatively inexpensive ISDN service, it may be your best option.

CABLE Rather than using the telephone network to connect to an ISP, you can use a cable television network to make that connection. This requires a different kind of modem from a telephone modem; it also requires a cable service provider who offers Internet access. This area is also changing rapidly.

FRAME RELAY Another technology that is available in many places uses a telephone technology called frame relay. It is most effective for the case in which you need a telephone line constantly connected to a given phone number. This would be the case when you want to be on line to your ISP at all times. Before the advent of frame relay, leased lines were used for these purposes. (One typical application is automated teller machines. They are always connected to their bank via a telephone line—they do not dial up when you stick your card in the slot. This permanent connection is done for reasons of efficiency and security.)

Like ISDN and cable, frame relay needs to be available in your area and must be supported by your ISP.

PERSISTENT CONNECTIONS Your ISP (like an online service) receives e-mail addressed to you as it arrives. When you connect to the ISP, you download your e-mail to your computer. If you receive a great deal of e-mail (or if you send a great deal of e-mail) you may need a persistent connection—one that is always available as opposed to one that is established only when you dial on. You may also need a persistent connection if you are using the Internet as part of other operations that need to happen continuously. For a persistent connection, you need an option such as a leased line or frame relay—maintaining a dial-in connection is impractical.

Everyone connected to the Internet has an IP (Internet Protocol) address, which consists of a quadruplet of digits (235.14.6.1, for example). Deep down in the depths of TCP/IP, communications are actually sent to these addresses rather than to the more easily understood addresses that use text (as in www.claris.com). Each time you dial into your ISP you are assigned an IP for that session. There are circumstances under which you may need an IP to be maintained persistently. (These occur most often when you are using the Internet for customized applications.) If you have a persistent connection with your ISP, you have a constant IP, but you can also often arrange to have a static IP address even with a dial-in connection. (Your ISP will often charge more for a static IP address.)

Domain Names

Addressing on the Internet is usually done using domain names such as claris.com (Claris Corporation), royal.gov.uk (the British monarchy), or philmont.org (the Philmont Public Library). Domain names are assigned by different organizations in each country (in the United States it is www.internic.net) to avoid duplication. The final parts of the name identify the type of organization (edu for education, org for nonprofit organization, net for network, com for commercial, etc.) as well as the country in which it is located (uk for United Kingdom, fr for France, etc.). Reflecting its origins in the United States, the absence of a country suffix implies that the organization is in the United States.

Internet computers maintain tables that translate domain names into quadruplets identifying specific computers on the Internet; this information is used to route messages as needed.

Files on the Internet are identified using a path that starts with the computer on which the file is located; that computer's name includes a domain name. Slashes separate parts of the path (directories or folders). Thus, www.claris.com is a computer at Claris.

E-mail can be addressed to individuals at a given domain. Thus, subscribers to America Online can receive e-mail addressed to them at the American Online domain—aol.com. If your e-mail address is johndoe and you subscribe to America Online, your e-mail address in full is johndoe@aol.com.

Similarly, if your name is still johndoe and your e-mail account is located at an ISP such as taconic.net, your full e-mail address is johndoe@taconic.net. The combination of e-mail account name and domain name must be unique.

Virtual Domain Names

If you use an ISP as opposed to an online service, you can use a virtual domain name. This is a domain name that you register (with Internic, in the United States) and that is assigned to the quadruplet of your ISP. Thus messages addressed to johndoe@johndoe.com are sent to John Doe's ISP.

John Doe would maintain an account at his ISP—perhaps account1045@taconic.et. The ISP automatically forwards mail that is addressed to johndoe@johndoe.com to account1045 @taconic.net. John Doe checks his mail at account 1045 just as any other customer would; he receives mail addressed to both johndoe@johndoe.com and addressed to account1045@ taconic.net.

You must pay an annual fee for a domain name (currently $50 U.S.); in addition, your ISP may charge you a small additional fee for setting up the forwarding mechanism described here. There are several advantages to having your own domain name:

- Some people believe that it looks more professional or serious to have their own domain name.

- If you switch ISPs, it is relatively easy to change the Internet records to reflect that change. You can keep your e-mail address (and your stationery and business cards) as you move to another provider.

- You can create your own Web site—www.john-doe.com, for example. This site would be located on your ISP's computer.

- If your needs grow, you can invest in a Web server—a computer that processes e-mail, Web requests, and other Internet protocols. In effect, with a Web server you become your own ISP. From the standpoint of domain names, this is the same as moving to another ISP. You need to have your own Web server if you are going to provide variable information from a database over the Web. Most individuals do not do this.

Creating Your Own Web Site

You can create your own Web site easily with ClarisWorks (the next chapter goes into detail). If you have your own domain name, that site is typically named www.yourdomain.com. If it is hosted on an ISP, you transfer the files that constitute the Web site to your ISP's computer and people access them via the Internet.

If you use an online service, you are likely to have the option of creating your own Web site within their domain. Such a site would have an internet address that contains the service's domain, such as www.aol.com/users/~johndoe.

If you are providing your own Web server, people access that computer directly.

Internet and Your Computer

Increasingly, Internet capabilities come preinstalled on computers. Automated installers make the process much easier than it was in the past. Still, establishing a connection to the Internet for the first time can be a daunting experience.

Online services and ISPs know that it may take several customer support telephone calls to work out the kinks in connections. Once it is done, they generally do not hear from customers again.

Tips for Making Internet Connections Easier

Here are a few tips that may make the process easier.

Use an Automated Installer

Mac OS 8 boasts a sophisticated installation mechanism that installs and configures your computer and network connections—including Internet connections. (This software was derived in large part from a previous product, the Apple Internet Connection Kit.) Installing Mac OS 8 on a Macintosh computer may be the easiest way to configure your Internet access.

Online services as well as ISPs (both national and local) often provide you with diskettes or CD-ROMs when you open an account. These install the appropriate software and set up your computer for the online service or ISP. This is the second easiest way to install Internet access on your computer if you do it yourself.

Don't Do It Yourself

It does not require great intelligence, manual dexterity, or imagination to connect your computer to the Internet for the first time. It is a task that most people perform very infrequently, and it is a task with many steps and many possible complications. Consider the number of elements involved—a telephone company (usually), the computer and modem (hardware), communications software (supporting TCP/IP), and applications software (a Web browser, e-mail, etc.). A rarely performed complex task is almost a guarantee of trouble. Some local ISPs provide a carry-in service in which they configure your computer for a small fee. Computer resellers often will install all appropriate software for the ISP you choose (the cost is usually about $50–$75).

Rarely is it necessary to do this. The installer disks are your best option. The only common case in which you do not use installer disks is when you are installing Internet software on an older computer that may require special tweaking.

Keep a Copy of Your Settings

With automated installation, it is easy to lose track of the settings you need to access the Internet. Just as you may forget your friends' phone numbers once you have programmed your telephone's auto-dial buttons, it is easy to forget settings and passwords once they have been set up.

However, hard disks crash, and other mishaps occur in your computing environment. Keep track of your installation disks, and write down everything that you have entered. It is very easy not even to know the number to dial to get to your ISP: most software saves the number and dials it automatically.

Writing down passwords is universally discouraged in the computer world. Anyone who finds your password can access your files and account. Some people are beginning to modify this advice, if only because the proliferation of accounts and passwords is creating problems. They rec-

ommend that you write down everything—*password, access number, etc., and place that paper in a very secure place (such as a safe deposit box). Of course, remember that keeping your passwords in a safe deposit box is of little help if you leave your computer unguarded and have your password stored in your access software.*

Getting to the Internet from ClarisWorks

In the previous chapter, you saw how URL links can be created and used to jump to an Internet location (see "URL Links" on page 107). ClarisWorks will automatically open the Web browser that you have selected and ask it to display the page. Your Internet connection will also be started by dialing the phone if necessary.

On Windows, you choose your default browser. On Mac OS, a small utility program called Internet Config records your choices. On Mac OS, you can launch Internet Config from the Internet tool bar in ClarisWorks.

On both Windows and Mac OS, automated installers set these values for you: you may never need to adjust these settings manually.

You can also just open your Web browser in ClarisWorks—a button in the Internet button bar launches the browser as shown in Figure 8-1.

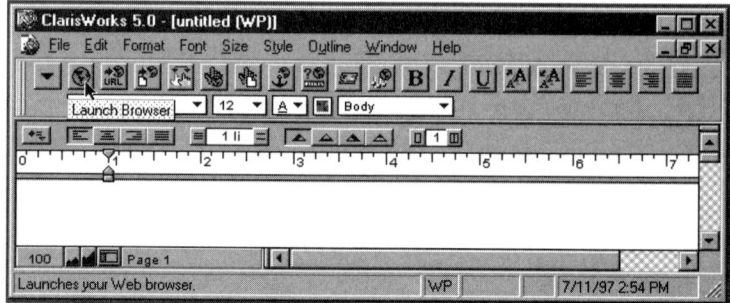

FIGURE 8-1. Launching Your Browser from ClarisWorks

Summary

This chapter provides a very high-level summary of the Internet. The specific technologies of the Internet are covered in the next chapter in a detailed manner.

The integration of ClarisWorks with the Internet is not superficial or cosmetic: with the Internet tool bar and URL links you can move seamlessly from the Internet to your desktop. The media-rich documents of the Internet (particularly the World Wide Web) are old hat to users of ClarisWorks.

ClarisWorks is particularly well suited to creating content for the Internet as well. While serious, heavy-duty Web authoring tools are available for people who spend their lives developing Web sites, for many purposes ClarisWorks is just dandy.

9

Creating Web Pages in ClarisWorks

You can create pages for the World Wide Web using Claris-Works. There is a wide range available to you when you decide to create pages for the Web: you can create simple, text-only pages; you can create dynamic Web pages that are generated on the fly by sophisticated software applications; you can write your own HTML code; you can use a visual editor (such as Claris Home Page); or you can use Claris-Works.

For heavy-duty Web authoring, you will probably want to use a tool like Home Page. However, for many routine (and fairly sophisticated) purposes, ClarisWorks is quite satisfactory.

You can certainly use ClarisWorks to put up a tacky and cheesy Web page—but then you can use many products to do so. Whether you are putting up Web pages (or doing anything else for that matter), decide how much time, effort, and energy you want to spend and do the best job you can within those constraints. There is a case study of putting up a Web site at "Posting the Newsletter on the Web" on page 259).

A ClarisWorks Web Page Example

Figure 9-1 is an example of a page created with ClarisWorks (you can find it on the Web at http://www.philmont-mill.com, but it may look different because its data changes periodically).

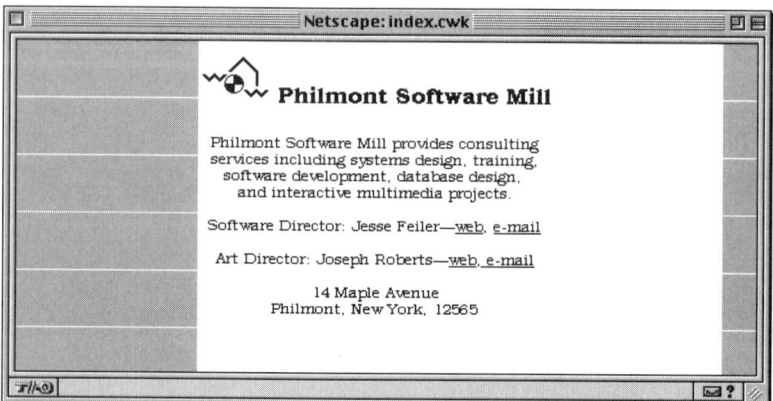

FIGURE 9-1. Philmont Software Mill Home Page

This is a basic site, but it contains a number of the features that go into any site:

- It contains a graphic (the logo at the top).
- It contains a background image (the gray bars at the left and right).
- Its text varies between header and body text.
- It contains links to e-mail and Web addresses.

Here is how it is done.

The Basics of Web Authoring with ClarisWorks

Web authoring with ClarisWorks lets you use ClarisWorks in two ways:

1. You can create components of Web pages with ClarisWorks (graphics, tables, etc.).

2. You can assemble an entire page from these components with ClarisWorks. (Of course, you can also use the components you create in other authoring environments. After all, the whole point of the Web is that its formats are interchangeable.)

Two Documents with Automatic Translation

When you create a ClarisWorks Web page, you start by creating a word processing document that has specific HTML styles in it. The easiest way to do this is to open the WWW [HTML] Document from the stationery folder. This is a blank document, but it contains the necessary styles for creating a Web page. (The styles are shown in Figure 9-2.)

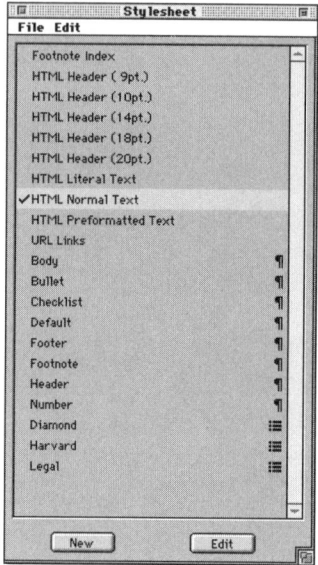

FIGURE 9-2. HTML Styles

You create your document as you would any word processing document; when you are finished, save it with a name that ends in .cwk. Then, immediately save it as an HTML document, which ends in .htm or .html. ClarisWorks will perform the necessary translation. (You can use the button bar to open the translated document in your browser without bothering to save it; this is convenient for testing.)

For files to be recognized as HTML files by a browser, they must end in .html or .htm. Some operating systems allow only a three-character suffix; for these, .htm is the necessary ending. You can find out which suffix you need by asking your Web manager or by looking at other Web pages on the same server. Use the same suffix they use. (If you are using an ISP and plan to upload your Web page to your own Web site, look at the ISP's home page—that will let you know what the server requires.)

Not all ClarisWorks formatting features are available for translation: you can use them in the document, but they will be removed on translation. The basics, though, will apply:

- font sizes and colors
- alignment (justification)
- embedded graphics
- embedded movies
- embedded tables (ClarisWorks spreadsheets)
- bulleted and numbered lists
- links

This covers a great deal of what you create on a Web page or in a ClarisWorks word processing document. There are really very few hidden features. In fact, there is only one that is a little unusual: to insert a horizontal line in the Web page, use New Section or New Page. In the ClarisWorks document, it will have its normal function; on the Web page, a horizontal line will be inserted.

Not everything can be translated to the Web page. For one thing, the nature of the Web is that each browser can be configured differently. In the example shown in Figure 9-1, the browser (Netscape) has been configured to use the font Bookman for text. The rule (of the Web) is that individuals can take precedence in this way; if this were not the case, Web page designers could specify fonts unavailable on people's machines and the results would be a mess.

If you look at the original page as created in ClarisWorks (Figure 9-3), you will note several differences. They have to do with spacing and—of course—with the fact that the font specified in the ClarisWorks document is different from the font specified in the user's browser.

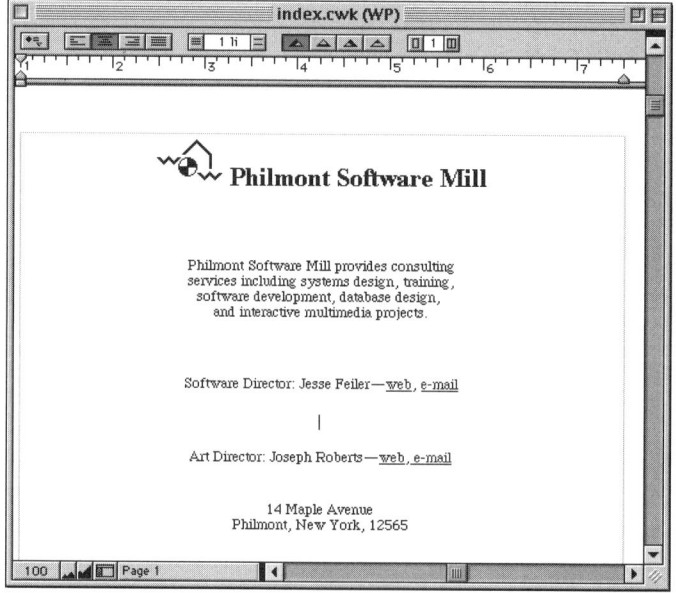

FIGURE 9-3. The ClarisWorks Version of the Home Page

These discrepancies are normal for all Web page designers. No matter what tool you use, you must verify that your page looks good in all major browsers and in all font environments.

Maintaining a Web Site with ClarisWorks

Just as you often do when using any tool to create a Web site, it is useful to place related files for your Web site in a single directory or folder. Already, as you can see, you will have a pair of files for each page: the .cwk file (which you edit) and the .htm or .html file (which is automatically generated and which you upload to your server).

ClarisWorks takes any graphics in your page and saves them as separate files which you must also upload: the HTML code that is generated refers to these files by name. If you do not keep a separate directory for each page, you will start to get confused as to which file is which.

What Can You Do?

Here is how to deal with some of the basic elements of a Web page.

Basic Text

The default style for a document opened from the WWW [HTML] Document is HTML Normal Text. All of your text should be typed with that style.

As necessary, you can make words, sentences, or paragraphs bold or italic by using the normal tools. You can also change other text attributes (color, for example). Try not to underline text: it can be confused with links by users.

You can also use the normal alignment tools to justify text.

Headers

ClarisWorks defines a number of headers for you in its style sheet for HTML (Figure 9-2). The best Web pages use a combination of different size headers to make it clear how the page is organized. If everything is the same size, it all tends to blur together.

If you want, you can italicize headers (as you would any text); you can also align them. Centered headers are very common.

Links

Links are the easiest part of creating a Web page in ClarisWorks. You just create a link as you normally would and ClarisWorks takes it from there.

Since you already saw how links work ("Making Documents Interactive—Using the Links Palette" on page 103), this should be easy for you:

- A bookmark is a link destination within a document (an anchor).

- A document link is a link that takes you to a book mark within the same or another document.

- A URL link is a link that takes you to an Internet address.

The only thing to remember is that if you create a document link to a document other than the current document (that is, to a document elsewhere on your computer or its own network), the converted HTML results are undefined—and probably will not work for anyone who is not using your computer.

Lists

A convenient way to organize information on a Web page is to create lists. You can use any of the outlining styles to create an outline and ClarisWorks will convert them to a list.

Often, elements of a list will be URLs or a combination of descriptive text and a URL. This is easier to read and to manage than a paragraph of text containing a number of URLs.

Graphics

Use ClarisWorks to create graphics that you place on your Web pages. When the conversion is done, ClarisWorks will convert all graphics to GIF or JPEG format (you can control which one—GIF normally takes up more space and JPEG is generally more visually complete). Each graphic will be saved in the appropriate format with an automatically generated name. The HTML will reference each graphic appropriately.

All that you have to do is to remember to upload these generated files when you upload your Web page. Each time you generate the HTML, ClarisWorks will ask you if it should overwrite existing graphics files. The safest thing is always to overwrite files; that way things will not get out of synch. (Of course, if you have a whole bunch of Web pages and their associated graphics in the same folder, who knows what you may be overwriting—that is why it is best to keep things separate.)

Tables

Whether you use a graphical HTML editor such as Claris Home Page or raw HTML, it is a big bore to create a table and specify all the parameters. With ClarisWorks, insert a table or spreadsheet or draw a spreadsheet on your document at the appropriate location.

It will be outputted correctly when the HTML is generated.

Backgrounds

Web pages can have two kinds of backgrounds: a solid color and a background image. In the page shown here (Figure 9-1), a background image is used.

Background images are replicated across and down the Web page by a browser until they cover the entire page area. Normally, background images are fairly small; as users resize their browser windows, more and more copies of the image are generated by the browser in order to cover the background.

When background images become large or complex, they not only take away from the foreground (the information on the page) but also start to degrade performance.

You can create a simple background image using Claris-Works. Here is what you do:

1. Create a draw document.

2. Draw the background image—keep it small and simple.

3. Save the draw document as a JPEG or GIF file.

4. Open the HTML Configuration from the button bar, and use the Set Background Image... button to locate the file. When the HTML is generated, ClarisWorks will make a copy of the file ready for you to upload.

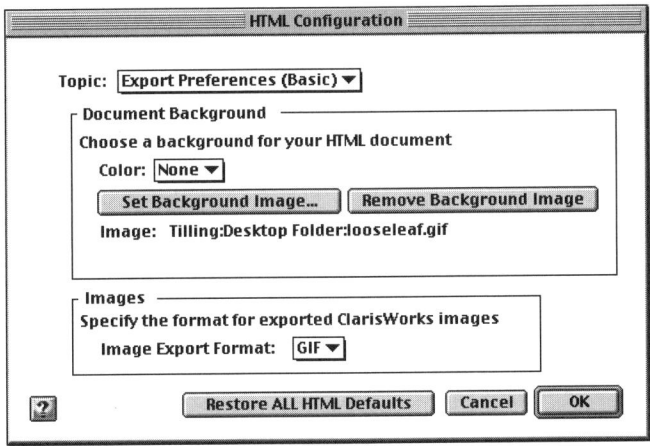

FIGURE 9-4. HTML Export (Basic)

As you can see from Figure 9-4, you could also use this window to set a solid background color for your Web page.

Since the background image is replicated over and over to fill the variable size of a browser, you should test how it looks as it is replicated. Often, these images are made very wide and not very high. If you look at Figure 9-1, you can see that the image is shown vertically six times; at the right, another set of six replications is partly shown.

Figure 9-5 shows the ClarisWorks draw document used to create this background image.

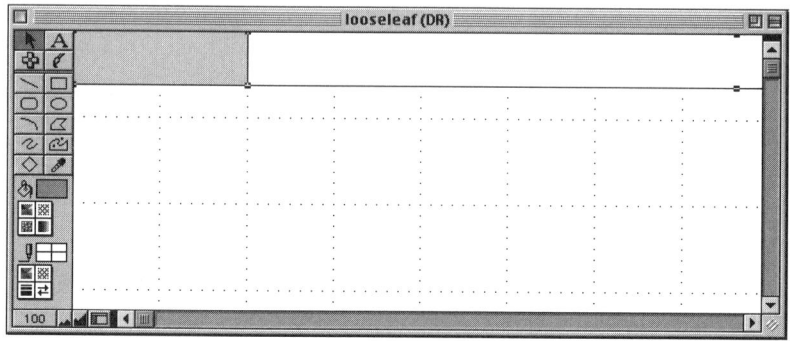

FIGURE 9-5. ClarisWorks Draw Document for Background Image

Note that the image is created simply from two rectangles (both are selected in Figure 9-5). If you want a solid bar down the left side of the page, the colored rectangle at the left should have the same color for its interior and for its border. In Figure 9-1, the border color (white) makes a contrast with the interior color, producing the lines. If you find this attractive (as many people do), that is how to do it. If you want a solid (boring) blob, make the colors the same.

Advanced HTML

For more advanced HTML features, you will probably use a visual editor like Claris Home Page. However, there are many cases in which you just want one or two advanced features. You may even have a section of HTML code that you just want to stick in without really knowing what it does (the image map in "Creating an Image Map in ClarisWorks" on page 193 is such a case).

You have two ways of expanding the basic ClarisWorks HTML.

First, you can simply paste the HTML code into your ClarisWorks document. Select the HTML code and style it with HTML Literal Text. It will be passed through intact.

The other way to modify ClarisWorks is to use the advanced HTML options as shown in Figure 9-6 (which can be opened from the button bar).

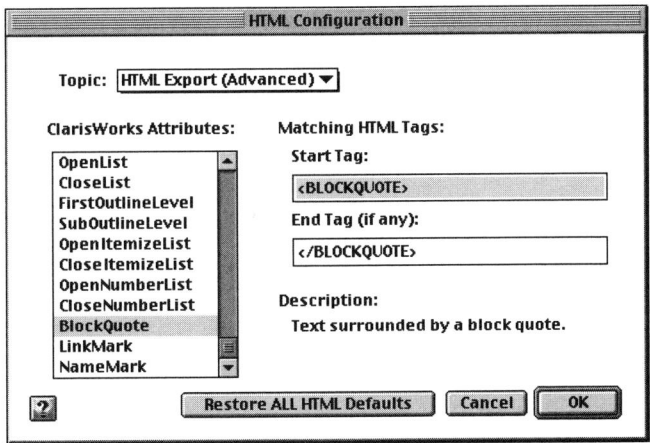

FIGURE 9-6. HTML Export (Advanced)

You can change how ClarisWorks editing attributes (on the left) are interpreted. To use this window, you need to know the basics of HTML—or at least of that part of HTML that you are using. If you don not know, then do not use it.

Summary

ClarisWorks lets you create basic Web pages of reasonable sophistication using the tools that you are familiar with. Although no one would try to create a 100-page Web site using ClarisWorks, you may very well find that your basic needs can be handled quite easily.

As with the rest of ClarisWorks, there is a tremendous benefit to its power and simplicity. It is much better to have a Web site that works (and that you control) than to have a sophisticated Web site with broken links, missing images—and a Web master who will be back from Xigaze shortly.

10

Multiple Solutions to Problems with ClarisWorks

One of the main attractions of ClarisWorks is its flexibility; there generally is no right or wrong way to do anything that you want to do—you do it in the way that is easiest and most intuitive for you. This chapter takes a very simple problem and demonstrates how you can approach it in ClarisWorks as a word processing document, a spreadsheet, a database, and as hybrid documents. It serves as a comparison of the different components of ClarisWorks and also as a review of some of their features.

From time to time you will come across dogmatic people who insist that—even with ClarisWorks—there is only one way to approach a problem. This book is designed to help you out in such situations: hit your interlocutor over the head with it. It is your data, your computer, and your convenience that matter. (The one exception to this statement is the case in which it is your boss's data, your boss's computer, and your boss's convenience that matter. You might want to take that into account. Of course, there is also the question of who actually is doing the work. Such a discussion is beyond the scope of this book.)

Finding the Right Document Type

Here is a simple example of what may be a counterintuitive document type. Presumably you have registered your copy of ClarisWorks—you were prompted to do so as soon as you installed it. Do you remember what happened?

First, a ClarisWorks assistant prompted you for appropriate information, as shown in Figure 10-1.

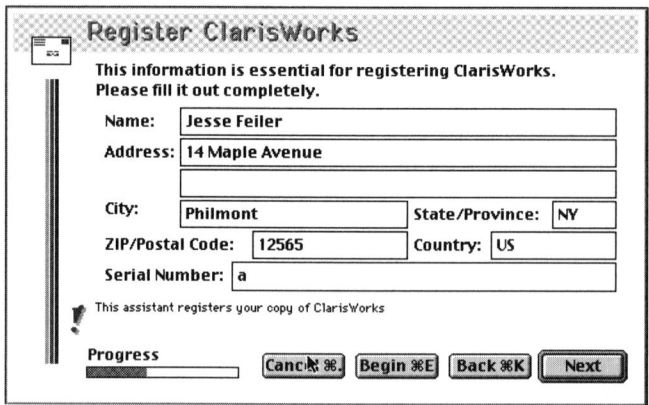

FIGURE 10-1. Claris Registration Assistant

After you have entered the information, the Assistant opens a document and inserts the text into it. You might think that it would be a word processing document—after all, you have entered only text. In fact, the document that is created is a ClarisWorks draw document, as shown in Figure 10-2.

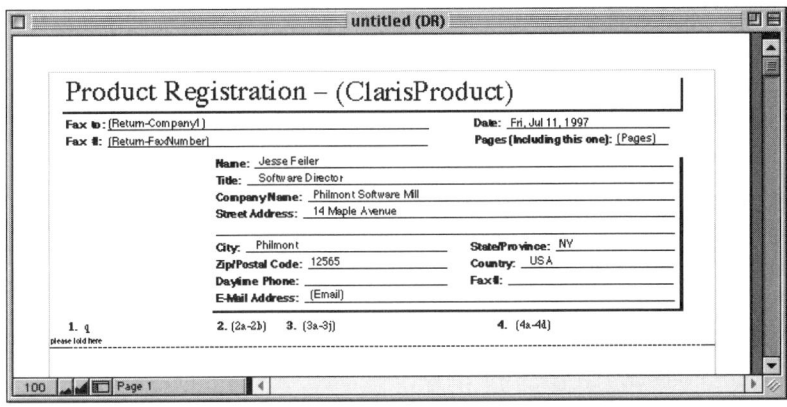

FIGURE 10-2. ClarisWorks Registration Document

The few additional lines that outline the text areas make the document more attractive (and easier to read). And in all the time that this registration process has been used, no one has complained that the registration document is (horror of horrors!) not a word processing document.

The Case Study

This chapter deals with a simple case study: a library's overdue book list. Whether they use an automated system, a manual system of cards, or the librarian's memory, most public libraries keep track of overdue books. They use this list in three ways:

1. When a patron wants to check out a book, the list is checked to make certain that the patron does not have overdue books. (Each library has its own policy as to the leeway that is allowed: usually one or two books a day or two overdue will not prevent you from checking out another book.)

2. When someone asks for a book that is not on the shelf, the librarian can check the overdue list to see if the book is overdue; if it is, a phone call to the delinquent patron may be of help.

3. Finally, the overdue list itself is used in an attempt to get the books back. It normally has a record of phone calls or letters that have been made and sent in order to retrieve the books.

This is a simple problem of the sort that organizations confront every day. Is it a word processing problem? A spreadsheet? A database? Here is how to address it in each format, with a summary of the pros and cons of each.

Word Processing

For many people, a word processing document is the simplest way of entering data. "You just type" is the mantra, and although that is not always the best way to do things, it has enough truth to it that it is a good place to start.

If someone is comfortable using a tool like a word processor, it has to be really inappropriate (or cause complications for others) to deny that person the use of the tool they like.

Figure 10-3 shows the overdue list as a word processing document. It is clear, easy to read, and works perfectly well. This section summarizes how it is created and can serve as a review of the ClarisWorks word processing tools.

Here are some of the features to note in the document.

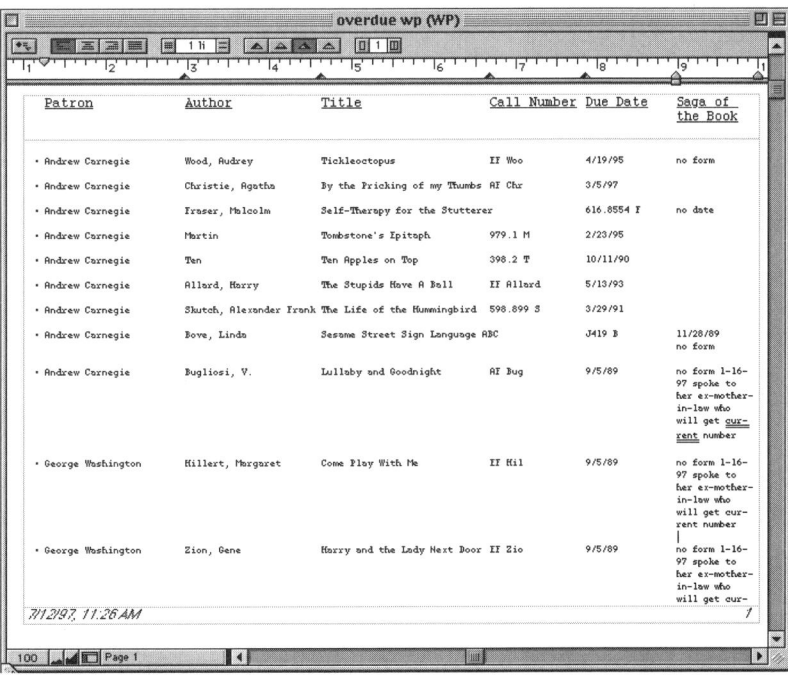

FIGURE 10-3. Overdue List as a Word Processing Document

Automatic Hyphenation

Look at Figure 10-3 and note the hyphenated word with the double underline in the lower-right. It may be a minor point to you, but all the issues involving pagination and hyphenation are handled easily in a word processing document.

You turn on automatic hyphenation as shown in Figure 10-4.

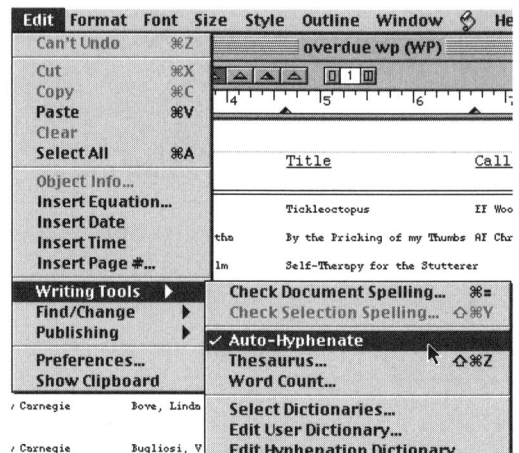

FIGURE 10-4. Hyphenation Menu

Automatic Headers and Footers

From the Format menu (shown in Figure 10-5), you can choose to add headers and footers.

The light gray lines at the top and bottom of the page outline the header and footer areas. You can type anything you want in them—the text will appear on each page. Here, column names are typed into the header.

In the footer, the date, time, and page number are shown. Since these are variable, you cannot just type them in. Instead, you enter them into the footer by positioning the insertion point where you want it and using the Edit menu to insert the date, time, and page number (refer to Figure 10-4 to see the Insert Date, Insert Time, and Insert Page #... commands).

The spacing of the footer is achieved as follows:

1. Align the text left (from the ruler).
2. Enter the date (from the Edit menu).
3. Type a comma and space after the date.
4. Enter the time (from the Edit menu).
5. Set a right-adjusted tab for the right-hand side of the footer. You select a tab from the ruler and then click where you want it to be located. The right-adjusted tab is highlighted in Figure 10-3; it is located just above the 4.5 inch mark in the ruler at the top of the window.
6. After typing a tab (to move to the right-adjusted tab stop), enter the page number (from the Edit menu).

This is a common type of footer.

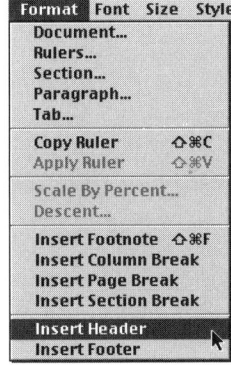

FIGURE 10-5. Format Menu

Margin Control

Word processing documents handle variable-length text very well. In this case, the saga of the book and why it has not been returned can be very lengthy (and sometimes very creative). Variable-length text is a necessity. Here, tabs are set to allow you to enter each of the items regarding the overdue book.

For the saga, however, it is assumed that this will go on and on and on. Note that the margins are set as follows:

- The first line of each paragraph (which starts with the patron's name) is at the left margin. (You may not think of each entry as a paragraph, but that is what it is.)

- Subsequent lines are indented to align directly under the tab stop at the 9 inch mark on the ruler (the margin indicator obscures the tab, but it is there). As you continue to type in the saga, the text will wrap (and be automatically hyphenated) in an bottomless column.

Outlining

The bullet preceding each entry is generated automatically by ClarisWorks: the Bullet outlining feature has been selected.

Pros and Cons

Setting up a form like this as a word processing document is very simple once you have done it a few times. It requires a familiarity with the basic word processing concepts, but once you have got them down, you are ready to go.

The advantages of using word processing for a task like this include:

- It is very easy to set up the document.

- Many people are familiar with word processing; once the document is set up, people with even less knowledge of ClarisWorks can use it with little training.

- The output looks excellent on paper.

- You do not have to worry about formatting in the vertical dimension—ClarisWorks takes care of page breaks, numbering, etc.

Disadvantages of using word processing for a task like this include:

- It is difficult to sort the document into a different order.

- Although you can use the Find/Change command from the Edit menu to locate specific information, computer-assisted navigation through the data isn't really possible.

- Although the output looks good on paper, it does not take maximum advantage of the computer's capabilities.

So, maybe this is a good task for a spreadsheet.

162 • Chapter 10: Multiple Solutions to Problems with ClarisWorks

Spreadsheets

The same information is shown in a spreadsheet in Figure 10–6. There are some differences and some similarities when compared to the word processing document.

If further proof were needed that the same data can be used in various ways, the spreadsheet shown in Figure 10-6 was created from the word processing document shown in Figure 10-3. You create a spreadsheet, then use the Insert... command from the File menu; if you insert a tab-delimited word processing document (that is, a document that consists of columns of data that are aligned using tabs), ClarisWorks converts the data to the columns of a spreadsheet. This works with a document containing tab-delimited columns: it need not be a ClarisWorks document.

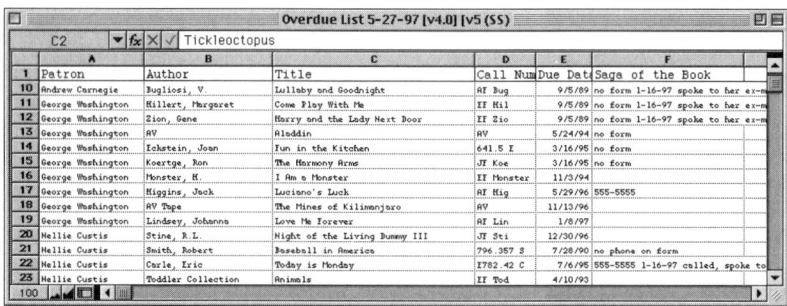

FIGURE 10-6. Overdue List as a Spreadsheet

Text Cells

The first difference is that this document is not paper oriented. Notice that the text at the right side of the page (in the Saga column) runs off the right side. Whereas the word processing document was able to create a bottomless column for this variable-length text, that is not the case with the spreadsheet.

The Wrap alignment option (from the spreadsheet Format/Alignment menu) lets you wrap the text as necessary to the next line, preventing the lengthy excursion at the right of the spreadsheet. However, lengthening the text within this cell means adding a lot of extra space—possibly several inches—at the bottom of all the cells on each row. In other words, the very nature of the spreadsheet's layout makes dealing with variable-length text problematic.

Titles versus Headers and Footers

You can create headers and footers on your spreadsheet just as you would on a word processing document. In addition, you can create titles for columns or rows. Titles provide constant text that is always visible at the top or side of your spreadsheet.

Creating a Title

In Figure 10-6, note that the first row (numbered 1 at the left) is followed by row 10. Row 1 is a title; it is always shown at the top of the spreadsheet, no matter what the window's size or shape or how the spreadsheet has been scrolled.

To create a title, select the row(s) or columns(s) at the top or left of your spreadsheet and choose Lock Title Position from the Options menu as shown in Figure 10-7. (To select an entire row or column, highlight its identifying number or letter in the spreadsheet's border.)

Titles are artifacts of the spreadsheet window; they are distinct from headers and footers, which are printed and are shown in page view.

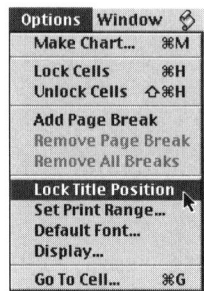

FIGURE 10-7. Options Menu

Making the Spreadsheet More Presentable

The spreadsheet shown in Figure 10-6 is quite clearly a spreadsheet. If you fiddle with a few options, you can produce a somewhat more pleasing version as shown in Figure 10-8.

Here are the changes that were made from Figure 10-6:

1. A header was added (Library Overdue List). This is shown in Page View and on printouts. You add a header to a spreadsheet exactly as you do with a word processing document (see "Automatic Headers and Footers" on page 158).

Spreadsheets • 165

2. The screenshot shows Page View from the Window menu selected. This shows the page images that can be printed, rather than the infinite rows and columns of the spreadsheet.

3. Using the Display window from the Options menu, the grid, row, and column headers have been turned off (see Figure 10-9).

FIGURE 10-8. More Pleasing Spreadsheet

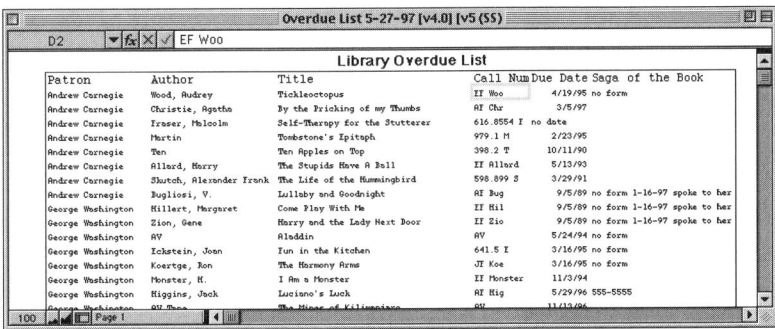

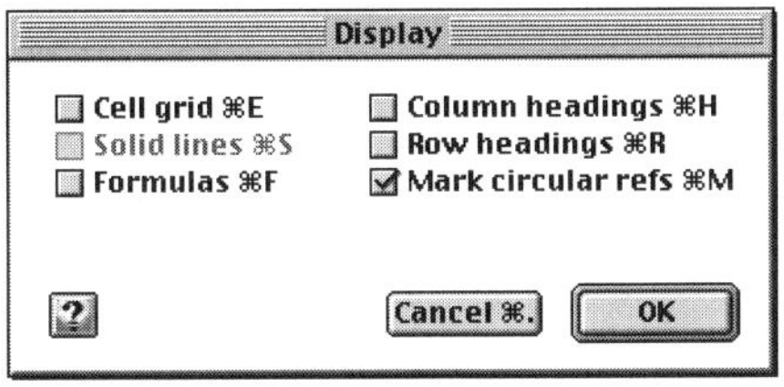

FIGURE 10-9. Display Window

Sorting the Spreadsheet

The main advantage to using a spreadsheet is that you can sort the contents on demand. To do so, select all the cells in the spreadsheet (Select All from the Edit menu), and then choose Sort from the Calculate menu. The Sort dialog shown in Figure 10-10 appears.

The range of cells to be sorted is shown at the top; you can modify it. By default it is the entire spreadsheet (since you chose Select All). The first row is excluded automatically in this case because it was set as a title. If it had not been set as a title, it would be sorted with all the other data.

The Order Keys section lets you specify up to three ways to sort. Here, only one key is used. The second column (B) is the author's name. The spreadsheet will be sorted by author in ascending order.

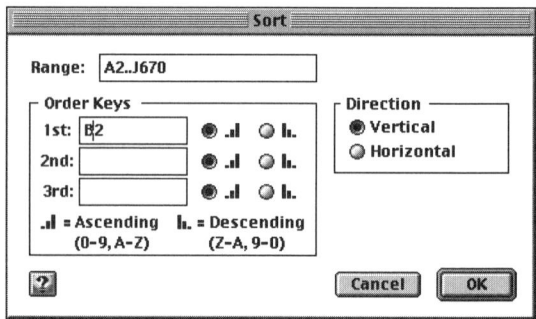

FIGURE 10-10. Sort Dialog

The sorted spreadsheet is shown in Figure 10-11: it is sorted on the second column (Author) as specified in the Sort dialog in Figure 10-10.

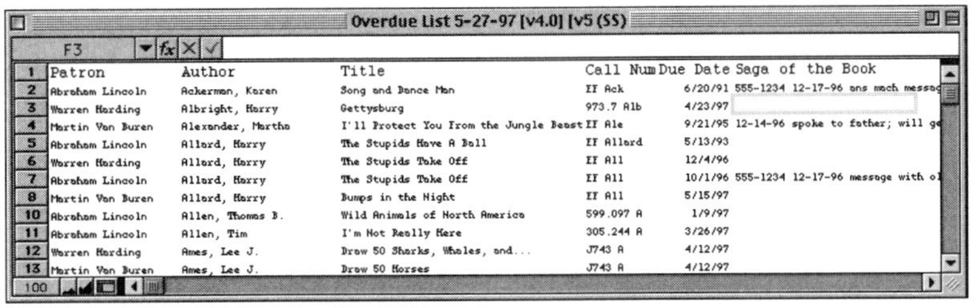

FIGURE 10-11. Sorted Spreadsheet

You can add up to two additional keys. When sorting by multiple keys, each additional key provides a finer sort. Thus, if you requested a primary key of Patron, a secondary key of Due Date, and a tertiary key of Title, you would get the overdue list sorted by patron; within all of a patron's listing you would get the books due on each date sorted together; and finally you would have the books due on each date for each patron sorted by title. (Needless to say, this hypothetical patron would have a lot of explaining to do.)

Using a Hybrid Document

You can create a hybrid document as shown in Figure 10-12. This is a ClarisWorks draw document with a spreadsheet frame shown within it.

168 • Chapter 10: Multiple Solutions to Problems with ClarisWorks

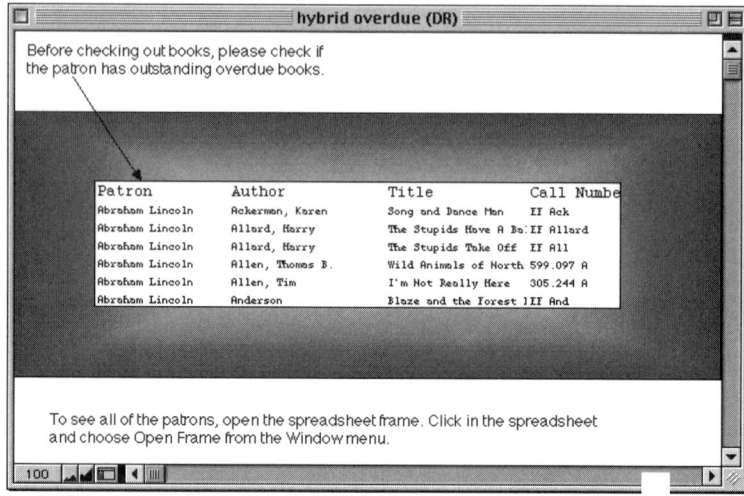

FIGURE 10-12. Hybrid Overdue List

This document truly cannot exist on paper: there is no way to see the contents of the spreadsheet frame except by opening it as directed to in the window. The advantage of this type of document is that it is simple, elegant, and easy to use.

In order to create a document like this, here is what you do. Steps 2 through 6 involve the use of the tools. They are keyed to Figure 10-13.

1. Create a ClarisWorks draw document.

2. Using the text tool, type the two sections of text.

3. Using the rectangle tool (a) and the gradient fill (b), draw the rectangle in the center of the window.

4. Using the spreadsheet tool, draw a spreadsheet frame within the rectangle.

5. Using Insert... from the File menu, insert the spreadsheet into the spreadsheet frame. You will get a warning that it is of a different size; you can ignore this.

6. Using the line tool (a), draw a line from the upper text to the Patron column of the spreadsheet. Using the arrow palette (b), select the appropriate arrow for the end of the line.

7. Using either the Display dialog from the Options menu or the Frame Info... dialog from the Edit menu, hide the grid lines and headers as shown in Figure 10-9. (In Figure 10-9, the cell grid as well as row and column headers are not checked—and therefore are not shown.)

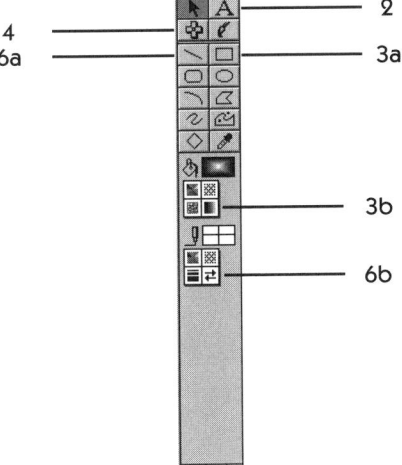

FIGURE 10-13. Tool Palette

> *Note that both commands open the same dialog. If you have activated the spreadsheet by clicking in a cell, use the Display dialog. If you have selected the spreadsheet so that its corners are highlighted, use the Frame Info... tool.*

As you can see, your choice of word processing document, spreadsheet, or hybrid document is certainly influenced by what you are trying to do; but the final choice should be based on what looks best to you and seems easiest to use. A major consideration is whether or not you need to print the information: in such a case, a hybrid document (and often a spreadsheet) is clumsy.

If you are going to be using the information on a computer, you do not need to display everything all the time. In fact, you can make a very elegant and simple display that shows only what you need to see. To do this, you can use a database.

Databases

The power and flexibility of the ClarisWorks database are very impressive. Unfortunately, many people tune out as soon as they hear the word "database." It is one of those words and phrases, like "cosine," "restrictive pronoun," and "charm," that remind many people of gaps in their education. (Sadly, many programmers are reluctant to use databases, preferring instead to reinvent a wheel with their own code.)

Even if you have played with databases before and decided that they are too much for you, take a moment to read this section: you will see how easy it is to do very practical things with databases. The ClarisWorks documentation both on paper and online provides details of all the database features; this section just covers what you need to create a simple but powerful (and attractive) database for the overdue list (see Figure 10-23 if you want a preview). The techniques are easily applied to other applications.

Why Use a Database?

A ClarisWorks database lets you manipulate the same data that has already been shown in a word processing document and in a spreadsheet. A database lets you combine some of the formatting features of word processing with the fairly rigid data storage formats of a spreadsheet.

A database also provides the ability to control data entry in a more sophisticated way than the other documents.

What Does the Database Look Like?

Just as before, each element of data has five components:

1. A patron name
2. An author name
3. A book title
4. A call number (a combination of letters and numbers that locates the book on the library shelves)
5. A due date

6. A saga recounting the attempts by library staff to locate the patron and the book as well as the (imaginative) responses to the question, "can you just return the book, please?"

In the case of the word processing document, each paragraph was divided into six parts by using tabs: the result (shown in Figure 10-3) was a document with six columns. In the case of the spreadsheet, each row consisted of six columns (as shown in Figure 10-6). In database parlance, each overdue book (paragraph in word processing, row in spreadsheets) is a record. Each of the six parts of a record (columns in both word processing and spreadsheet parlance) is a field. This variation in parlance has absolutely no effect on the data.

Note that relational databases (such as FileMaker Pro) sometimes refer to a record as a row—just as in a spreadsheet.

Creating a Database

When you create a new database from the File menu, ClarisWorks opens the window shown in Figure 10-14. You can define the fields in your database here. You type in each field name in the Field Name box and then select a field type from the pop-up to the right. Figure 10-14 shows the window as it is after entering all of the fields for the overdue database. At this point, you close the window by clicking the Done button.

This is a moment when many people give up. Don't! Create any fields you want: you can add to them or modify them later—you can even delete fields. If you have thought about your data, you probably know what fields you will want to use and what types they are; if you have not, just define one or more fields that you might want and change them later.

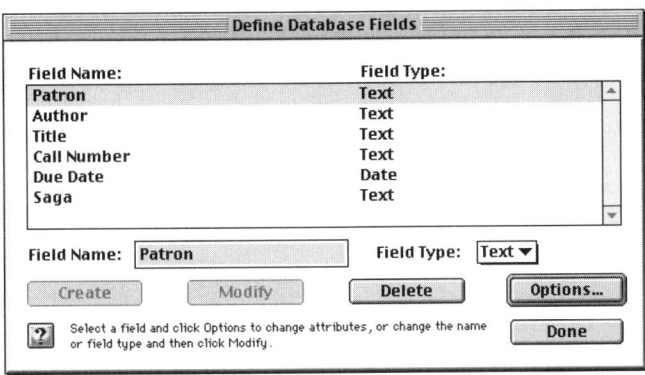

FIGURE 10-14. Creating Fields in a Database

When you have defined your fields and clicked Done, ClarisWorks creates the database for you and opens the database window as shown in Figure 10-15.

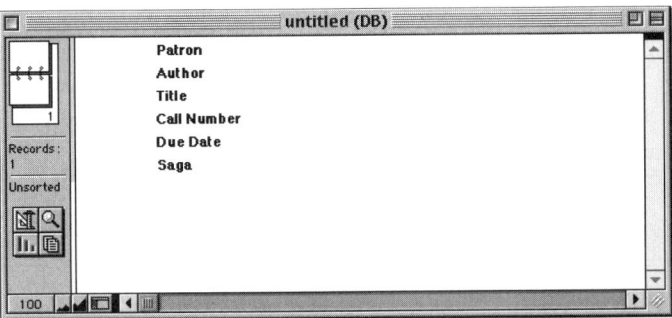

FIGURE 10-15. A Basic Database Layout

This is another moment when people sometimes give up. What is this thing? What do you do with it?

The answer is that this is a default layout for the database, consisting of all of the fields and their names as you entered them in the field definitions (Figure 10-14). You do not have to use this layout—you can rearrange things and create new layouts.

From the Edit menu, you use New Record to create each additional database record. Just as with a spreadsheet or word processing document, you type the appropriate information into each record. What is nice about the database is that instead of knowing that the second column is for the author's name, ClarisWorks puts the field name right on the layout for you so that you do not have to guess what goes where.

But you can do better, modifying the layout yourself.

Modifying a Database Layout

It is very easy to transform the default layout that Claris-Works creates for you to an easy-to-use data entry form as shown in Figure 10-16.

In order to convert the layout from Figure 10-15 into that of Figure 10-16, you need to do the following:

1. Enlarge the size of each record (the highlighted area in Figure 10-16).

2. Move the fields and their labels.

3. Enter the descriptive text.

4. Add the highlight behind "Enter overdue information here."

Here is how you do it.

Databases • 175

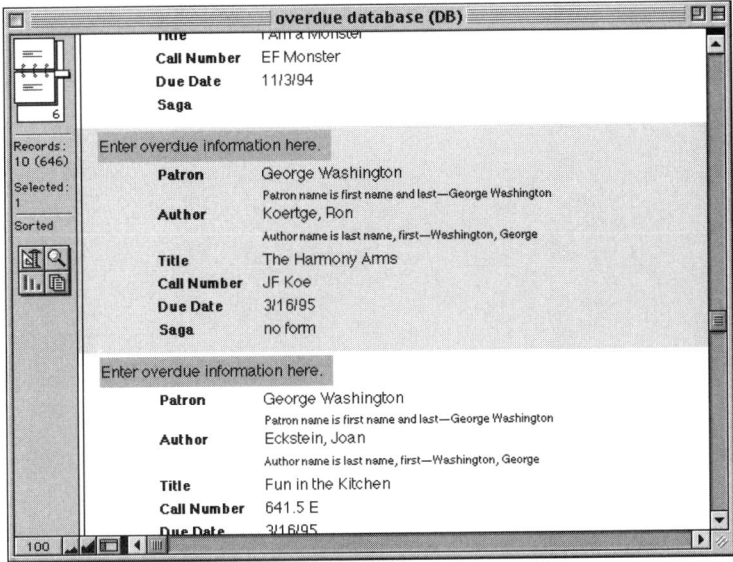

FIGURE 10-16. Browse Mode from the Layout Menu

First, you need to be in Layout mode (from the Layout menu, shown in Figure 10-17).

FIGURE 10-17. Layout Menu

176 • Chapter 10: Multiple Solutions to Problems with ClarisWorks

When you select Layout mode, the window changes to the Layout display, shown in Figure 10-18. Note that instead of data, the name of each field is shown within the data entry boxes.

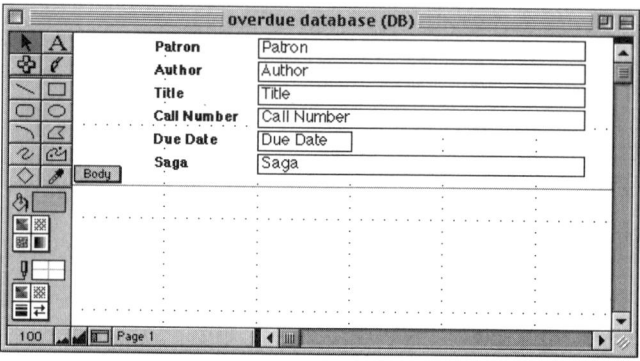

FIGURE 10-18. Layout Mode from the Layout Menu

There is only one record visible in Layout mode—it is the template record that will be used for each record in the database.

The first step is to enlarge the body of the Layout. For now, do not worry about the terminology—"body" is the main part of the layout. As shown in Figure 10-19, enlarge the Body part by dragging the lower limit down.

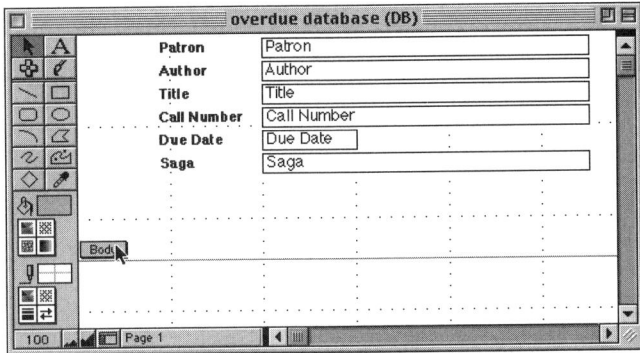

FIGURE 10-19. Enlarging the Body of the Layout

Next, move the fields and labels as shown in Figure 10-20.

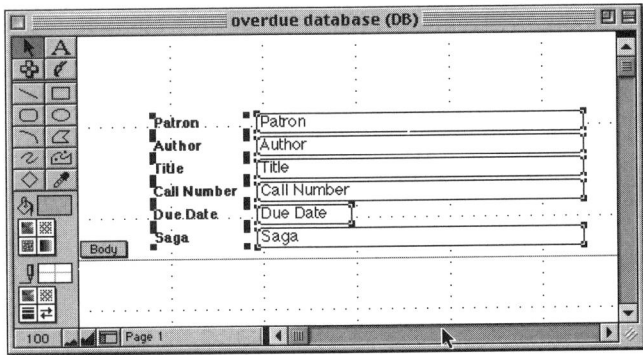

FIGURE 10-20. Moving the Fields and Labels

The simplest way to do this is to choose Select All from the Edit menu and use the arrow tool to draw them to the bottom of the Body part. Then, select individual fields and their labels and make further adjustments.

Note that at this point you can resize and reshape each field. The Saga field clearly should be larger than the other fields. This is a case in which the word processing document, with its ability to wrap words across many lines, was superior to the spreadsheet, which suffers from the fact that each cell is a specific size. Here you can have the best of both worlds.

Finally, use the text tool to enter instructions and use the rectangle tool to draw a shaded rectangle to highlight the main instruction ("Enter overdue information here."). The result is shown in Figure 10-21.

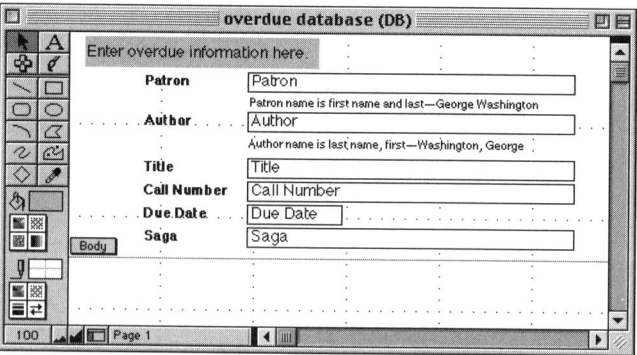

FIGURE 10-21. Adding Instructions to the Layout

Choose Browse from the Layout menu to see what the Layout looks like in Browse mode (the mode you use to view, enter, and edit data). Figure 10-22 shows what this looks like.

You can use the New View command from the Window menu to open a second window onto the same data (this applies at any time in any ClarisWorks document). If you do this, you will be able to see the results of your modification to the layout as you work: you can keep one window in Browse mode and the other in Layout mode.

Entering and Editing Database Data

Figure 10-22 also shows how you enter and edit database data. When you click inside a data entry field for a database record, all of the fields for that record are outlined for data entry.

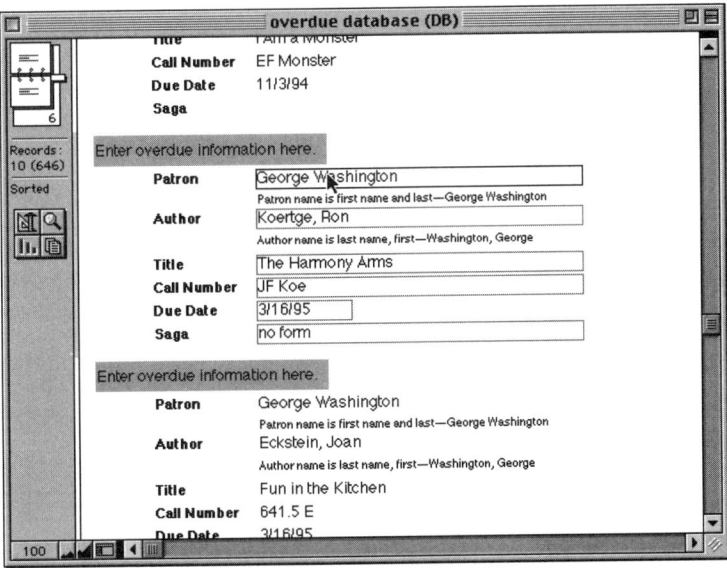

FIGURE 10-22. Entering Data in Browse Mode

Compare this to the highlighting shown in Figure 10-16: that is what you see when you click in a database record anywhere except within a data entry field. The difference is that in Figure 10-16 the mouse click selects the entire record (as for deletion); in Figure 10-22 the mouse click select a character or section of a single field's text for manipulation.

Creating a New Layout with Sub-Summaries

The balance of this chapter will show you how to create a new layout that is rather sophisticated but easy to create and use.

Figure 10-23 shows the data from this database in a new layout.

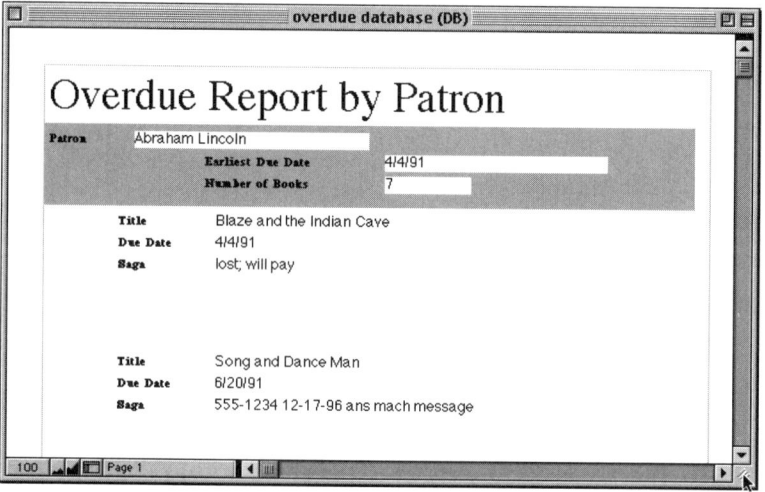

FIGURE 10-23. Database with Sub-Summary

Sorted by patron, it shows the patron's name, the earliest due date for all of the books (that is, the most overdue book), and the number of overdue books. This sub-summary is the grayed area in Figure 10-23.

You can create sub-summaries that either precede or follow their detailed records. This one precedes the details. Summaries can manipulate information in the detailed records—often adding it up. In this case, the sub-summary counts the number of books overdue and calculates the earliest date. (Often summaries that add up information from the detailed records follow them, but it does not make any difference to ClarisWorks.) Some people like to see them in one format, others in another.

Sub-summaries are summaries that apply to a certain group of records in the database—in this case, an individual patron. Summaries are summaries that apply to all records in the database. For sub-summaries to work, you must have sorted the database so that all of the records in the group are together. The next section covers this.

In order to create this new layout, here is what you do:

1. Create a new layout.

2. Organize the Body part of the layout using the same techniques you used previously.

3. Add a sub-summary part to the layout.

4. Create summary fields for the earliest due date and patron name.

5. Add the summary fields to the sub-summary and draw the gray background.

Creating a New Layout

Choose New Layout from the Layout menu (Figure 10-17) to create a new layout. As you will see when the new layout window (Figure 10-24) opens, you can name the layout; there are also a number of basic layout types that you can choose—you want a standard layout for this case.

Name the layout and then click OK.

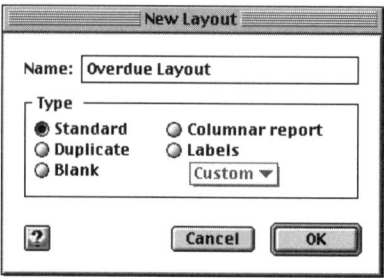

FIGURE 10-24. New Layout Window

Organizing the Body Layout

This is the same process that you did previously ("Modifying a Database Layout" on page 174). Note, however, that you will not need all of the fields. The body of the layout (the non-grayed portion of Figure 10-23) contains only the title, due date, and saga—together with their text labels. Select the other fields and their labels and delete them. Arrange these fields as you see fit.

Now you are ready for step 3—adding a sub-summary to the layout.

Adding the Sub-Summary Part to the Layout

From the Layout menu, choose Insert Part.... ClarisWorks opens the window shown in Figure 10-25 to let you choose the type of part you want.

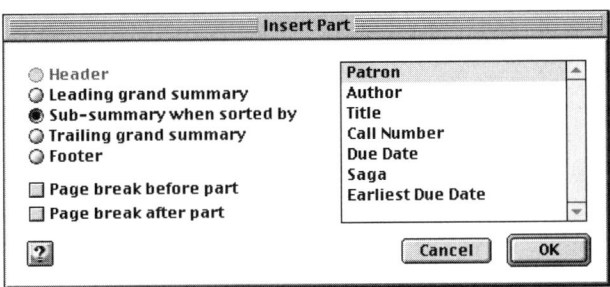

FIGURE 10-25. Insert Part Window

You can create grand summaries for the entire database: a leading grand summary is printed before the data; a trailing grand summary follows the data.

In this case, you want a sub-summary, because you want the data to be summarized for each patron. As noted previously, the database must be sorted so that all of the data for the sub-summary is together. As you can see from Figure 10-25, if you choose sub-summary, you also specify the field by which the database must be sorted.

You then are asked to choose if the sub-summary should precede or follow its data, as shown in Figure 10-26. In this case, choose Above.

184 • Chapter 10: Multiple Solutions to Problems with ClarisWorks

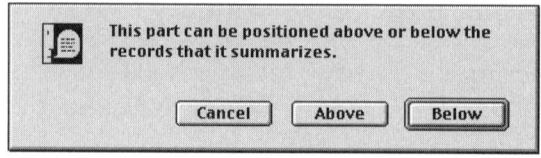

FIGURE 10-26. Part Placement Window

That is all you have to do to create the sub-summary.

Creating Summary Fields

The sub-summary will display three elements of data:

1. The name of the patron

2. The earliest due date for all books

3. The total number of overdue books

The first of these (the name) is easy enough: since the sub-summary applies to records for only one patron, you can simply insert the patron name field into the sub-summary (you will see how in a moment).

The other two fields, however, are trickier. They must be computed for all of the records in the sub-summary. Claris-Works lets you create summary fields in your database; you will need two of them.

Define Fields... from the Layout menu opens the window shown in Figure 10-27 (the same one you saw when you first created a database—Figure 10-14).

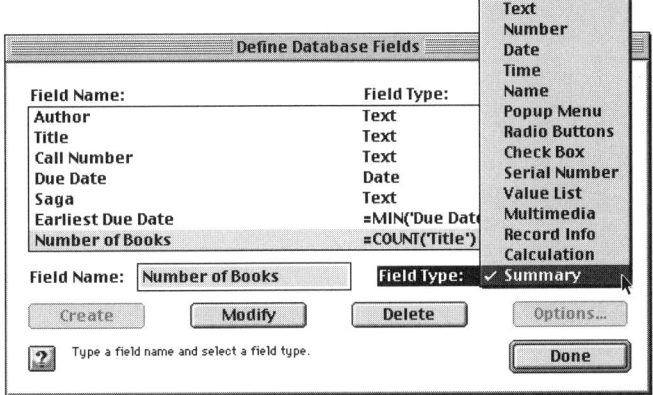

FIGURE 10-27. Define Database Fields

You will see that among the field types is a Summary type: enter the name of the field that you want to create and choose Summary from the pop-up menu.

Since a summary field must be computed for all the records in the summary, ClarisWorks immediately opens the window shown in Figure 10-28 to let you specify the computation.

You can combine fields, operators, and functions to create a formula (just as you would in a spreadsheet—for more information see the basic ClarisWorks documentation on paper or online).

Note that you can specify the format of the result. In this case, the formula is used to compute the minimum value of the Due Date field. The result must be formatted as a date.

A Summary data field is calculated by using the values of all of the records within the summary of sub-summary; in this it differs from a Calculation data field, which is part of each individual record and is calculated from other input fields.

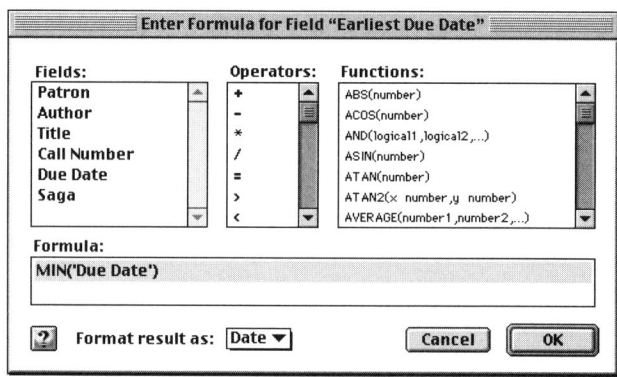

FIGURE 10-28. Field Formula Window

Adding Fields to the Layout

Now all you need to do is to add the summary fields to the layout. To do so, choose Insert Field… from the Layout menu (remember to make sure you are in Layout mode first). The Insert Fields window opens as shown in Figure 10-29.

The fields from the database that have not yet been added to the layout are shown here. Note that you can place a field only once in a layout—be it in a body part, a sub-summary part, or a summary part.

Add the two summary fields that you created as well as the patron field. The window shown in Figure 10-29 appears as it would after you have added the due date summary and count summary fields. The Patron field is about to be added;

the Author and Call Number fields will appear nowhere on this layout and therefore will remain in the Insert Fields window.

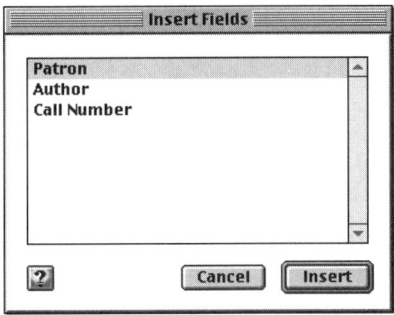

FIGURE 10-29. Insert Fields Window

Using the New Layout

To use the new layout, you choose it from the Layout menu—it will be added at the bottom. The default layout that was created by ClarisWorks will be called Layout 1 (unless you have renamed it with the Edit Layouts... command from the Layout menu).

Since the layout relies on sub-summaries, you must make certain that the database is sorted by Patron (remember that you specified this in the Insert Part window—Figure 10-25).

Sorting the Database

You can sort a spreadsheet by up to three sort keys (see Figure 10-10). A database, however, can be sorted by all of its data fields. When you choose Sort Records... from the Organize menu, the Sort Records window opens, as shown in Figure 10-30.

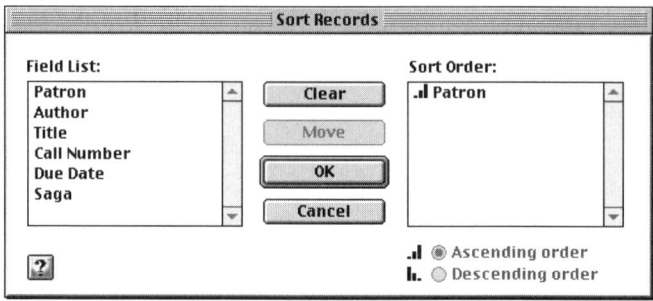

FIGURE 10-30. Sort Records Window

Whenever you want to sort records, you click on the fields you want to sort on and move them one by one (with the Move button) to the Sort Order part of the window.

For example, if you want to sort by Patron in ascending order, you click on Patron, then Move and the Ascending order at the bottom right of the window. The window would look at that point as it does in Figure 10-30. You could then specify a second-order sort (a sort within a sort).

If you chose Due Date, then clicked Move, and then Descending order, your database would be arranged by patron; for each patron, the books would be listed in descending order of due date—that is, latest first.

For your layout to work, you must have sorted the database by Patron (with possibly additional keys, but the first one must be Patron).

Check that you are in Page View (from the Windows menu), that the new layout is selected (from the Layout menu), and that Browse mode is selected (also from the Layout menu). You can then scroll through the database.

Finding Data and Displaying It

You can use this layout to display selected parts of your database. The easiest way to do this is to open a New View from the Window menu. This will give you two windows onto the database.

Each window can have its own layout and display mode, but the underlying database is the same in both windows. Set one window to browse your new layout; set the other one to browse the default layout (which may still be called Layout 1 if you have not renamed it).

Click on the original layout, and choose Find from the Layout menu. You will see the Find window shown in Figure 10-31.

As with the Layout mode, this window shows only one record at a time; all data is blank—you enter what you want to search for.

Most likely you would want to search for a specific patron. Enter the name (or part of the name) in the Patron field. Click the Find button at the left of the window. All records that match that name will be found. (You can limit the search, but in this and many other cases you want to search from all records, not just the visible ones—the controls at the left of the window should appear as they are in Figure 10-31.)

You can change the layout of this window to your new layout to see the results—but you have a second window open whose layout is already set properly. Use the two windows to alternately find data and view it.

190 • Chapter 10: Multiple Solutions to Problems with ClarisWorks

FIGURE 10-31. Find Window

You may wonder why two windows are involved here. In fact, this is a very common situation. The field on which you want to Find information—Patron—does not appear in the layout that you have created. If it did, it would appear for each record. Patron is shown only in the sub-summary records. In order to be able to find on a field, you must be able to enter a value for it—which means that it must be in the body of a given layout. If you wanted to search by Title, you could do your finding and browsing within the single layout, since the Title field is in the body of that layout. Experiment for yourself and you'll see quickly how it works.

Summary

This chapter has shown how you can use three types of documents to accomplish the same task. You choose whichever is most convenient for you.

ClarisWorks has little problem converting data from one format to another. In fact, the data used in the examples for this chapter actually came from a ClarisWorks 4 spreadsheet. ClarisWorks 5 read that spreadsheet and was able to import its data into a word processing document and a spreadsheet.

There is no one right way to present and manipulate data. ClarisWorks is flexible and easy: you are in charge.

Creating an Image Map in ClarisWorks

You can use ClarisWorks to prepare information to be used in other applications. Whether it is finished text or graphics or supporting information such as a database or spreadsheet that you use in research, ClarisWorks can be used as part of a larger project.

This chapter shows how you can use ClarisWorks to create an image map for a Web page. This is a useful task in and of itself; it can also serve as a review of some of the ClarisWorks graphics tools.

About Image Maps

Image maps are a common addition to Web pages; they are a convenient interface for users and are often used to tie together the various pages on a single Web site. The image map is a graphic with a variety of hot spots that take you to specific locations. Figure 11-1 shows an image map in a browser.

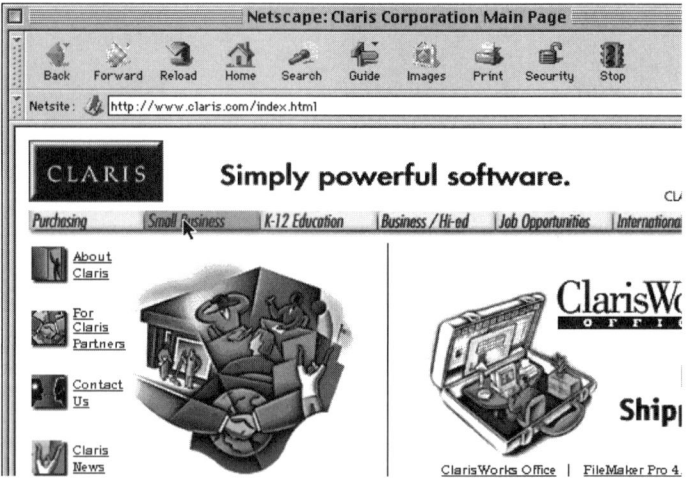

FIGURE 11-1. Image Map (Client Side)

This is from the Claris home page. The bar across the top (with the words "Purchasing," "Small Business," "K-12 Educaction," etc.) is a single image. As you move the cursor along the image, a click sends you to different places. At the bottom of the window you can see that with the cursor positioned over Job Opportunities a click would take you to http:/www.claris.com/about/hr/jobs.html.

Client and Server Side Image Maps

The Web page itself contains a reference to the graphic (which, like all Web graphics, is in a separate file). The Web page also contains a map—a list of areas of the graphic and where a mouse click should take you if you click there.

This is called a client side image map: the Web page has all the information needed to route your mouse click. Accordingly, your Web browser processes the mouse click and sends you to the appropriate destination.

Client side image maps are now very common and most browsers support them. Early browsers did not support client side image maps and instead implemented server side image maps. Figure 11-2 shows a server side image map.

This Web page (from *The New York Times*) has an image map at the left: the Sections area is a single image (containing text) that is mapped to various locations. The implementation here, however, is a server side image map. If you look at the bottom of the browser, you can see that instead of a regular URL, as you move the cursor its coordinates on the image map are shown. Furthermore, there is a reference to a file (index.map) on the Web site that contains the map to match specific mouse clicks to given URLs. This means that the browser does not have enough information to route the mouse click directly to the destination: the server has to do that. (In fact, the server has to run a little program to accomplish this.)

You can tell the difference between client side and server side image maps by whether the URL at the bottom of the screen shows coordinates (as in Figure 11-2) or URLs (as in Figure 11-1).

FIGURE 11-2. Image Map (Server Side)

You can implement image maps in either manner; you can also implement them in a composite fashion so that if people have a browser that supports client side image maps they will use that feature and use server side image maps only if the browser cannot support client side image maps.

Good Web page design dictates that you also provide the information in the image map in a plain text version (often at the bottom of your page). This is for people who do not have graphical browsers.

Many people today implement only client side image maps: most browsers have accommodated them for years, they do not require a small program to run on the Internet server, and they reduce Internet traffic slightly. You can build both client side and server side image maps with ClarisWorks; this section just deals with client side image maps.

How to Do It

It is very easy to create a client side image map with Claris-Works. There are three steps:

1. Create the graphic that you want for the image. Add text to it if necessary.

2. Locate the hot spots for mouse clicks and supply a URL for each one.

3. Modify the HTML code for your Web page. Although most people today use graphical Web authoring tools (such as Claris Home Page) or ClarisWorks itself, the change to support image maps is a very simple one: you just have to paste something into the HTML file.

Creating the Graphic

First decide what your image map will look like. Browse the Web and see how various organizations do this. You will find that many sites use an image map on each of their pages to provide a common interface and shared identity. The bar on the Claris pages that is under the cursor in Figure 11-1 is one such example (which may well have changed to another image by the time you read this).

The major concern in designing an image map is its size and shape. As it will probably appear on many pages, it will determine the design of the rest of each page. The Claris horizontal bar is one approach. Figure 11-3 shows yet another image map design.

FIGURE 11-3. Vertical Image Map

The basic image of your image map should be fairly simple: it will appear on many pages and should not overpower those pages' contents. Also, remember that the more complicated the image, the longer it will take to download.

The image in Figure 11-3 is very simple. As shown in Figure 11-4, just draw a rectangle and choose the gradient you want to fill it with. (You could also choose a single color or a pattern.) This step is shown in Figure 11-4.

Then, type in the text for the choices you want to appear in the image map. You can use simple text or you can augment (or replace text entirely) with other graphics. In this case, since the background is fairly dark, the color of the text is set to white so that it is easily read.

Next, save the file. That is all there is to it. You add it to your Web page just as you normally would add any other image to it.

To create Web pages in ClarisWorks, see "Posting the Newsletter on the Web" on page 259.

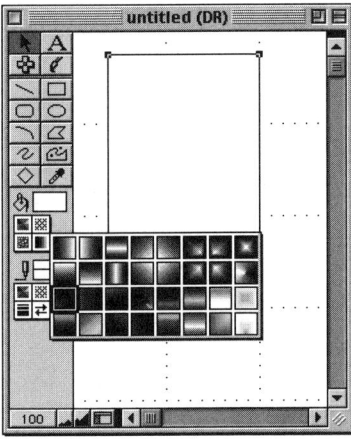

FIGURE 11-4. Image Map Step 1

Locate the Hot Spots

In this step, you will locate the hot spots on your image map. Reopen the graphic file.

Set the Rulers to Points

You need to show the rulers in units of points:

1. If the rulers are not shown, choose Show Rulers from the Window menu.

2. Set the rulers for points: use the Format/Rulers... command to open the Rulers window as shown in Figure 11-5. Set the Graphics ruler type to points as shown.

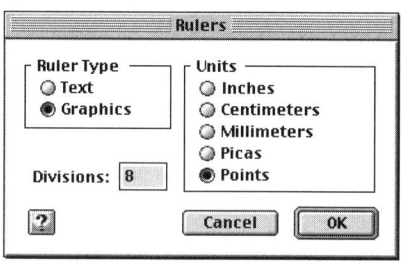

FIGURE 11-5. Format Rulers Window

Place the Graphic at Coordinate 0,0

Now, move the graphic so that it is at the upper left of the window (at coordinate 0,0). An easy way to position a graphic accurately at a specific location is with the Size window. Choose Object Size... from the Options menu to open the Size window as shown in Figure 11-6.

Set the values for the first two items to 0. You will see that as soon as you tab out of each field (or click on another) the object moves to the location you have just entered.

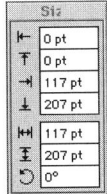

FIGURE 11-6. Size Window

Draw the Hot Spots

Open a ClarisWorks text document and type in the following. Yes, it is HTML, but just type it in:

```
<MAP NAME="mymap">

<area shape=rect coords= "" href="">

</MAP>
```

The quotes are straight quotes, not the curly smart quotes normally used in word processing documents. Turn off smart quotes by using the Preferences… command from the Edit menu. Select Text in the pop-up and turn off smart quotes, as shown in Figure 11-7.

You can name your map anything you want. "Mymap" is a poor choice because it is not very descriptive. Choose a more useful name.

Now, copy the second line (area shape) and paste it into the document once for every hot spot you will have. For each hot spot, type in the URL that it will go to by typing between the quotes following href=.

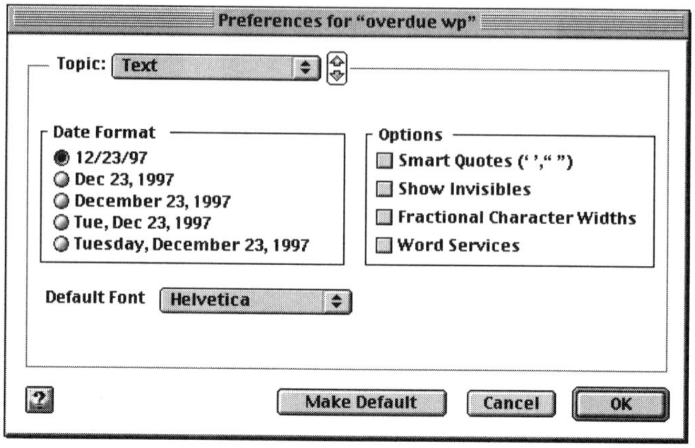

FIGURE 11-7. Text Preferences Dialog

For each URL, locate the coordinates of the hot spot as follows. On your image, draw a rectangle that you want to be hot. Using the Size window, type its coordinates between the quotes following rect coords =. In Figure 11-6, the Size window shows the size of a rectangle that covers the entire graphic. The coordinates are the first four numbers shown (0, 0, 117, and 207). To make that rectangle a hot spot for the Claris home page, you would wind up with a line that reads:

```
<area shape=rect coords="0,0,117,207"
   href="http://www.claris.com">
```

You should have one such line for each hot spot. Each hot spot has its own coordinates and its own URL.

Copy all of the text in the text document. You will paste it into the HTML file.

Modify the HTML Code

Finally, you need to modify the HTML code for your page. If you used ClarisWorks to create your Web page, open the .html or .htm file. If you have used another authoring tool (such as Claris Home Page) choose the menu option called Edit HTML Source (or its equivalent).

Just for insurance, save a copy of your HTML file before starting to work.

Find the code that inserts your graphic into the page: it starts with <IMG SRC (for image source). <IMG SRC may appear in the middle of a line, preceded by other HTML code. The line of code might look something like this:

```
<IMG SRC="image.gif" WIDTH=102HEIGHT=279 ALIGN=bottom>
```

The name of the image file is shown in this line of code; you may have named it or your authoring tool may have named it for you. (If you have multiple images on that page, you must make certain that you are modifying the correct one.)

Just before <IMG SRC, paste in the lines of text that you typed. You may have to add a carriage return afterward to get <IMG to start on its own line. Extra carriage returns do not hurt.

In the <IMG SRC line, add a reference to the map that you created and that you just pasted in. You will need the name ("mymap" or whatever you named it). Add the underlined code to the <IMG SRC line as shown here:

```
<IMG SRC="image.gif" usemap="#mymap" ISMAP WIDTH=102
HEIGHT=279 ALIGN=bottom>
```

The pound sign (#) within the quotes is required to precede your map name. Do not change any of the other text in the <IMG SRC line (even if it does not quite match the text shown here).

Save and upload the file to your Web site as usual, and you should be set.

Summary

Creating a client side image map is very simple; some Web authoring tools provide map-making tools for you, but using ClarisWorks to create the image and to make the map is very simple. Even modifying the HTML is not particularly difficult.

Part III

ClarisWorks in the Real World

12

Creating a Newsletter

This part of the book presents several real-life scenarios mostly centered around creating a newsletter and distributing it. The point of this presentation is not so much to describe the actual practice of creating a newsletter but rather to put the features and capabilities of ClarisWorks in focus in the context of an ordinary operation.

The ClarisWorks documentation (on paper and online) is organized primarily around the functional areas of ClarisWorks; this section ties together disparate ClarisWorks features in the way that you might actually use them. Not every feature is presented, nor are all the options for the features described. The idea of this section is to give you a sense of what you can do with ClarisWorks and how to begin to go about things that you may not have thought of doing so far.

About Newsletters

A newsletter is a good project to use to explore ClarisWorks. A newsletter can be a weekly or monthly bulletin that you send out to staff or customers; it can be an annual report to shareholders—or an annual holiday greeting to your friends. Newsletters can be informational or entertaining (or some combination thereof).

They can be distributed by being left in a pile by the water cooler; they can be sent through the mail with preprinted labels or by merging their contents with a mailing list (see "Sending the Newsletter Out" on page 233). They can be converted to HTML and posted on the Internet (see "Posting the Newsletter on the Web" on page 259). A newsletter can also serve as the basis for a presentation that you give to colleagues or staff (see "Presenting the Newsletter in Person" on page 281).

Whatever it is, and however it is produced, a newsletter has the following characteristics (which are addressed in this chapter with ClarisWorks features):

- A newsletter typically contains a number of different articles, stories, or other items; in this it differs from a simple memo or flyer which deals with only one issue.

- A newsletter may combine text and graphics.

- Newsletters generally are part of a series—they are issued weekly, annually, or periodically—rather than being a one-time document.

- Often, several people contribute to a newsletter.

- The person putting a newsletter together may have other responsibilities.

A typical newsletter might look like the illustration in Figure 12-1.

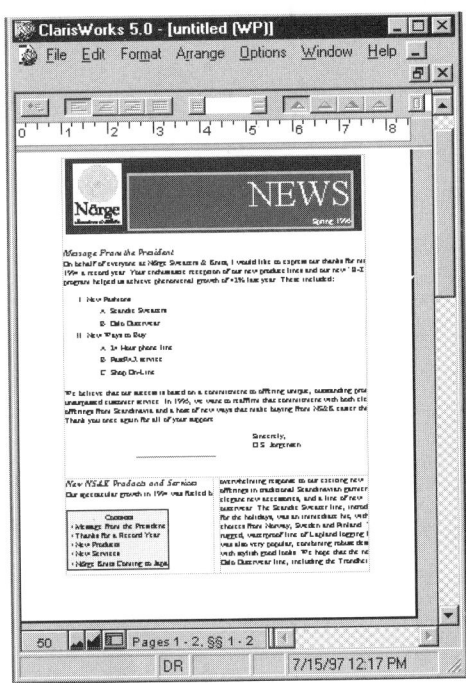

FIGURE 12-1. Newsletter Stationery—Page 1

What This Chapter Covers

These are the ClarisWorks features that are discussed in this chapter:

- Assistants and Stationery—They make it easy for you to create a newsletter even if you are not experienced at doing so.

- Style Sheets—They help you provide a constant look for your newsletter, even if several people are working on it.

- Publish and Subscribe—They let you incorporate material from other documents without changing it. While cut-and-paste lets you copy information and then modify it yourself, publish and subscribe keeps the information intact (although you can change its formatting). You can worry about its presentation while someone else worries about keeping it up to date.

- Linked Text Frames—You can link text frames together, letting text flow from one frame to another. In a newsletter—with a number of different articles and with pictures and other material on the page—you often want to continue a story on another page of the document.

Assistants and Stationery

ClarisWorks provides two primary tools for helping people do tasks that they do not often do (and hence need help

Assistants and Stationery • 211

with). These tools are the ClarisWorks assistants and the stationery that is provided with ClarisWorks.

Stationery

Newsletter stationery is provided with ClarisWorks. The two pages of this document are shown in Figures 12-1 and 12-2. (Note that stationery documents are always opened as untitled copies of themselves; the stationery documents themselves remain unchanged as you work on your copies.)

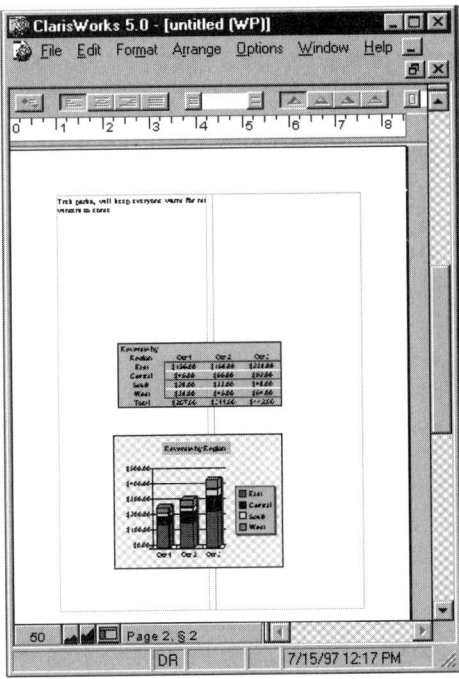

FIGURE 12-2. Newsletter Stationery—Page 2

In Figure 12-2, even more than in Figure 12-1, you can see that the layout consists primarily of a template into which you can type or paste your information. The newsletter stationery is a word processing document.

Assistants

The assistant for newsletters walks you through questions about the number of pages you want, the style you want, and whether you want the layout to accommodate blank space for a mailing label. When you have answered the questions, the assistant prepares a newsletter such as in Figure 12-3.

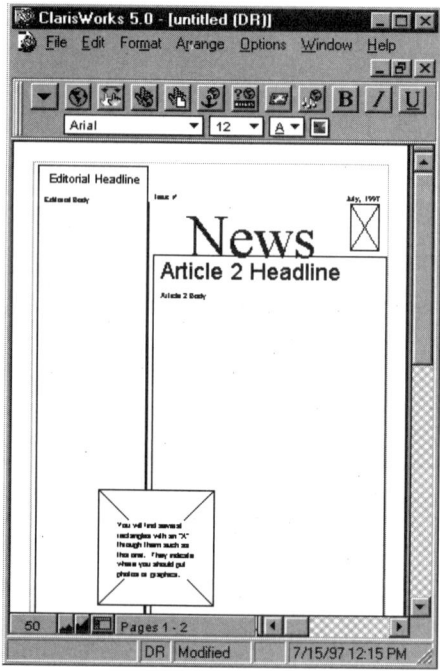

FIGURE 12-3. Newsletter Assistant

The Newsletter assistant produces newsletters that are draw documents (as opposed to the word processing documents from the stationery). Also, since the assistant asks you a number of questions, a great variety of newsletter templates can be produced automatically by the assistant.

Finally, the assistant produces a helpful newsletter of Tips and Hints as shown in Figure 12-4. Not only does this provide useful information, but you can use it as a jumping off point for your own Tips and Hints. You can customize it for your own organization and use it as a style sheet for yourself and others.

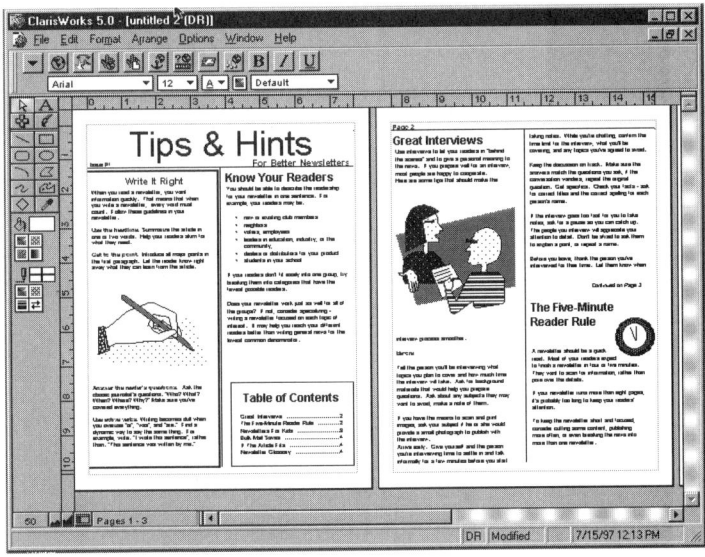

FIGURE 12-4. Newsletter Tips and Hints

Whether you use the Newsletter stationery, the Newsletter assistant, or create a document on your own, it is easy to start a newsletter in ClarisWorks.

Now what?

As a practical way of working, many people start to gather the material that will go into a newsletter far in advance of a deadline. You (and others) can create graphics, ClarisWorks text documents, and much of the rest of the newsletter. Then, when it comes time to put the newsletter together, you can take either the Newsletter stationery or the document created by the Newsletter assistant (or something of your own creation) and insert the prepared text and graphics into it.

Style Sheets

Of course, it is likely that each of the documents that you insert uses a different font, size, margins, etc. You can try to enforce standards, but these efforts are usually fruitless. Even if you are preparing the newsletter solely by yourself, you need a variety of fonts, sizes, margins, etc. for your other work.

What to do?

You can create styles for your newsletter: styles combine a variety of formatting options into a single combination called a style. No matter how people have formatted their material, when you incorporate it into the newsletter you can just restyle it (instead of having to change fonts, margins, tabs, etc. individually). First, open the Stylesheet from the Window menu as shown in Figure 12-5.

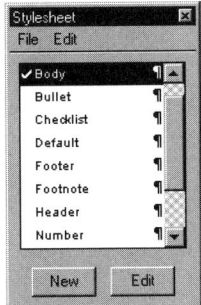

FIGURE 12-5. ClarisWorks Stylesheet

The Stylesheet for each document lists all of its styles. You can add and remove styles from the Stylesheet; you can also edit them. (The File submenu within the Stylesheet lets you import and export styles; this can be a big help when you need to use common styles for several documents—such as for various issues of your newsletter.)

If you click the Edit button at the bottom of the Stylesheet window, you can edit the styles—as shown in Figure 12-6.

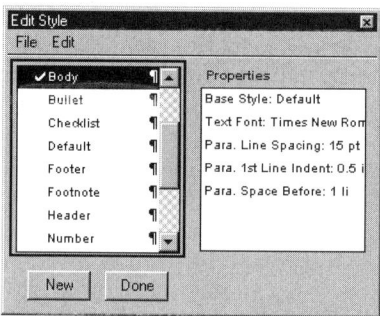

FIGURE 12-6. Editing a Style

At the right, you see the properties of this style. You use the normal formatting features of ClarisWorks (the button bar, the menus, keyboard equivalents, etc.) to modify the properties of the selected style. While the Stylesheet window is open, all formatting commands affect the selected style—not the document itself.

For example, a common customization of a style is shown in Figure 12-7. The default spacing of most fonts is not ideal. A 12-point font is usually displayed in lines that are 12 points high. This is normally considered not high enough. As a result, many designers prefer to display 12-point text in lines that are 15 points high. The Paragraph window shown in Figure 12-7 is used to set line spacing to 15 points. (You can see the Edit Style window behind the Paragraph window, so you know that the editing change is affecting a style rather than a document's text.)

This style also indents the first line of each paragraph by half an inch. As you can infer from the pop-up menus, you can specify the spacing in points, lines, inches, and other units.

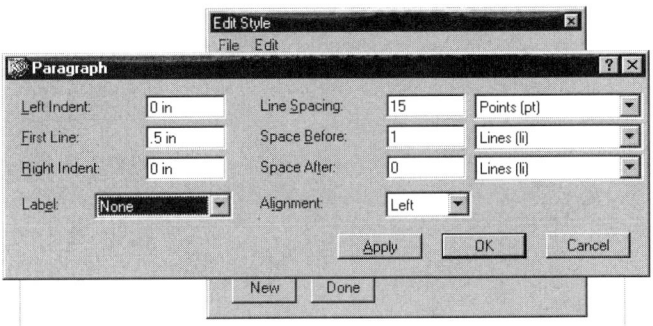

FIGURE 12-7. Formatting Paragraph

For an example of this spacing, consider the fact that the text of this book is set in 11-point type spaced on 13-point lines. The text in this note is 10-point type spaced on 11-point lines.

Publish and Subscribe

It is easy enough to incorporate information from various documents in your ClarisWorks newsletter, but sometimes you want to have more control over that information.

Publish and Subscribe (on Mac OS) let you do that. On Windows, OLE lets you do similar things.

The point of both Publish and Subscribe and OLE is to have information in one document that is displayed in another—but which is modified only in the original document. The example in Figure 12-8 may make this clear.

218 • Chapter 12: Creating a Newsletter

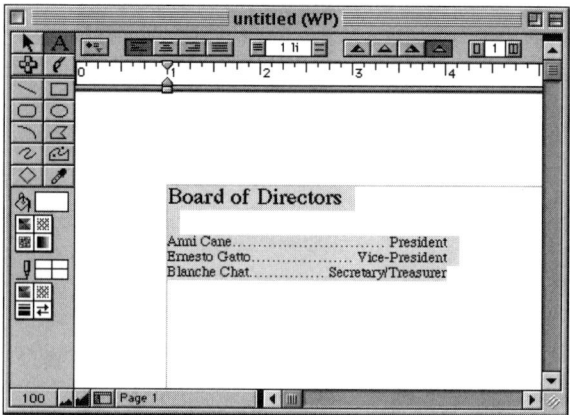

FIGURE 12-8. Publish and Subscribe

Here is a document that contains a list of a board of directors. This information may need to appear in your newsletter—as well as in many other documents. It is very easy to copy the information into each document, but if there is a change to the board then each document needs to be manually changed.

If you publish this information from the original document, any number of other documents can subscribe to it. Changes made in the original document (the publisher) are reflected in the other documents. When you consider that you can publish and subscribe over a local area network, it is clear that you can save a lot of time and effort on routine types of information. In addition to staff lists such as this, you can publish hours of operation, staffing schedules, cafeteria menus, etc. Various documents can subscribe to them without knowing what their specific contents are. If you create a weekly newsletter, you can simply type

```
This week's menus are:
```

and then subscribe to a menu document somewhere on your network. Every time you open your document, you will get the latest version of the menu—without worrying about it.

There are two parts to this process: publishing and subscribing.

Publishing Information

You select information, publish it, and specify a file for the published information to be stored in. Then you save your document and you are done.

Once you have entered your information, select it (as shown in Figure 12-8). Note that you can publish only some of the information in a document—you need not publish the entire document.

Then choose Create Publisher... from the Edit menu as shown in Figure 12-9.

On Mac OS, publish and subscribe is supported by many applications; you can publish from ClarisWorks documents and subscribe to them from other applications. Similarly, you can publish from other types of documents and subscribe to them from ClarisWorks documents.

---

220 • Chapter 12: Creating a Newsletter

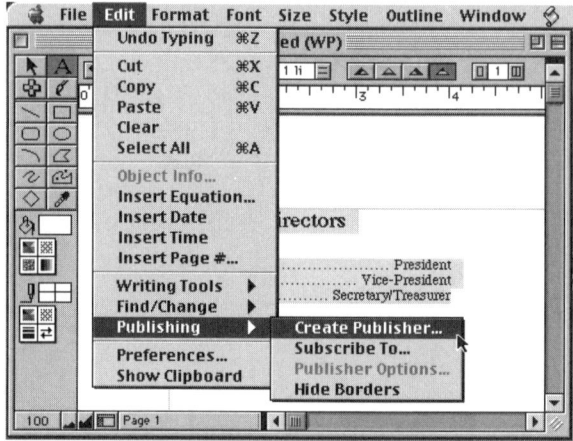

FIGURE 12-9. Publish Command

You will be asked to specify a file for the published material (the "edition"); if you place this file on a shared disk on a file server, you and others can subscribe to it from anywhere on your network. (The basic document need not be on the file server.) Figure 12-10 shows the dialog in which you are asked to name the edition that you are publishing.

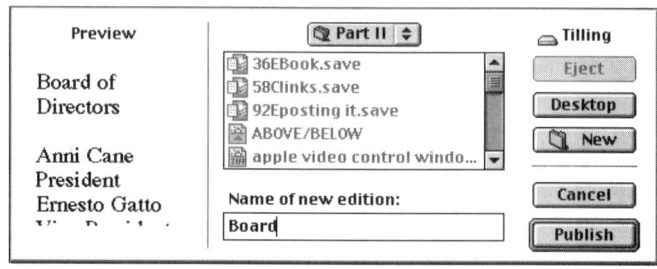

FIGURE 12-10. Naming an Edition

Subscribing

The next step is to subscribe to the information. (In the case of the newsletter, you are probably only subscribing to information: someone else may have published it.)

Choose Subscribe To... from the Edit menu as shown in Figure 12-11.

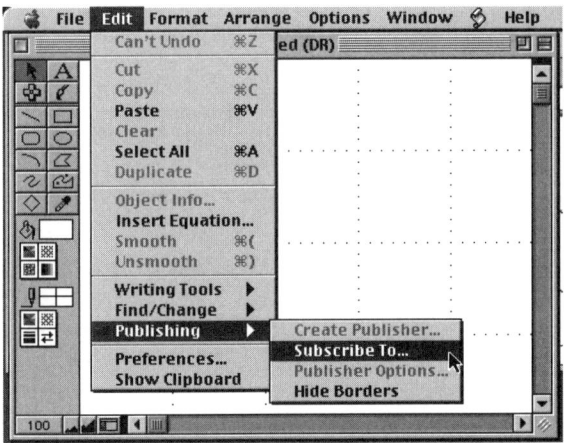

FIGURE 12-11. Subscribe To

The information is shown in your document as in Figure 12-12. Notice that you cannot tell what part of the information is in this document and what part comes from elsewhere. It all looks like one.

222 • Chapter 12: Creating a Newsletter

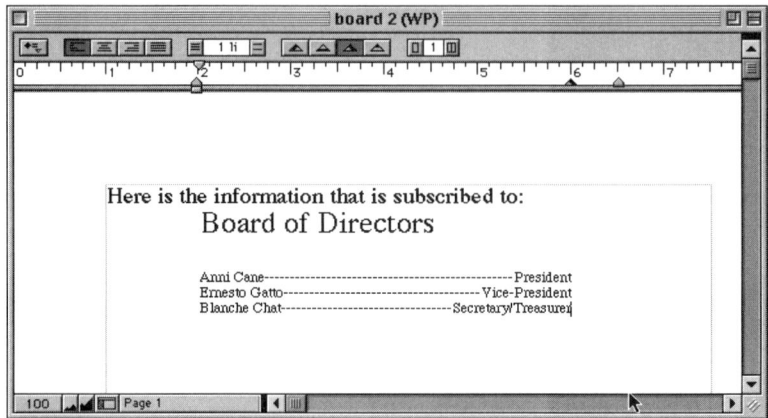

FIGURE 12-12. Publish Subscribe Embedded

If you click in the information that you have subscribed to (or if you choose Show Borders from the Publishing submenu of the Edit menu shown in Figure 12-11), you will see a special border as illustrated in Figure 12-13. The Show Borders command toggles with the Hide Borders command as you change this option.

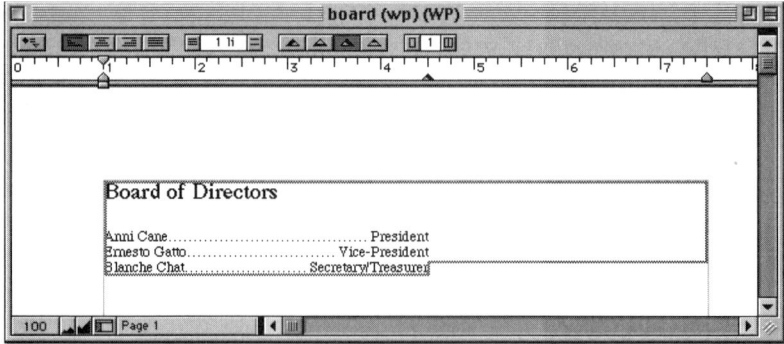

FIGURE 12-13. Publish Subscribe Edition

You cannot edit this information in this document, but if it is edited in its original document, the changes will be reflected here.

Figure 12-14 shows both documents. In the foreground is the document that publishes the information. Note that a change has been made; the document in the background does not yet reflect that change.

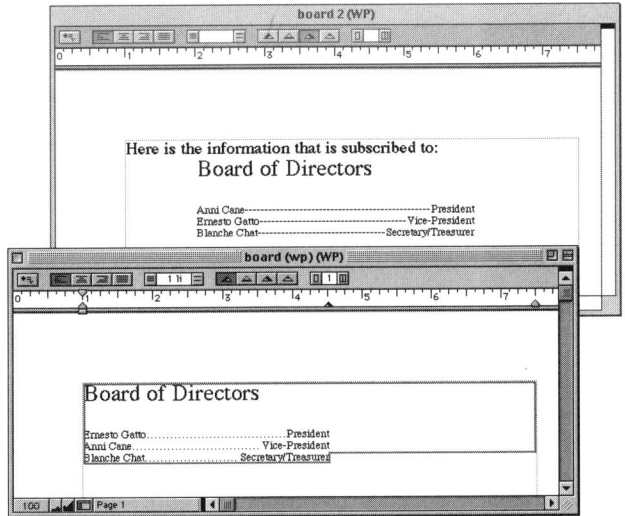

FIGURE 12-14. Changing a Publisher

As soon as you save the publisher (the document in the foreground), the subscribed automatically changes, as shown in Figure 12-15.

If you are creating a newsletter (or any of many other types of documents that relies on information from other sources in your organization), think of the time that you can save by subscribing to other documents!

The publish and subscribe mechanism is very robust and handles accidents very well. For example, if the publisher disappears—which can easily happen on a network—the subscriber simply uses the last version of the data that it has. Whatever happens, things will not break.

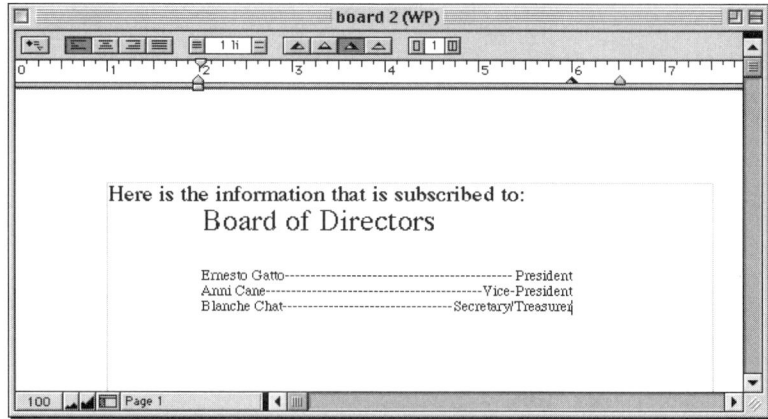

FIGURE 12-15. Updating

These examples have all used word processing documents: you can publish and subscribe to or from text frames within draw documents. (You can also publish and subscribe graphics.)

For example, Figure 12-16 shows the same information subscribed to from a draw document. Notice the four handles that outline the text frame; within it you can see the border of the subscribed text.

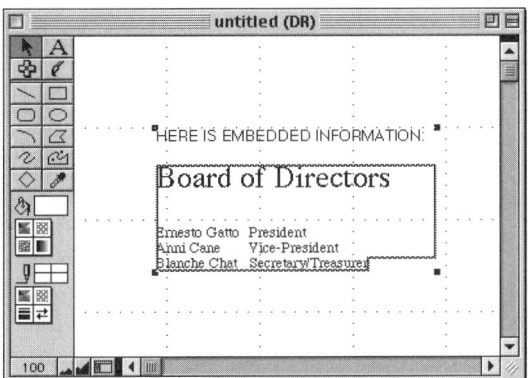

FIGURE 12-16. Embedded in Draw

The information is what is subscribed to. In Figure 12-17, the font and other formatting information of the text frame have been changed. This is done in the receiving document only.

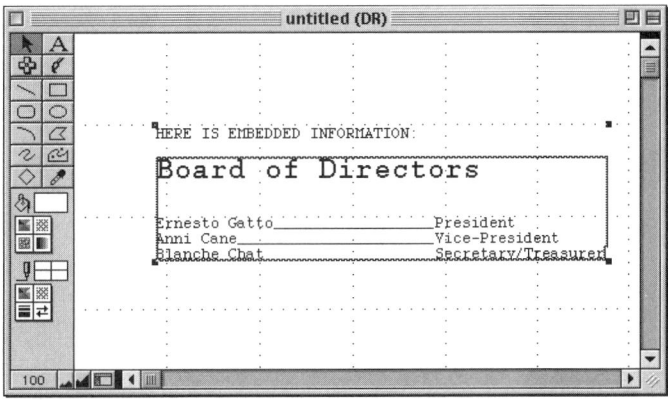

FIGURE 12-17. Embedded in Draw with Changes

When you subscribe to information, you can format it and style it just as you would any text.

You may notice that the tabs have changed between Figures 12-16 and 12-17. Figure 12-18 shows you how to change this format. If you double-click on a tab in the ruler, you can open the Tab formatting window. Notice the Fill character options at the upper right: you can vary them (as well as the alignment of the tab in the upper left). This seems to be one of the things that a lot of people miss—and it is very useful.

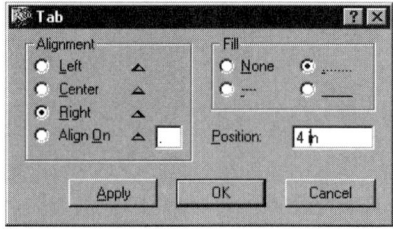

FIGURE 12-18. Formatting Tab

Linked Text Frames

Another issue that comes up in newsletters is the need to split text frames across columns or pages. This section shows you how to do that.

In Figure 12-19, you see a text frame within a draw document. It is selected (the four corner handles are highlighted).

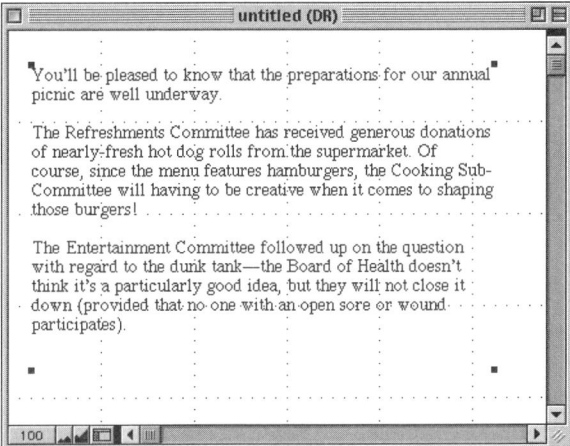

FIGURE 12-19. Frame Links 1

If you choose Frame Links from the Options menu (Figure 12-20), the outline of the text frame changes to that shown in Figure 12-21.

FIGURE 12-20. Frame Links Command

Here, in addition to the four handles at the corners, you see two additional features:

1. At the top is an indicator showing that this is the top of the frame.

2. At the center of the bottom is an indicator showing that there is a continuation for the text.

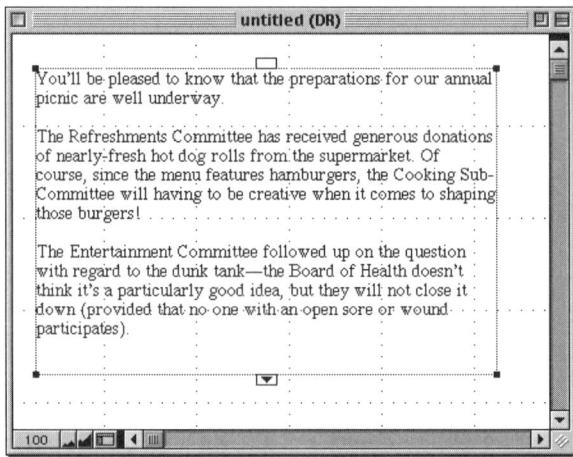

FIGURE 12-21. Frame Links 3

If you resize the text frame (as shown in Figure 12-22), all of the text can no longer be shown within the frame. The little X in the lower right corner shows that the text overflows the frame.

You can flow the text into another text frame as follows:

1. Click on the continuation indicator (under the mouse in Figure 12-22).

2. Click anywhere else in your document to create a new text frame that continues the flow (Figure 12-23).

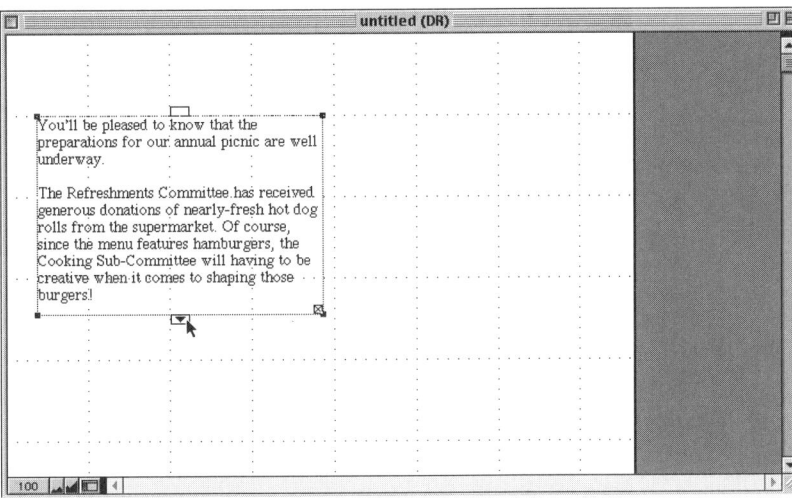

FIGURE 12-22. Text Frame with Overflow Indicator

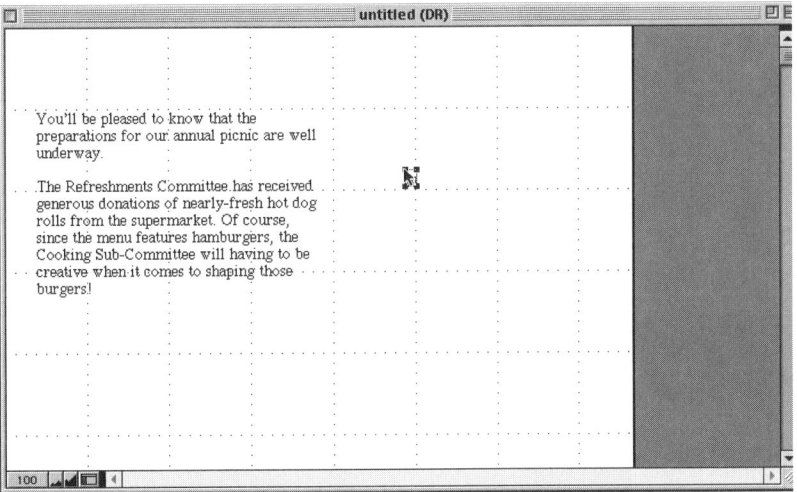

FIGURE 12-23. Overflow Text Frame Created

You can then resize and move each of the two linked frames independently. If necessary, as you resize each one the text will reflow from one to the other.

Figure 12-24 shows the new text frame resized; the text flows into the resized frame. You can see that the resized text frame is still not big enough to contain all of the text: a third text frame can be created using the same steps outlined here.

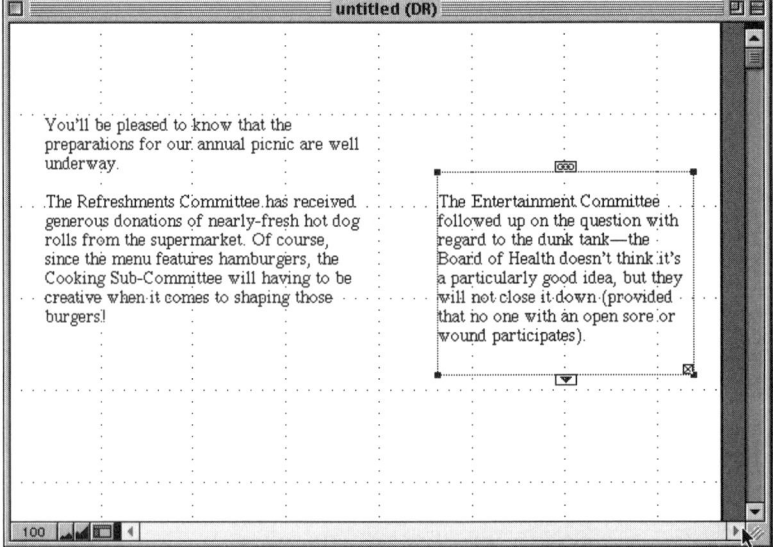

FIGURE 12-24. Text Frame Resized with Flowing Text

Summary

In the context of preparing a newsletter, this chapter has shown you how you can take advantage of assistants and stationery, style sheets, publish and subscribe, and linked text flows. (Obviously these features are useful in many contexts in addition to newsletters.)

The next chapter continues the newsletter adventure, addressing the issues in sending it out: preparing labels, maintaining a mailing list, and dealing with mail merge.

13

Sending the Newsletter Out

There are many ways to distribute your newsletters. The easiest is to hand them out or place them in a pile at a central location. However, if the recipients of your newsletter are in any way scattered, you are going to have to rely on some other means of distribution.

The most common is the mail system—and here is where you run head first into the need to keep track of the recipients and print their addresses on demand. Maintaining mailing lists is the sort of thing that computers do very easily. In fact, one of the early selling points of personal computers to small organizations was that they could manage mailing lists.

Unfortunately, the tools that were promoted for the task were far too complicated. A mailing list really requires a word processor and a database. Attempts to use word processors alone to manage mailing lists are extremely awkward. Their two major failings are precisely the points that are made easy in ClarisWorks:

1. Word processors often have trouble formatting output that must be placed exactly on a page. Desktop publishing applications and drawing programs are used to the need to place an item at a specific location; word processors deal with a continuous flow of characters across a line and then down to the next. Even when graphics are interspersed, they are placed within this essentially linear and one-dimensional structure.

2. Word processors are not databases. They handle words and characters together with the marks of punctuation that accompany them. Information about the meaning of the words (which one is a name, which one is an address, etc.) has to be added on in one awkward way or another.

ClarisWorks has no difficulty whatsoever with these issues. Maintaining a mailing list and printing it out on demand are very simple. You may well have been burned before and have sworn never to touch another mailing list and never to lick another stamp or envelope. Although ClarisWorks cannot do anything about the paper cuts and messiness attendant on actually doing a mass mailing, it can—and does—make the mailing list itself trivial. If you have given up in the past, try it again. You may even enjoy it!

This chapter covers the two basic parts of mailing out your newsletter: creating and maintaining a database with the names and addresses and laying out the labels and producing the addresses (either as labels or printed directly on the newsletters). The process of creating labels or other printed addresses from the database into another ClarisWorks document is called mail merge (as it is in most other applications as well).

Creating the Mailing List/Contact Database

Notwithstanding the fact that you can use the different ClarisWorks document types to handle various problems in different ways (see "Multiple Solutions to Problems with ClarisWorks" on page 153), some problems are more appropriate to one document type than another. Managing a mailing list is definitely a problem for which you should use a database.

About Databases

Some of the specific database features that make it appropriate for this application are:

- format flexibility
- meta-data
- sorting
- selecting

Together, these attributes largely define what a database is.

Format Flexibility

A database stores data and allows you to print it out in any number of ways: the data layout is distinct from the data storage. In ClarisWorks, you can have multiple layouts for a database, allowing you to view or print it in any number of ways. In both word processing documents and in spreadsheets the format and the data are closely intertwined.

You can coerce a spreadsheet into storing name and address data and even into printing labels, but you will then have to rearrange the spreadsheet in order to print out the information in a different format. (Note that this is not the same as rearranging a layout in a database: rearranging the order of the rows or columns in a spreadsheet does affect the data.)

Meta-Data

A database stores data as well as information about the data (meta-data, if you want to impress your friends with you knowledge of Greco-Latin jargon). Meta-data matters because you can specify that you want specific elements of the database to be dealt with in specific ways.

For example, you can construct a mailing label that specifies where the first name goes, where the last name appears, where the postal code is printed, etc. You cannot do this (at least not easily) with other types of documents.

Sorting

Databases are designed to be sorted and resorted as the need arises. In most cases, the sorting information is stored separately from the data, so that the data itself is undisturbed by the order in which it is presented.

If you are mailing newsletters out (or anything else, for that matter), you may need to sort them by state, postal code, etc. in order to get the best postage rate. It is much easier to have the computer sort the addresses so that the labels and addresses will be generated in the correct order than for you to sort the envelopes at the end.

Selecting

With a database, you can select records based on any criteria that you devise. When you use a database as input to a mail merge command, only the currently selected records are used.

Creating Your Database

For all of these reasons, a database is the right tool to use to manage your mailing list. Your choices within ClarisWorks are three:

1. Create a database document from scratch and enter your data.

2. Use the Contact Database stationery that comes with ClarisWorks to create your mailing list.

3. Use the Address List assistant that comes with ClarisWorks.

Because you can always modify a database, it is best to use either the stationery or the assistant; if your needs are not covered by those documents, you can modify them. Starting from scratch does not prove that you are a database expert: it proves something else entirely.

Both the stationery and the assistant are described in the following sections.

Mailing List Stationery

If you open the Contact Database stationery that comes with ClarisWorks, you will see the window shown in Figure 13-1.

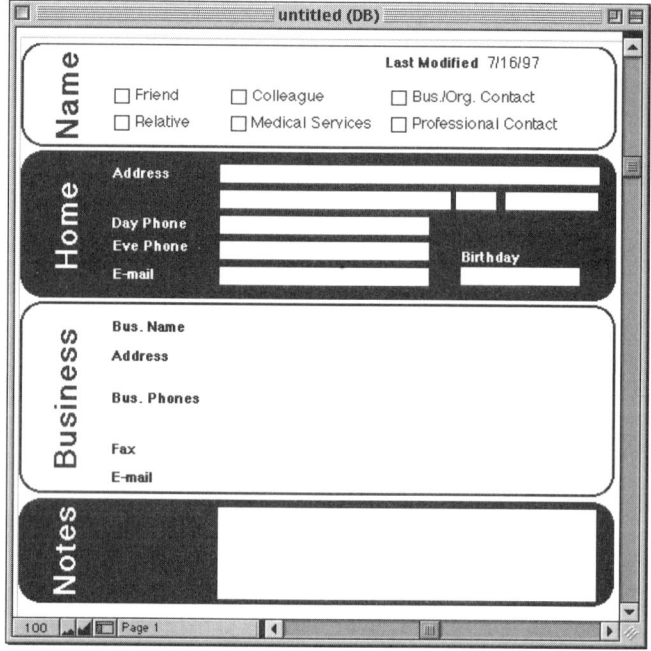

FIGURE 13-1. Contact Database Stationery

This is a reasonable place to start. There may be some additional fields that you need for your own purposes (see "Additional Fields You May Need" on page 245); in addition, there are some fields here that you may not be familiar with (such as the modification date at the top, which is a Record

Info field—see "Using Record Info Fields" on page 247). On the whole, however, most people find this basic database to be a good starting point.

Built into this document are several features that are particularly useful in maintaining your mailing list.

As shown in Figure 13-2, there are two predefined searches that you can access from the tools at the left of the window.

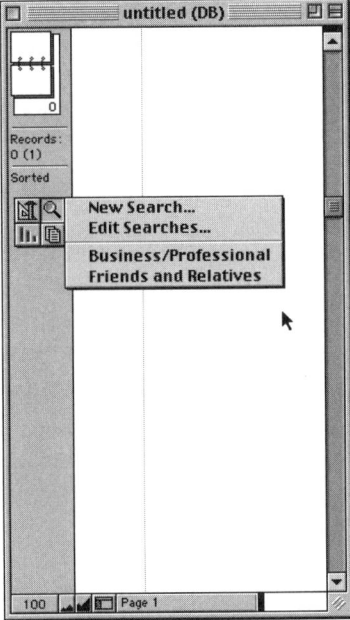

FIGURE 13-2. Search Popup

As noted previously, the database provides many additional services over and above simply storing data. This is one of them.

Another is the layouts that you can define for the database. In the case of the Contact Database stationery, several layouts have already been defined, as shown in Figure 13-3.

Among these layouts are several that are particularly useful to you if you are printing mailing labels. The Avery labels are commonly used self-adhesive mailing labels that you can put through your printer. Once they are printed, you peel them off and put them on your newsletter, envelope, etc. (Avery is a brand name, and these numbers are the Avery product numbers. Other brands are available—including generic and store brands, which often are keyed to these numbers.)

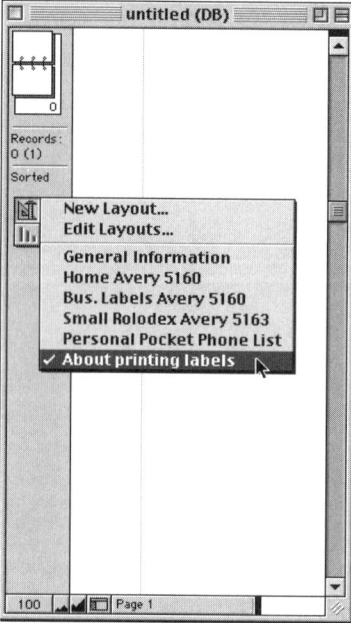

FIGURE 13-3. About Printing Labels Menu

Given this database with its fields, its predefined searches, and its layouts, you can do much of your mailing list work.

All you have to do is open the stationery and start to enter your information. (When you first open the stationery, check to see if sample data has been provided—it often is. Delete any records that have been shipped with the stationery before you enter your own data.)

Before you set to work retyping a long mailing list, check the sections in this book about data transfer and data conversion—"Databases" on page 170 and "Spreadsheets" on page 162). If you already have your mailing list in a word processing document or a spreadsheet, you probably do not have to retype it.

While you are exploring, you might take a look at the About Printing Labels layout, which is selected in Figure 13-3 and which is shown in Figure 13-4.

This is an interesting use of a layout: it does not display any information from the database. This is a clever way of keeping descriptive information with the database. Particularly if you are designing a ClarisWorks database that will be used by several people, you might want to consider creating a one-page layout like this with basic instructions.

242 • Chapter 13: Sending the Newsletter Out

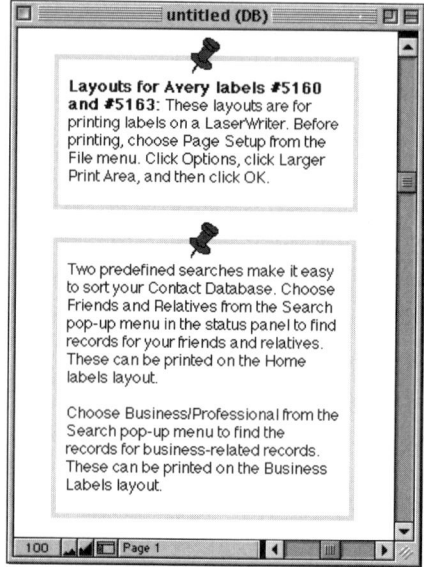

FIGURE 13-4. About Printing Labels Layout

Using an Assistant

Rather than using the Contact Database stationery, you can use the Address List assistant to create a database. From the Assistants button bar, click on the Address List assistant as shown in Figure 13-5.

Creating the Mailing List/Contact Database • **243**

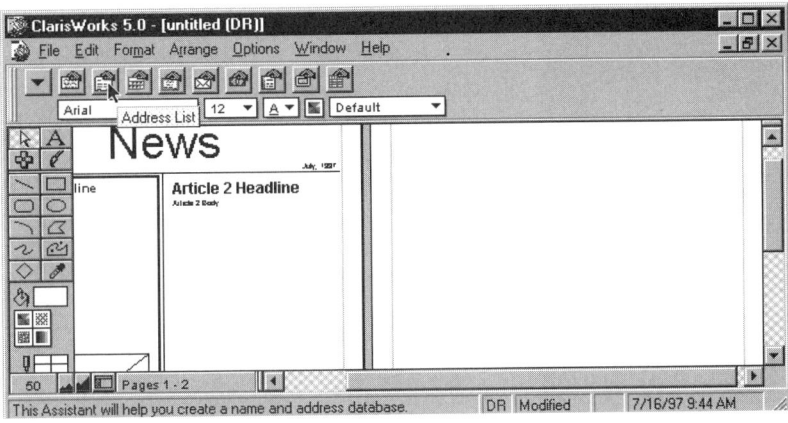

FIGURE 13-5. Name/Address Database Assistant from Assistant Button Bar

After an introductory screen, you will see the screen shown in Figure 13-6. You can choose from a Business, Personal, or Student database—as you choose each one, you see a preview of the fields to the left of the window. The Business and Personal databases each have two versions—a long and a short one. The Add More Fields check box in the assistant lets you add a set of additional fields to each database. Of course, you can always add even more fields yourself once the database has been created.

After you have chosen the type of database you want, you click the Create button and ClarisWorks creates the database for you. It opens it with a layout such as that shown in Figure 13-7 (the layout depends on which database you have chosen to create).

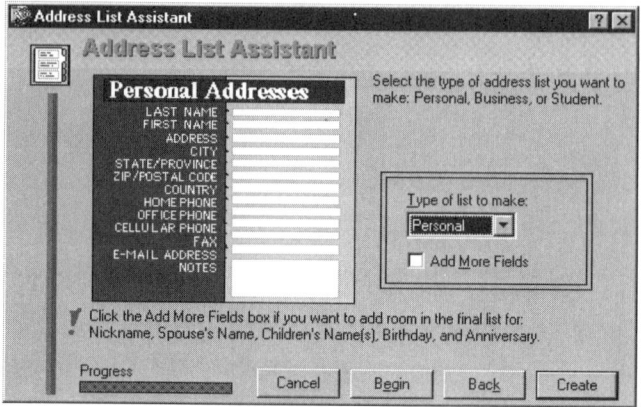

FIGURE 13-6. Address List Assistant

At this stage you can add more fields if you want; you can also rearrange or redesign the layout.

As with the Contact Database, this database comes with a few records already created. Switch to Browse mode, delete the records in the database, and start to add your own data.

As noted previously, before you start typing away, consider using one of the data import options. You can insert from a spreadsheet, a tab-delimited table in a word processing document, or from tab-delimited files produced by other applications.

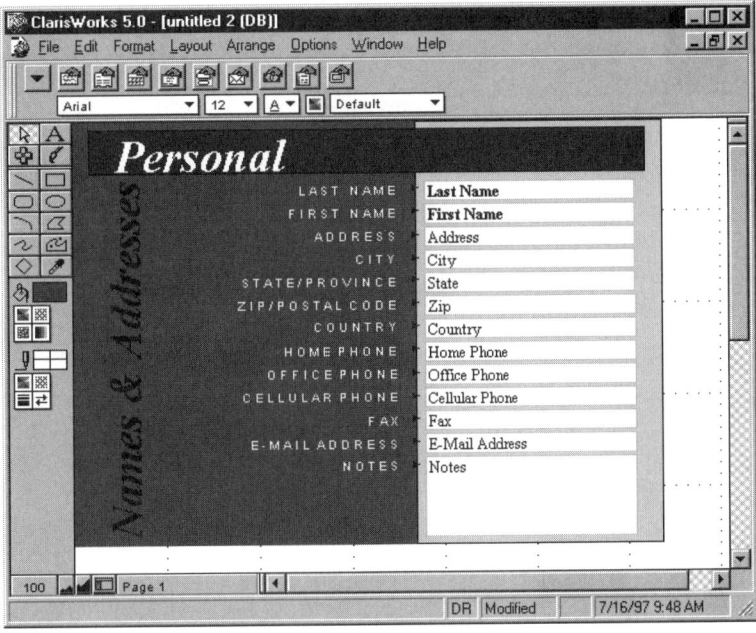

FIGURE 13-7. Database Entry Layout

Database Niceties

There are a number of features of databases in general and ClarisWorks databases in particular that may be of use to you in this project. Here are a few of them.

Additional Fields You May Need

You may want to add additional fields to your database. These fields may contain information not already in the database, or they may break down existing fields into smaller divisions; they also may contain calculated information.

As a general rule, you should have separate database fields for any field you want to search or select; you also need database fields for any field that needs to be printed on an address label.

ADDING NEW FIELDS If you look at the Contact database as well as at the Address List database, you will notice that neither contains a field for an honorific (Mr./Ms./Dr.). Depending on your database and the purpose to which it is put, you may need to add such fields.

Remember that the layout with which you view the database is totally independent of the database itself. You can add such fields whenever and wherever you want and display them as needed—or not—in various layouts.

BREAKING DOWN EXISTING FIELDS An example of breaking down a database field is the case in which you want to divide the address field into two or more parts. If someone's address contains an apartment or suite number or a mail stop, you may want to be able to select or sort by that part of the address. (You would want to do this when preparing a mailing that needs to be presorted for delivery either by the post office or within your organization.)

If the apartment or suite number or mail stop is part of the address field, it is hard (although not impossible) to sort or select on that portion of the address. The solution is to add a new field called something like Apartment/Suite/Mail Stop. Once that field exists, you can do your sorting and selecting on it.

USING CALCULATIONS It is very easy to sort or select data from your database when you can use an individual field to do so. The Contact Database stationery provides two calculated fields which it uses in its searches.

As you can see in Figure 13-8, there are two calculated fields—CityStateZip and BusCityStateZip. Each field is calculated by concatenating the values from three other fields together. When you want to select or search, you can just use the calculated fields rather than having to go about doing the calculation as part of your selection or search.

Do not go overboard with such fields: they can degrade the performance of your database. For most people, though, with modern computers, you do not have to worry about performance. And, fortunately, you can always remove these fields without destroying data: as they are calculated from the data which is entered, they can always be recreated.

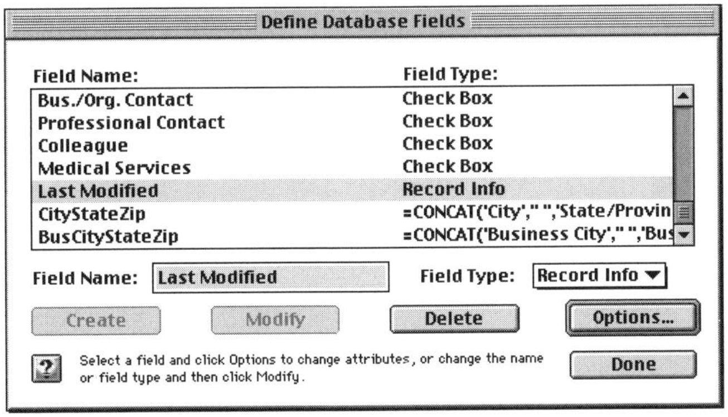

FIGURE 13-8. Define Fields

USING RECORD INFO FIELDS The ClarisWorks database lets you create fields of type Record Info. Last Modified (in Figure 13-8) is such a field; if you click on Options in that window for a Record Info field, the window shown in Figure 13-9 opens.

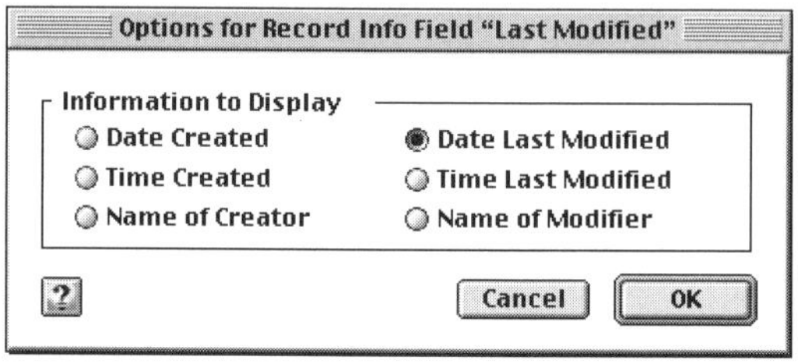

FIGURE 13-9. Options

These are special field types that are maintained by ClarisWorks. You can add them to your database and to your layout as you see fit. They require no data entry, but you can display them as you want. (The Last Modified field is displayed at the top of the layout shown in Figure 13-1.)

These fields are maintained by ClarisWorks based on information from the computer the database is running on. The name of the person creating or modifying the data as well as the dates involved may be wrong if the computer is set incorrectly. If you are using a database over a network where machines may have varying dates and times, you should be careful about using these fields in important reports. In particular, relying on dates and times to sequence records is very risky. What is "before" another event may vary, as the clocks on different machines have different times.

Automatic Editing of Data Entry

Another feature of the ClarisWorks database can come in handy as you modify your mailing list database. For any field in the database, you can set options as shown in Figure 13-10. (You open this window by clicking Options in the Define Fields window shown in Figure 13-8. This set of options is available for fields that you enter; other options—such as those shown in Figure 13-9—are available for other types of fields such as Record Info fields.)

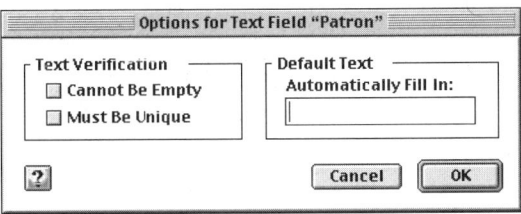

FIGURE 13-10. Setting Options for Fields in a Database

For your contact database, you might want to set the Last Name field to Cannot Be Empty. You also might want to fill in Country to be Italy (if most of your contacts are Italian). And so on.

The Must Be Unique option is important when you use a field as a unique key: that is the final database issue that is discussed here.

Unique Keys

A unique key is a database field that never has the same value for two different records in one database. Although you may have a number of Last Name fields that contain Chang, if you give each of your contacts an ID number, you should never have the same ID number in two different fields. In such a case you would mark the ID field as Must Be Unique in the Options window.

You use a unique key when you need the ability to locate a particular record unambiguously. Although the combination of first name, last name, address, etc. probably uniquely identifies most of the people in your database, it need not do so. (John Smith, Jr. may live at the same address as John Smith, Sr., and they may not identify themselves as Jr. and Sr.). This ambiguity is the source of what many people call computer mistakes. In fact, they are not computer mistakes at all—they are examples of the flexibility of the human brain and the relative inflexibility of computers.

An advantage of using ID numbers rather than names to locate people is that you can control the ID numbers. People do change their names for reasons of matrimony and felonious activities, among others. An ID number remains constant.

Many databases contain both an ID number and the name. You can devise your layouts in such a way that you search by name and use the ID number only if the names do not provide unambiguous identification.

Mail Merge

Once you have created your database, you need to set up your mail merge operation. It is literally only a matter of a few mouse clicks.

You have three basic choices when it comes to sending out your newsletter (or any other mailing, for that matter):

1. You can print the names and addresses on the folded newsletter and mail the newsletter.

2. You can print the names and addresses on envelopes and put the newsletters into the envelopes.

3. You can print the names and addresses on labels and affix the labels to either newsletters or envelopes.

There are pros and cons to each approach. Although it is often easiest simply to print the names and addresses directly on the newsletter, remember that after a relatively small number of copies it is more economical to photocopy or print your newsletter than it is to print it on your computer printer. Although prices vary, it often is the case that for a few hundred copies, offset printing is cheapest; for 50 or so copies to a few hundred, photocopying is cheapest; and for under 50 copies printing directly from your computer—while not necessarily cheaper—is certainly so much easier that it is worth doing.

This section shows you how you can print the names and addresses directly onto the newsletter. To print them onto envelopes, create a draw document and choose the paper size of the envelope you are using. Proceed as in these steps. To print them onto labels, use either a layout already defined in the database (either the stationery or the assistant) or create a similar one for your labels.

Preparing the Merge

There are three steps to setting up a mail merge:

1. Open the Mail Merge windoid.

2. Select your database.

3. Format the fields on your document.

252 • Chapter 13: Sending the Newsletter Out

Starting the Mail Merge

From the File menu, choose Mail Merge as shown in Figure 13-11.

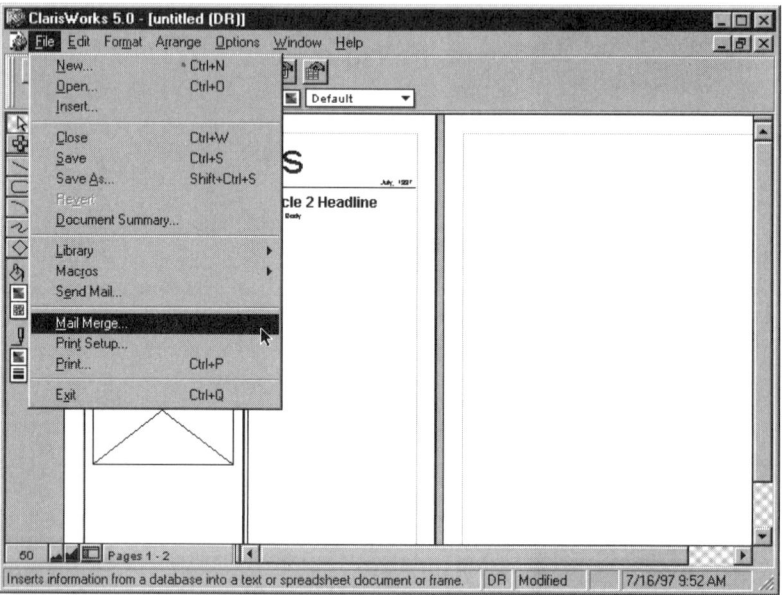

FIGURE 13-11. Mail Merge Menu

The Mail Merge windoid (Figure 13-12) will open. Use this to select your database—you do that by clicking the Switch Database button.

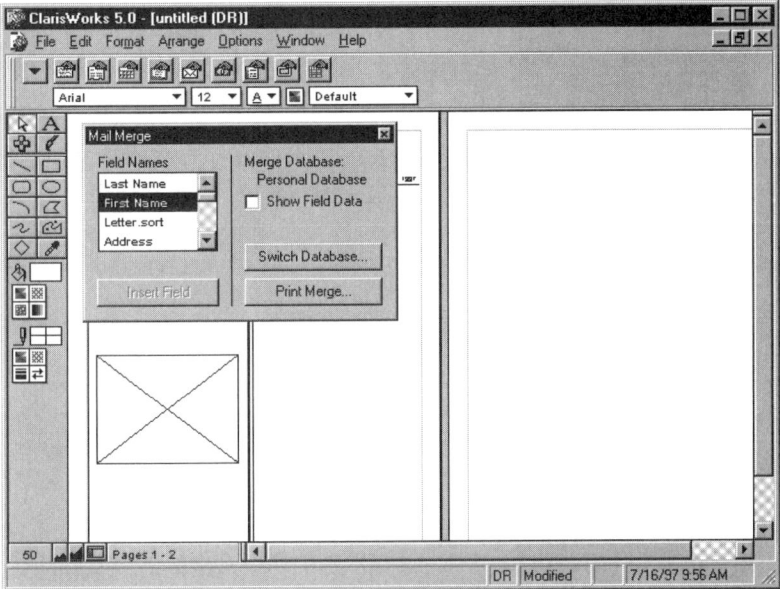

FIGURE 13-12. Mail Merge Windoid

Selecting Your Database

Select the database you want to use just as you would open any file—Figure 13-13.

If you are printing directly onto your newsletter, you probably should type a return address on the document in the appropriate location. If you used the assistant to create the newsletter, you were given the choice of leaving part of the newsletter blank so that address information could be placed on it when the newsletter is folded. If you did not do that, you may need to do some rearranging at this point.

You now specify the fields from the database that you want to be printed out. Using the text tool, click where you want the first field to be printed.

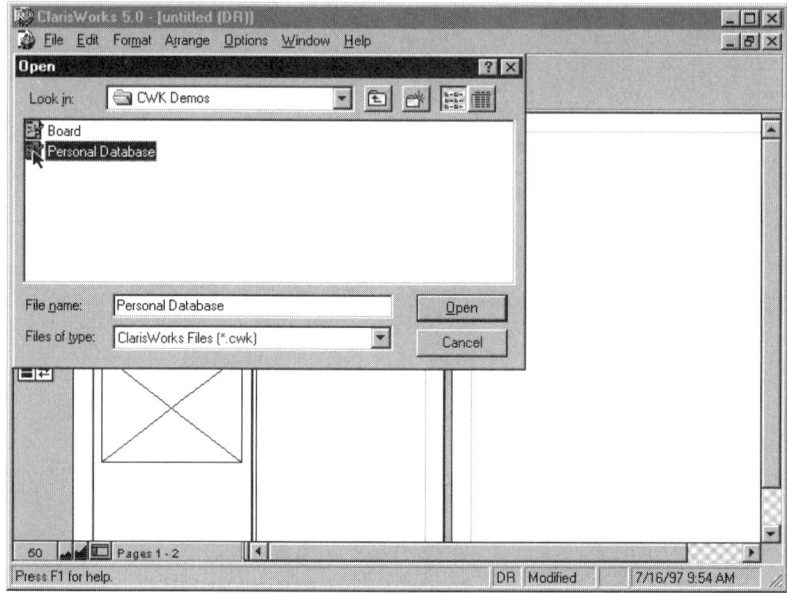

FIGURE 13-13. Select Personal Database

In Figure 13-14, you can see the results of the process described here.

For each field, select the field from the list at the left of the Mail Merge windoid, and then click Insert Field. The name of the field surrounded by << and >> will be placed in your document. You can format the text just as you would any other text that you had typed in. You can add spaces and commas as desired. Close the Mail Merge windoid when you are done.

In Figure 13-14 you can see that there is a space between the first and last names; a comma has been typed after the city, and two spaces precede the ZIP code (as requested in standard post office addressing practices).

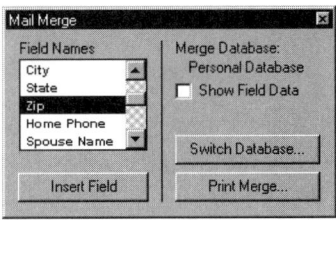

FIGURE 13-14. Completed Merge

At any time, you can check the Show Field Data checkbox in the Mail Merge windoid, as shown in Figure 13-15.

This displays actual data in the document. You can use the arrows to scroll through the data, viewing how each name and address will be displayed.

You should look through several records in this way before finalizing your document: fields in the database have a tendency to be bigger than you expected. If you live in Reno, you may not be expecting Maidenhead Thicket (in England) for the city name: your text box may be too small.

When you save the document, its connection to the database is saved (you have to save the database separately if you have made changes to it). You can modify the database independently of the document in which the names and addresses will be printed; but, of course, if you delete fields that are used in the mail merge you will cause problems. Often, one person will maintain a database and other people will use it for inclusion in their own documents.

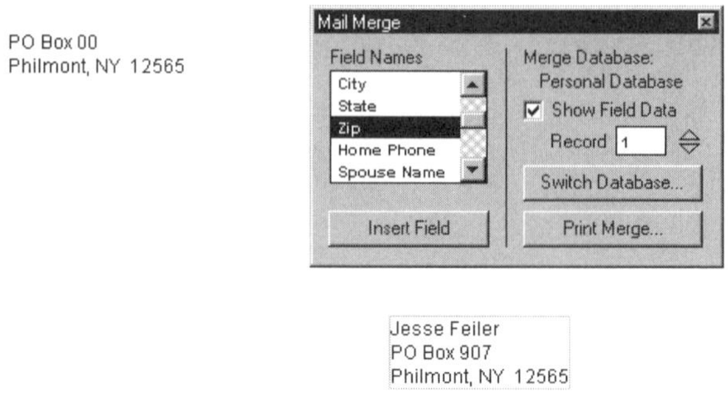

FIGURE 13-15. Completed Merge with Data

Printing the Merged Data

When you are ready to print, nothing could be simpler. Open the newsletter (or the envelope document, if you are printing on envelopes), choose Mail Merge again from the File menu, and then click Print Merge in the Mail Merge windoid. The document will be printed once for each name and address in the database.

Before printing, you can sort the database; the way in which the database is sorted determines the order in which the documents will be printed. You can also select records from the database (using Find in the database). Only the records currently selected in the database will be printed.

Summary

By now you should be reasonably comfortable with databases: they are not the horrors that many people think. Likewise, the mail merge nightmare is substantially reduced when you use ClarisWorks.

The stationery and assistants for newsletters and databases further simplify your life: all you really should worry about are the content of your newsletter and the things that you want to do.

If you want to simplify your life further (and save a tree in the process), you can do away with the paper-based newsletter entirely. You can post the information on the Web and be done with it.

From a practical point of view, this may not be possible. You may have to do both. It is not hard to take your paper-based newsletter and modify it for the Internet.

14

Posting the Newsletter on the Web

The newsletter saga can continue as you post it on the Internet. The key to using the Internet successfully in your projects is to integrate it as much as possible with your normal operations. Creating a newsletter for the Web is a great idea for keeping in touch with clients, suppliers, friends, and so forth; but the effort involved in creating and maintaining a Web site is not insignificant. Particularly if you also have to publish a paper-based newsletter, this project can easily start to take over your life.

Since ClarisWorks has built-in HTML filters and since it lets you save documents as HTML files, you can work from your paper-based newsletter in creating a Web-based newsletter. This saves time, effort, and a lot of aggravation.

This chapter focuses on what you need to do to convert a newsletter to a Web site; it also touches on some of your other Web publishing options.

Reviewing the Newsletter on Paper

The newsletter shown in Figures 14-1 and 14-2 is the Department Newsletter stationery that ships with ClarisWorks.

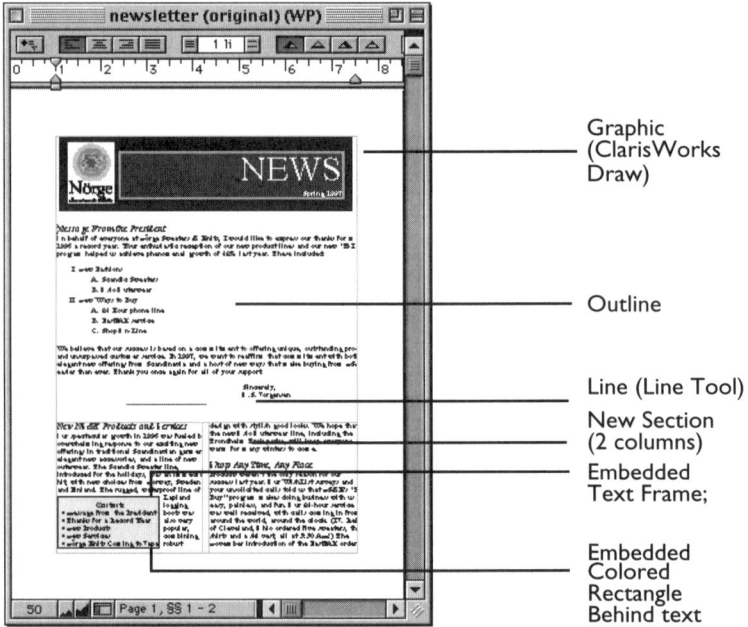

FIGURE 14-1. Department Newsletter (Page 1)

The elements of the newsletter are typical ClarisWorks features. Most of them translate very easily to the Web. The nature of HTML and the Web is different from that of ClarisWorks and paper; some adjustments will necessarily have to be made (but they are very few).

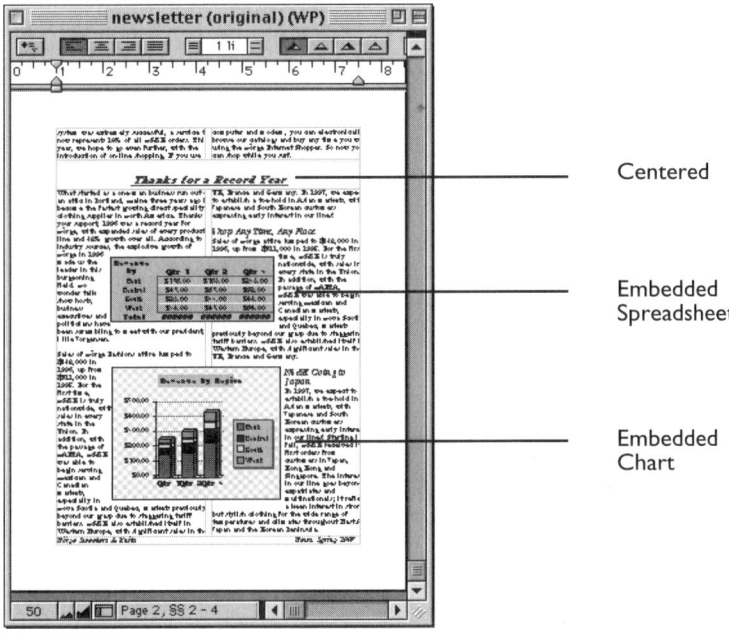

FIGURE 14-2. Department Newsletter (Page 2)

Of the newsletter's elements shown in Figures 14-1 and 14-2, ClarisWorks will automatically convert the following:

- the text
- the graphics (including the embedded chart)
- the spreadsheet

- the outline

That covers most of the newsletter—and a great deal of sophisticated material that will make for a fine Web page. The following section shows you how to do this—and how to deal with the few things that ClarisWorks will not convert.

Preparing the Newsletter for the Web

As discussed in "Posting the Newsletter on the Web" on page 259, preparing an HTML file from a ClarisWorks document is a two-step process:

1. Create a ClarisWorks document and name it with a name that ends in .cwk.

2. Save the document again as an HTML document with a name that ends in .html.

File Structure and Storage

You edit the .cwk document and save it as you normally would. When you are done with it, you resave a copy of it with the .htm or .html suffix; ClarisWorks creates the html version at this time. It is the .html document that will be uploaded to the Web.

Each graphic on the Web page will be stored as a separate file in the same folder as the .html and .cwk files. ClarisWorks automatically names these graphics files and references them as appropriate from the .html file. Since you will have a number of files that together make up the Web site, it is a good idea to create a separate folder to hold them all.

In this case, you might want to create a folder that contains both the paper- and Web-based versions of the newsletter. You will have three basic files:

1. Save the newsletter in its paper form as newsletter.

2. Resave it as newsletter.cwk—the version that you will modify for the Web.

3. Generate a newsletter.html file for posting to the Web.

ClarisWorks will generate its graphics files as needed within the folder.

What You Have to Modify

There are four general areas that you have to worry about when you convert ClarisWorks documents to the Web:

1. Lines drawn with the Line tool do not convert; they should be replaced with HTML lines (using the New Section or New Page command).

2. Embedded text frames do not convert—they have no counterpart in HTML.

3. Multiple column sections do not convert to columns—columns are not supported in HTML. (The data will be converted, but the formatting will probably not be what you intended.)

4. Formulas in embedded spreadsheets will be carried forward as formulas: if you want their results to be shown, you need to reenter the data for the cell with the formula as its result. (In other words, replace SUM (A1..A3) with 153.52 if that is the sum of those cells.)

The newsletter shown in Figures 14-1 and 14-2 is shown again in Figures 14-3 and 14-4 with the modifications necessary to put it on the Web.

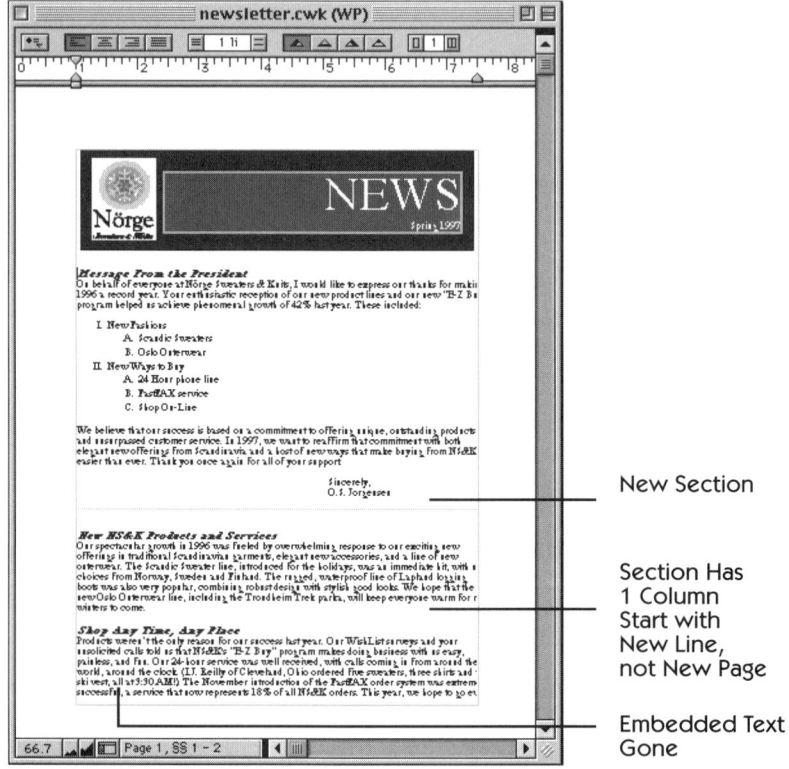

FIGURE 14-3. Department Newsletter with Web Modifications (Page 1)

The changes are very simple to make. First, select the line that was drawn with the Line tool, delete it, and replace it with a New Section (which will convert to an HTML line).

You may want to format the Section to start with a New Line (rather than a New Page)—this will make it easier to view the page.

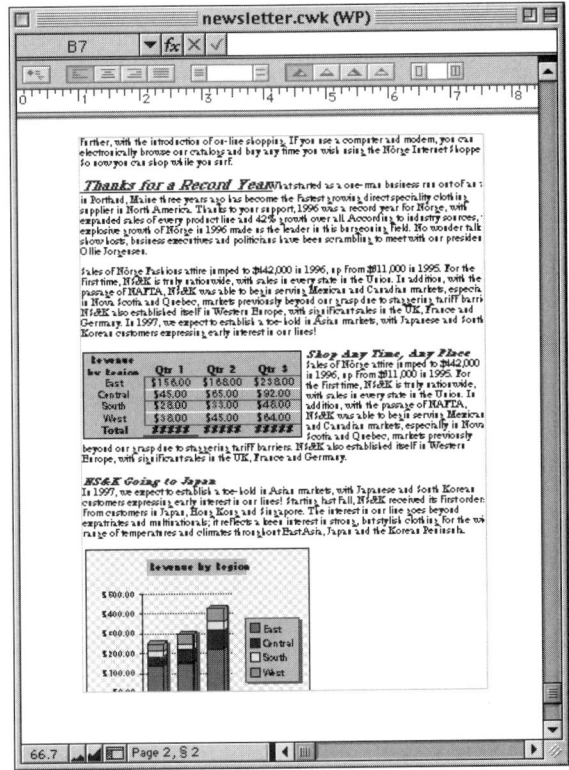

FIGURE 14-4. Department Newsletter with Web Modifications (Page 1)

To format the section choose Section... from the Format menu as shown in Figure 14-5.

FIGURE 14-5. Format Menu

The Format Section window (Figure 14-6) lets you modify where the section starts as well as the number of columns it has.

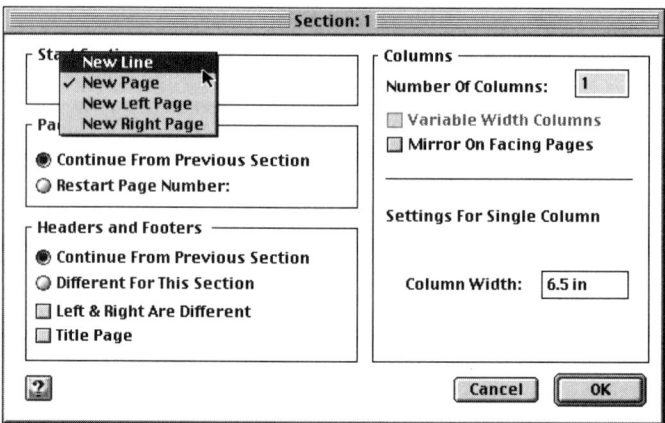

FIGURE 14-6. Section Window

Next, reformat the second section so that it has only one column.

When you have changed the columnation of the second section, you may want to move the embedded spreadsheet and chart so that they are not in the middle of paragraphs. At the same time, you can remove the formulas from the spreadsheet. The bottom row of the spreadsheet contains SUM() functions: they need to be replaced with the values shown in the spreadsheet. Just retype the numbers.

Finally, save the .cwk document and then resave it as an HTML file with a .html suffix. You can then open it in a browser and you will see the results shown in Figures 14-7 through 14-9.

In Figure 14-7, you see the HTML line that was created where you inserted the New Section in the .cwk document. You can also see that ClarisWorks converted the outline without a problem.

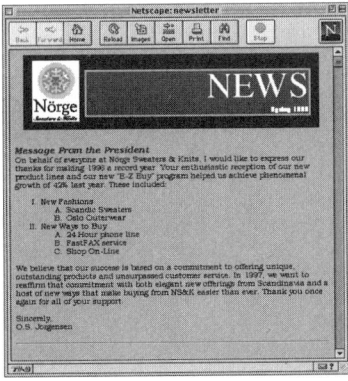

FIGURE 14-7. Department Newsletter in Netscape Browser (First Part)

In Figure 14-8, the embedded spreadsheet has been converted into HTML. Cells that were bold in the ClarisWorks document retain their bold style.

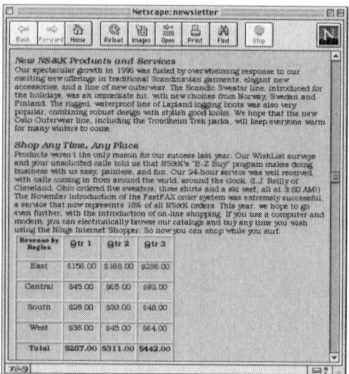

FIGURE 14-8. Departmenet Newsletter in Netscape Browser (Second Part)

The chart is converted as a graphic in Figure 14-9. There is really very little for you to worry about.

Nevertheless, as with any automatic conversion of data, there will be a few tweaks you may want to do. In the case of this document, there were two additional steps:

1. The centered heading shown in Figure 14-2 needed to be uncentered (aligned left).

2. The spreadsheet and chart needed to be repositioned in the .cwk document so that they came out between paragraphs. ClarisWorks tries very hard to keep things where they are—and sometimes that can result in less than perfect placements.

As you can see, these are minor adjustments. Generating the HTML version of the two-page newsletter can easily be done in under half an hour—and you never have to look at the HTML!

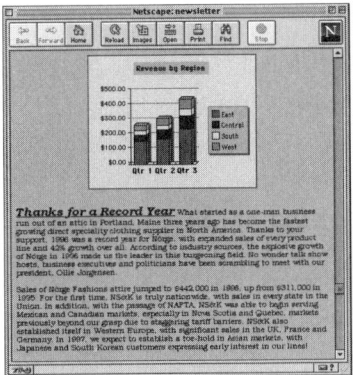

FIGURE 14-9. Department Newsletter in Netscape Browser (Third Part)

Adding Links and Other Web-Based Features

If you want to, you can add some more features to the Web-based version of the newsletter. One obvious thing to do is to replace the Table of Contents which was removed (because it was an embedded text frame). The Table of Contents for the paper-based newsletter is shown in Figure 14-10.

This does not make sense for a Web-based document; what would make sense is a series of links—a "hot" table of contents.

Using ClarisWorks links, it takes just a few moments to add these to the document.

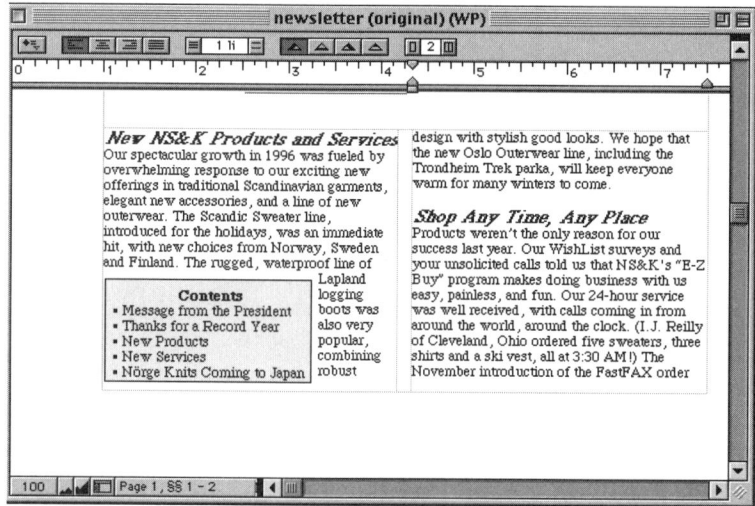

FIGURE 14-10. Table of Contents (Paper-Based Version)

Links within a document have two parts:

1. Book marks are link destinations.

2. Document links are link sources—what you click on to go to a book mark.

Creating the Book Marks

Open the Links windoid (as shown in Figure 14-11).

1. Choose Book Marks from the pop-up menu.

2. Next, highlight the destination of the link.

3. Choose New Link from the Links menu in the windoid. The New Book Mark window will open as shown in Figure 14-11.

4. Type the name of the book mark; if you want to leave it named with the text you have highlighted, just click OK.

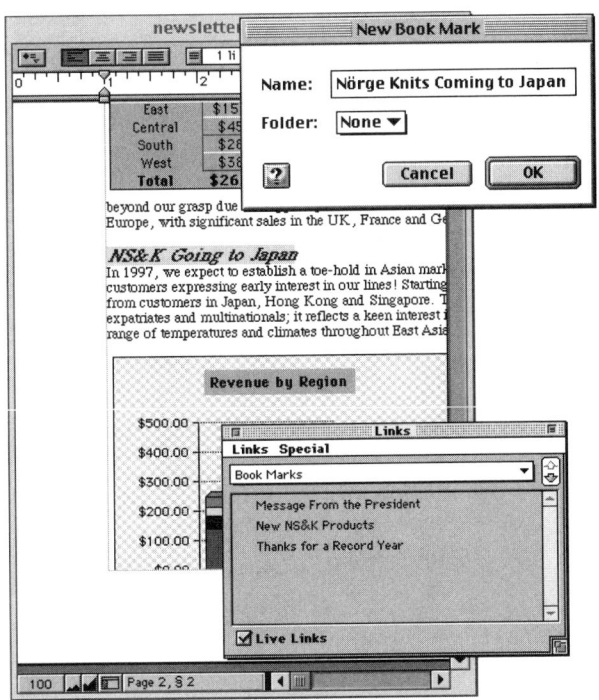

FIGURE 14-11. Adding Book Mark Links 1

Creating the Links

Next, type the text that will be hot into the document. Figure 14-12 shows the links at the top of the document—a convenient place for most people to find them.

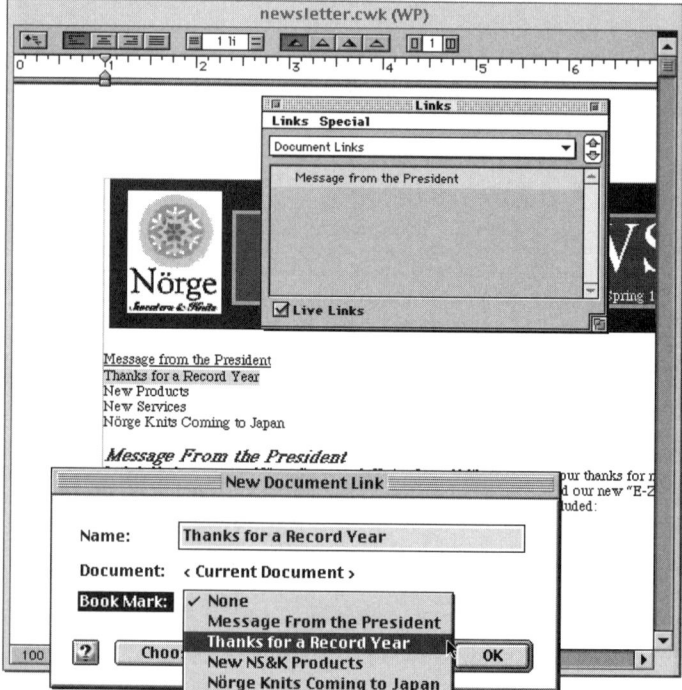

FIGURE 14-12. Adding Book Mark Links 2

1. Highlight the text that will be hot ("Thanks for a Record Year" in the background document of Figure 14-12).

2. From the Links windoid, choose Document Links.

3. Choose New Link from the Links menu in the windoid.

4. In the New Document Link window, select the book mark to which you want to link.

That is all there is to it. After you save the .cwk file and regenerate the .html file, you can open the .html file in your browser as shown in Figure 14-13: there the links are, just as if you were an HTML expert.

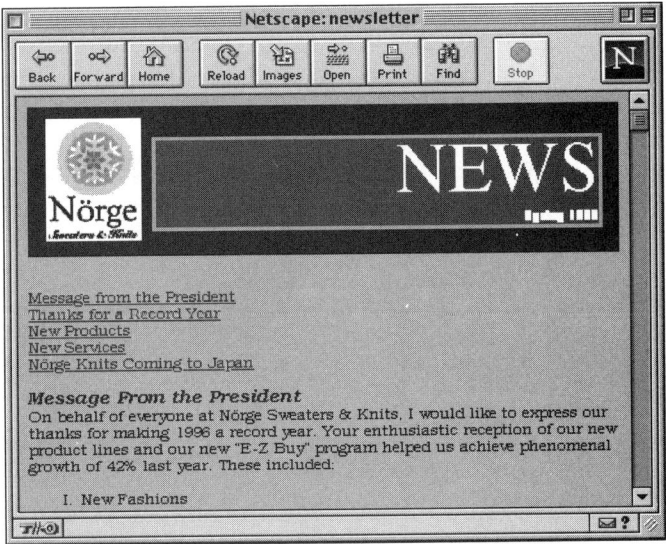

FIGURE 14-13. Adding Book Mark Links 3

Other Web-Based Features

You can add a background image to your Web page (see "Backgrounds" on page 148). You could also consider adding a QuickTime movie to your Web page—it would not make any sense for your paper-based newsletter, but from the point of view of ClarisWorks, converting an embedded graphic is the same as converting an embedded QuickTime movie.

Posting the Newsletter as a Portable Digital Document

Sometimes you want to distribute your newsletter over the Internet in the same format in which it was seen on paper. There are two ways of doing this:

1. You can post the ClarisWorks file to the Internet. You can also save the file in one of the many conversion formats so that people with other types of software can open it.

2. You can post a digital version of the printed image of the newsletter document to the Internet. This differs from the previous method in that the digital version cannot be modified; furthermore, people do not need to have ClarisWorks (or any other particular application). They need the ability to read PostScript or .pdf files—and the software for that is widely available.

To create a digital image of any document, print it and send the output to a file. On Mac OS, use the Print dialog to change the destination to a file as shown in Figure 14-14.

Posting the Newsletter as a Portable Digital Document • **275**

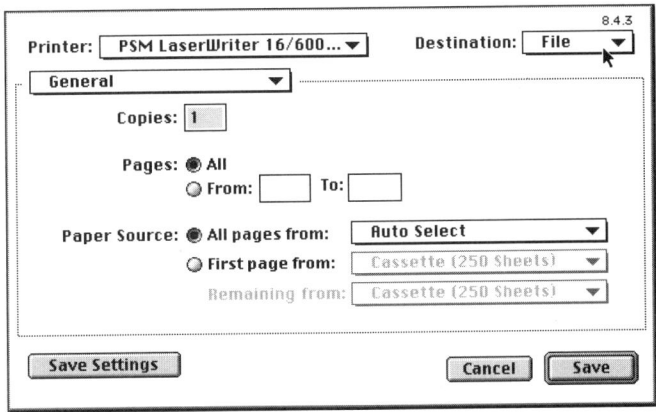

FIGURE 14-14. Print to File (Mac OS)

From the pop-up menu at the left (beneath the Printer pop-up) you can choose Save as File options as shown in Figure 14-15.

In most cases, the default options (as shown) are sufficient. The only option that you need to concern yourself about is the Font Inclusion option.

Printing to a file prints the entire image of your document to the file. You can control which fonts are included in the file (and that is what the Font Inclusion pop-up does). These files are usually pretty big—and including a large number of fonts in them makes them even bigger. If you know that the output file will be read on a computer that has the fonts that you used in the document, you can select None. If you are the least bit worried about what fonts the reader of the file has, you should include All. The other two options let you include most of the fonts except for common fonts; if you understand the wording of those two options, you can use them. If not, stick with None or All.

If you do not include the necessary fonts and if the computer where the file is read does not have those fonts, the document may be distorted as the computer substitutes fonts that may or may not be appropriate.

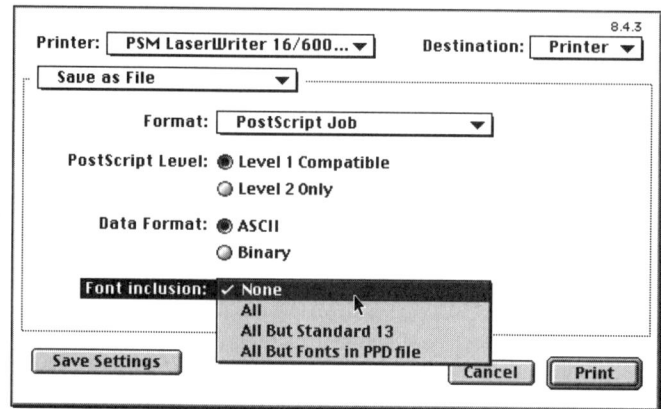

FIGURE 14-15. Save as File Print Options

You will be asked to name the file to which the output is printed as shown in Figure 14-16.

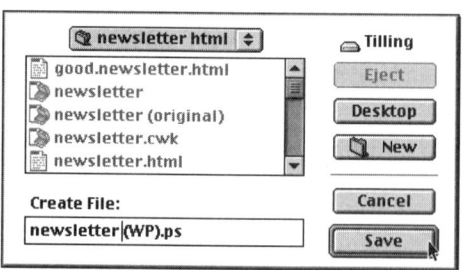

FIGURE 14-16. Naming a Print File

On Windows, the Print dialog has a checkbox that lets you select file output for the print job as shown in Figure 14-16.

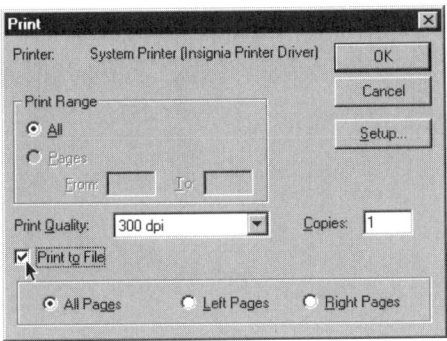

FIGURE 14-17. Print to File (Windows)

PostScript and PDF Files

The output will be saved in a PostScript file. PostScript files are the files from which PostScript printers actually work. They tend to be fairly large. For this reason, they are not normally posted on the Web or sent via e-mail.

PDF files (portable digital format files) are produced by Adobe's Acrobat Distiller application. They can be read by Acrobat Reader, which is widely available (it comes bundled with a number of Internet browsers). If you have Acrobat Distiller, you can read the PostScript file and it will automatically create a—much smaller—pdf file. If you are going to be publishing digital images of documents, you should probably invest in Acrobat Distiller.

Posting Files on the Web

These files—either your .html file, your PostScript file (with suffix .ps), or a .pdf file—need to be posted on the Web. Your Internet service provider or Web support staff will tell you how to do this. Since it varies from provider to provider, there is no common procedure that you can follow.

The basic steps, though, are the same:

1. You log on to your ISP—sometimes using a different account than the one you use for your e-mail and Web browsing.

2. You use an FTP program (such as Anarchie, Archie, Fetch, or Cyberdog) to move your file to your Internet account.

3. You use a browser to check that the file looks as it should when it is accessed.

Browsers rely on file suffixes—a period and a few letters—to identify the kind of file that they are dealing with. Thus, for browsers to display your Web pages correctly, they should be named with a suffix of .htm or .html. For digital images of printed pages to be correctly processed, they should be named with a suffix of .pdf for Acrobat files (from Acrobat Distiller) or of .ps (for ordinary PostScript).

Internet file servers and browsers have different ways of interpreting special characters in filenames—particularly blanks. Although it looks ugly, you are safer constructing filenames that are relatively short and which have no embedded blanks. It will save you grief later.

Summary

In this chapter, you have seen how to move a paper-based newsletter to the Internet—either as a Web document (HTML) or as a digital document. The power of ClarisWorks is that it makes this additional step relatively easy, since it automatically converts most of a word processing document to HTML for you.

But there is more.

You can take that very same newsletter and convert it into a presentation to give to your boss or to your staff. If you have got something important to say, the combination of paper, Internet, and an in-person presentation should get the message through.

If it does not, try retyping the message on small pieces of paper and putting them in fortune cookies.

15
Presenting the Newsletter in Person

ClarisWorks has built-in presentation capabilities to let you create and give presentations. You can use these features to present your newsletter in person. This chapter shows you the ClarisWorks presentation features, explores some of the presentations available (as assistants and stationery), and then reviews the use of the image libraries—something you often may do in preparing slides for presentations.

About Presentations

Of course, a newsletter on paper (or on the Internet) is a very different thing from an in-person presentation. On paper (or the Internet), headlines and layout help readers understand the scope of what is being presented and where they are in the newsletter's information.

An in-person presentation relies on graphics to emphasize the high points of the presentation and to keep people informed as to where they are.

Presentation Formats

There are three commonly used presentation formats that are supported in ClarisWorks:

1. You can use the computer monitor as a slide show. Every time you touch the space bar or an arrow key the next (or previous) page is shown. If you type q (quit), the presentation is over. During the presentation, each page is shown as a full-screen image: no menu bar, desktop, or other images are seen on the screen.

2. You can create overhead transparencies with ClarisWorks. There are two significant differences between slides and transparencies. First, slides use a landscape orientation (since most monitors and screens are wider than they are high) and overheads use a portrait orientation (since overhead projectors project a taller and narrower image than slides). Second, the background of overhead transparencies is usually clear: the text is dark; with slides, this is not necessarily true, and it is often reversed with dark backgrounds and light-colored text.

3. Finally, you can use ClarisWorks to prepare paper-based presentations for use as handouts. These may augment or replace slides and overhead transparencies.

Things to Watch Out For

There are many books and other training materials to assist you in preparing and giving presentations. Here are a few tips:

- Slides, overheads, and handouts should contain topic or agenda points; save the details for your presentation or for other documents that you hand out.

- Use a common format for your visuals so that the presentation has a unified look to it.

- Keep the background of your presentation in the background: use the strongest images and brightest colors for the content.

- Practice out loud—preferably using the equipment you will be using during the presentation. Most people are comfortable (as speaker and as audience) with one slide every one to two minutes.

The Mechanics of a Presentation

If you use ClarisWorks to prepare paper handouts or overhead transparencies, you do not have to worry about the mechanics of the presentation. If you are using a computer to present, here are your options:

- If your computer has video output (as from a digitizing card), you can plug a large-screen video monitor or projection TV into the video out plug.

- If your computer allows you to plug a second monitor in, you can connect an image converter device into the monitor plug; the output from the image converter will be a video signal that can go into a large-screen or projection TV.

Remember to do this plugging and unplugging when the equipment is turned off; when you turn it on, turn it on toward the computer: monitor first, image converter (if any) next, then the computer. If the other devices are not powered up fully, the computer may not recognize them.

As with any prop for a presentation, try to practice in advance and have a backup procedure ready.

Presenting a Document as a Slide Show

Any ClarisWorks document can be presented as a slide show by choosing Slide Show... from the Options menu as shown in Figure 15-1. When you choose Slide Show..., the window shown in Figure 15-2. opens.

You can select each page in the document from the list at the upper left of the window. For each page, you use the panel at the lower left to specify whether it is opaque, transparent, or hidden. (These icons toggle as you click on them for each page.) The meanings of these values are:

- Opaque pages are shown on their own.

Presenting a Document as a Slide Show • **285**

- Transparent pages are shown as if they were on transparencies; the page previously shown is visible through the current page.

- Hidden pages are not shown.

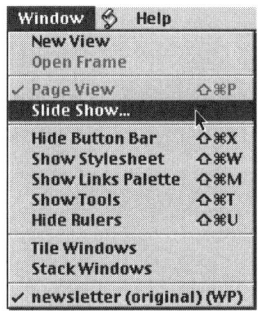

FIGURE 15-1. Window Menu (Slide Show)

You use the options at the right of the window to control how the slide show is presented. (If you want to make a self-running slide show for a trade show or demo, click Loop and Advance every _ seconds.)

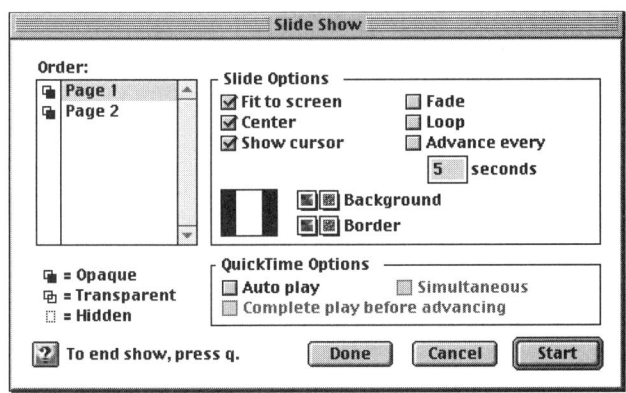

FIGURE 15-2. Slide Show Options

The background and border options let you determine how the area of the screen not filled by the slide's image is displayed. (If your document uses landscape mode small American letterhead, there will be no borders on common computer monitors.)

Creating a Presentation with an Assistant

You can use the Presentation assistant to create a presentation in ClarisWorks. As you can see from Figure 15-3, the assistant allows you to choose among a number of styles and presentation media.

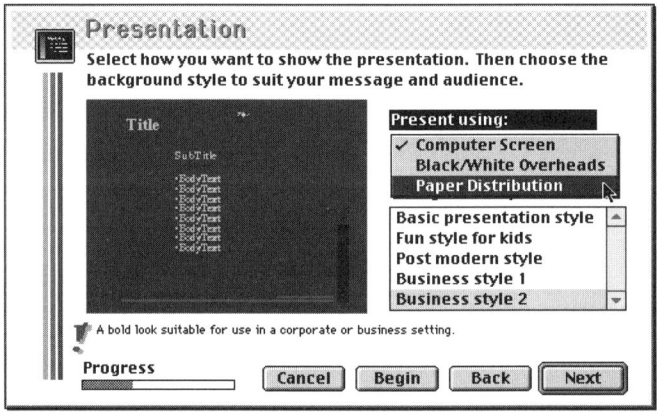

FIGURE 15-3. Presentation Assistant (1)

Two of the advantages of using the Presentation assistant are shown in Figures 15-3 and 15-4:

1. A number of common formatting issues are taken care of for you.

2. The Helpful Hints provide tips that are very useful in preparing your presentation—particularly if you do this sort of thing infrequently.

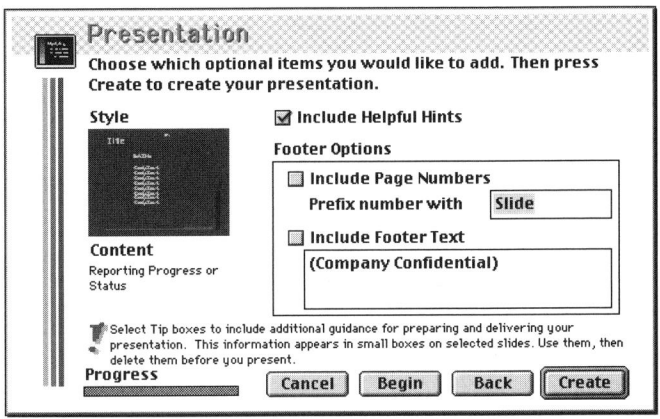

FIGURE 15-4. Slide Show Assistant (2)

Modifying the Presentation

Once ClarisWorks has prepared a presentation template for you, you can modify it with your own data; you can also change its basic appearance.

Figure 15-5 shows a slide prepared by the Presentation assistant before it has been customized with someone's own data.

As you can see, ClarisWorks has prepared a template and filled in the basic information that may be useful to you. You are under no obligation to use this structure or format, but many people find it helpful.

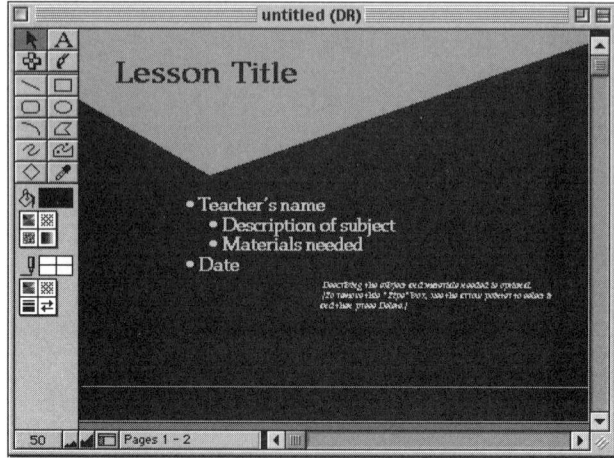

FIGURE 15-5. Lesson Slide 1

Editing the Master Page

You can change the appearance of the master page in your presentation, thus affecting all slides. Choose Edit Master Page from the Options menu (Figure 15-6), and you will see the window shown in Figure 15-7.

Creating a Presentation with an Assistant • **289**

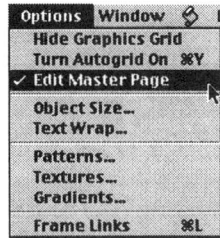

FIGURE 15-6. Options Menu

Compare Figure 15-7 (the master page) with Figure 15-5. You can see the elements that are on the master page and those that are on individual pages.

FIGURE 15-7. Lesson Template

Any change that you make to the master page will be reflected on all pages that use that master page. Note that this presentation is a multipage ClarisWorks Draw document: master pages are available in all Draw documents, not just in presentations.

290 • Chapter 15: Presenting the Newsletter in Person

Creating a Presentation from Stationery

If you would rather use stationery to prepare your presentation, ClarisWorks has Presentation stationery in the form of a teacher's research paper assignment as shown in Figure 15-8.

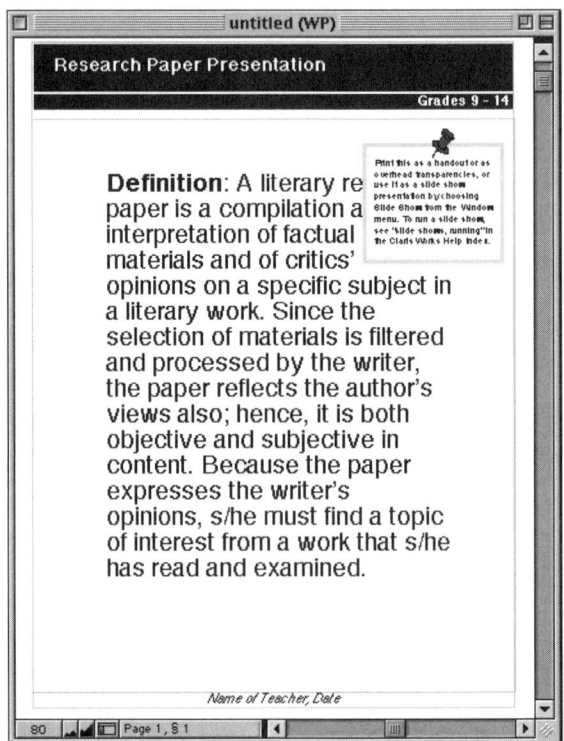

FIGURE 15-8. Presentation Stationery

This presentation is designed for use in an overhead projector: note the vertical orientation and the clear background compared to the previous presentation.

Note also the note outlined in yellow and shown with the tack in the upper right of the window. This is a note to you; when you delete it, the full presentation window is shown. Creating and using such notes and graphics like the tack are very simple: the next section walks you through the process.

Using Image Libraries

Figure 15-9 shows a close-up of the top of the Presentation stationery, with the note selected.

FIGURE 15-9. Tacked Note

Many people think of clip art only as the balloons they put on party invitations or the arrows they put on announcements. True, much clip art is used in a pretty gross and unappealing way, but the ClarisWorks libraries of images let you create simple graphics such as the tacked note shown here.

For the tacked note to work, a graphic (the tack), text, and the text's yellow outline need to be grouped into a single object that can be selected as shown in Figure 15-9. If you simply press the delete key, the entire image is removed, and the text of the presentation underneath is visible.

Here is how to create such a graphic:

- Create a Draw document.
- Type the text for the note.
- Change its border to yellow.
- From the Business Images library, select the tack and paste it onto the box.
- Rotate the tack.
- Group the tack and text box.
- Paste the grouped image onto the presentation.

Using Image Libraries • **293**

Figure 15-10 shows how you create the text. In a new Draw document, choose the Text tool and type the text.

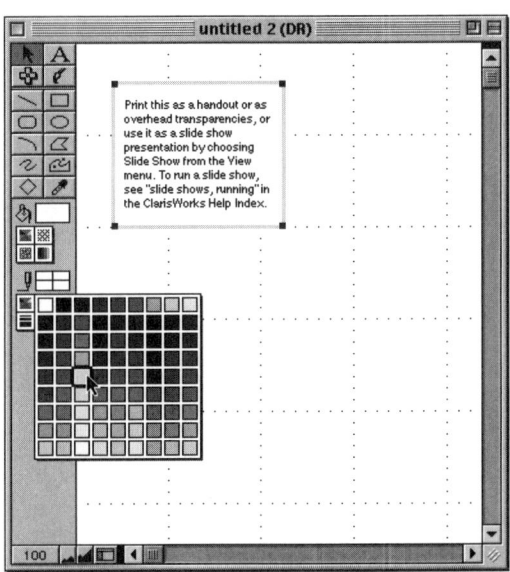

FIGURE 15-10. Creating the Text

Select its border with the Arrow tool, and then use the border color palette to change the border to yellow.

You open the image library from the File menu as shown in Figure 15-11.

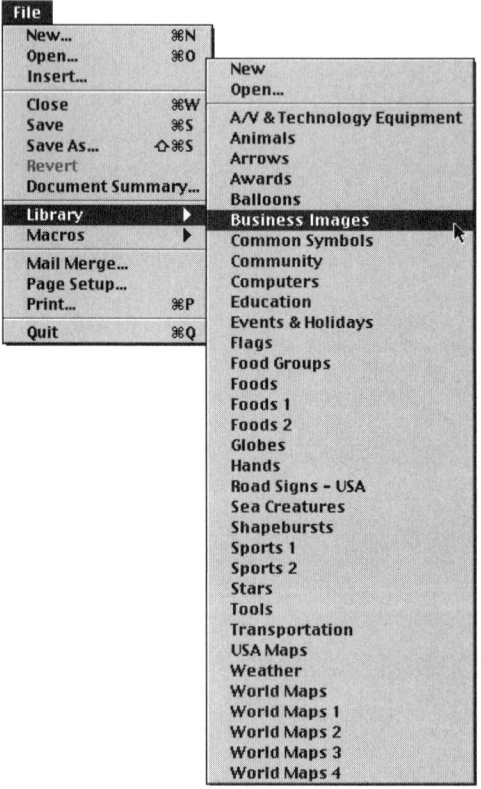

FIGURE 15-11. Library/Business Images

There is a wide variety of images in the libraries that come with ClarisWorks. In Figure 15-12 you can see the Business Images library with the Tack selected.

Copy and paste it into the Draw document as shown in Figure 15-13.

Using Image Libraries • 295

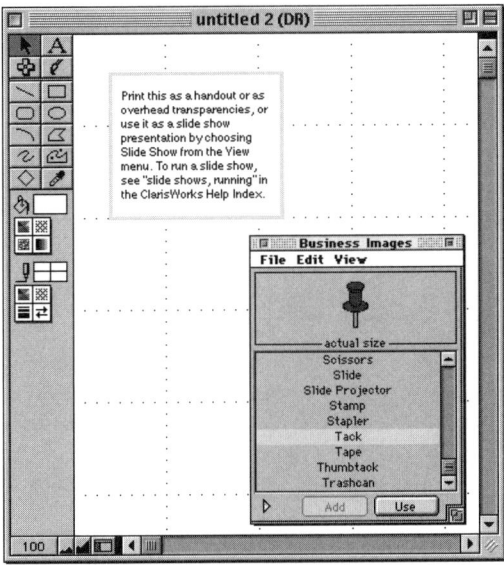

FIGURE 15-12. Tack Selected

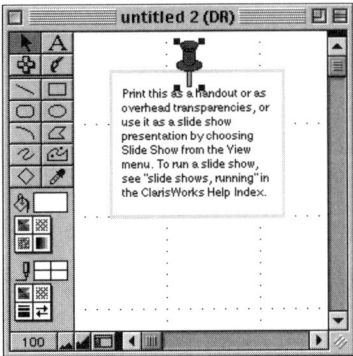

FIGURE 15-13. Tack Pasted

You use the Arrange menu (Figure 15-14) to rotate objects. Choose Free Rotate from that menu and rotate the tack by dragging any of its corner handles.

296 • Chapter 15: Presenting the Newsletter in Person

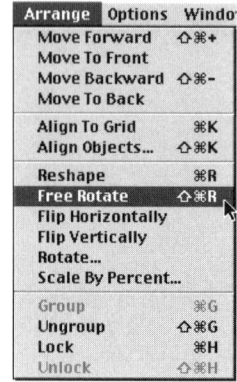

FIGURE 15-14. Arrange Menu

With the tack rotated and positioned as you want it, choose all of the elements of the drawing (Select All from the Edit menu), as shown in Figure 15-15.

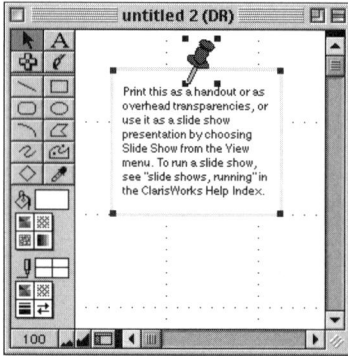

FIGURE 15-15. Ready to Group

From the Arrange menu, choose Group, and you will have a single object. Copy it and paste it onto your word processing document as shown in Figure 15-16. (Note that the four handles show you that this is only one object.)

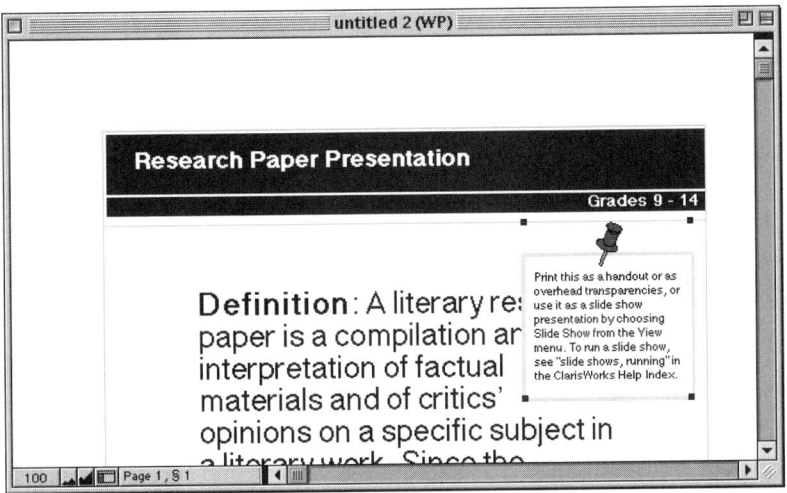

FIGURE 15-16. Tack Note Pasted

When pasting the completed tacked note into the word processing document, make certain that the Arrow tool is selected: this will paste it on top of the text—as shown in Figure 15-16. If the Text tool is selected, the graphic will be inserted into the text flow—that is, between two characters of the text flow. That result is shown in Figure 15-17.

298 • Chapter 15: Presenting the Newsletter in Person

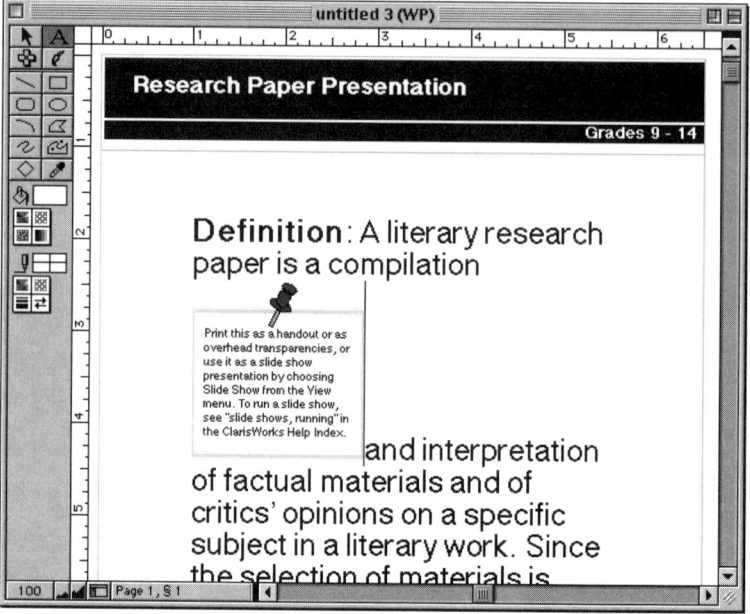

FIGURE 15-17. Tack Note Pasted into Text Flow

Summary

In this chapter, you have seen the ways in which you can create presentations in ClarisWorks as well as how you can display any ClarisWorks document as a presentation. The discussion of the creation and use of the tacked note is a review of the use of image libraries, grouping, and the use of images within word processing documents (both as layers and within the text flow).

You certainly should have enough information about newsletters from these chapters to be able to create a few of your own! The newsletters techniques, though, are common to many activities that you do with ClarisWorks—whether for home, school, work, community groups, or just play.

The following chapter steps back to take a look at the office environment ClarisWorks often finds itself in. Things have changed over the years—have you?

16

Running the Small Office/Home Office with ClarisWorks

The small office/home office (SOHO) environment is very common these days. Telecommuting has made it possible for many people to work out of their homes—even when they work for large corporations. Even within large corporations, there are many attempts to recreate the environments of small work groups, which are often more productive than large corporate behemoths.

This chapter summarizes the main points of running a small/home office (at least from the computer point of view). Things have changed in the last few years; if you are doing things the way you did them five years ago, you may want to reconsider.

The main topics in this chapter are:

- ClarisWorks features for business use.

- Keeping your computer on—energy-saving computers no longer should be turned off.

- Backups and archives.

- Networking.

- Issues for laptops and PowerBooks.

ClarisWorks Features for Business Use

ClarisWorks Office (the product that incorporates ClarisWorks 5.0) ships with many additional tools and features that make life for everyone easier. (See "What's in ClarisWorksOffice" on page 337.) Most of these additional tools are stationery items that help you handle all sorts of situations—both common and uncommon.

Most small organizations do not have the support resources of large corporations. While a SOHO organization may in fact be a law firm (eliminating the need for a corporate legal department), that same SOHO law firm likewise does not have corporate resources such as a facilities management staff, bookkeeping, and presentations preparation. Still, in one way or another, these tasks need to be done.

The stationery that comes with ClarisWorks is no substitute for an experienced professional, but many small organizations find that preprinted forms and basic handbooks can guide them through many tasks. Before you light out for the local office supply store to stock up on preprinted forms for a variety of uses, look at what you already have with ClarisWorks—you will probably be able to create those forms (and more!) with the business tools provided.

Even if the tools and templates are not sufficient for your needs, they will often will be very helpful to you in organizing your thoughts so that when you do meet with accountants, lawyers, graphic designers, or management planners you are ready to make the best use of your (and their) time.

Using the Business Templates

Start by exploring the templates. Choose New from the File menu, and select Use Assistant or Stationery at the right of the window, as shown in Figure 16-1.

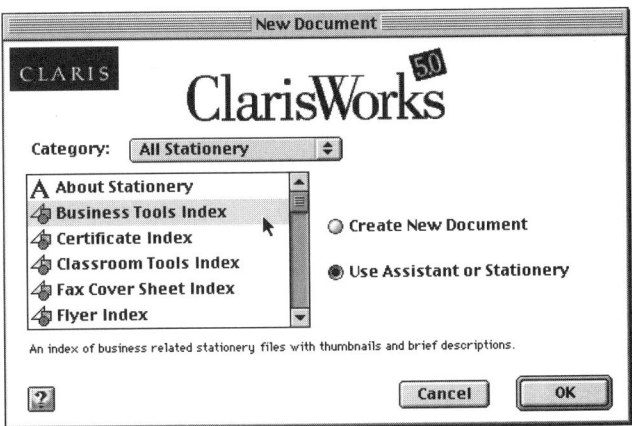

FIGURE 16-1. Stationery

304 • Chapter 16: Running the Small Office/Home Office with ClarisWorks

Business Tools Index

For the Category in the pop-up menu at the top of the screen, choose All Stationery; highlight the Business Tools Index item and click open (or just double-click Business Tools Index). You will open the document shown in Figure 16-2.

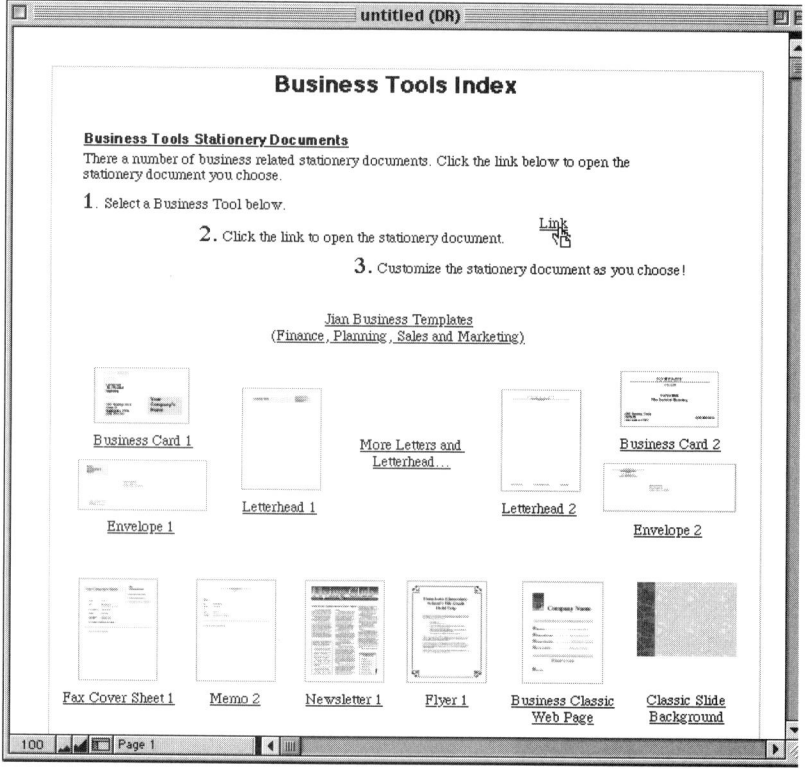

FIGURE 16-2. Business Tools Index

This document is interesting not only because it is a guide to the business tools that ship with ClarisWorks Office but also because it demonstrates the use of links and documents that transcend paper.

CLARISWORKS FEATURES AT WORK You can certainly print this document, but if you just look at it on paper, you will miss several important points about it:

- It is stationery. Changes that you make to it will be saved in a new file, unless you explicitly use Save As… and give it the name of the original document (note that its name is "untitled").

- It lists—and shows thumbnail views—of the various business tools. Although there is plenty of text, it is a draw document. A document that looks like this is usually easiest to create as a draw document.

- It does not provide the names of the documents to which it refers. That's because they are all links. (See "Making Documents Interactive—Using the Links Palette" on page 103.)

POSSIBILITIES WITH THE BUSINESS TOOLS INDEX Before proceeding to the various tools shown in the index (there are two pages of them), consider a few possibilities that are open to you:

- You can modify this document adding some standard documents of your own and deleting some of these. (For instance, you might want to remove Letterhead 1, Letterhead 2, and More Letters and Letterhead…, replacing them with Our Letterhead. If you modify this document (saving it as stationery named Business Tools Index), you will overwrite the standard document.

- You can modify this document and save it under other names. Perhaps some people in your organization care about some types of documents and others care about others. Make several versions and store them under appropriate names.

- You can even make this a start-up document: instead of launching ClarisWorks, open this document (or your version of it) to create appropriate documents.

The only thing to bear in mind is that since there are so many links on this document, you probably should store your new versions of this document in the same location—ClarisWorks Stationery. That will prevent any links from accidentally breaking. Remember also that before you edit the document, you should turn Live Links off (in the Links palette); you want to be able to select the links and copy, paste, or modify them without activating them.

JIAN Business Basics

If you click on The Business Templates at the center top of the Business Tools Index, you will open the window shown in Figure 16-3—the JIAN Business Basics. Once again, this is a draw document, and it is stationery—it is opened as an unsaved new copy (named "untitled").

Each of the templates is listed, together with a brief description. Some may not be needed—you may have a separate program to prepare invoices, or you may not issue invoices. Others, however, can be very helpful. Just reviewing the documents can provide a helpful overview of some of the issues involved in running an organization. The Meeting Agenda, document, for example (shown in Figure 16-4), helps you organize meetings—something you may not have given much thought to. You can use the Meeting Agenda document as the basis for subsequent minutes of a meeting rather than starting afresh with a blank word processing document when it comes time to write up the minutes.

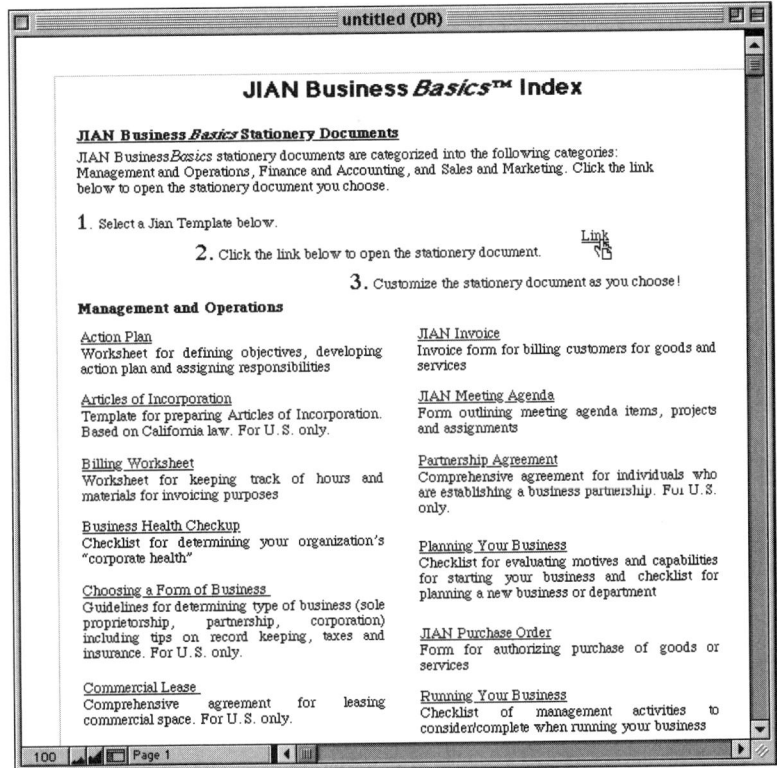

FIGURE 16-3. JIAN Business Basics™ Index

CLARISWORKS FEATURES AT WORK The Meeting Agenda in Figure 16-4 also demonstrates several important points about ClarisWorks:

- Once again, the document type may not be what you would expect. Surely an agenda is a word processing document—think again, this is a spreadsheet.

- On this (and all of the other JIAN templates), instructions and comments are shown in square brackets [] and are colored blue. This makes it easy to spot them—and to remove them before the document is printed.

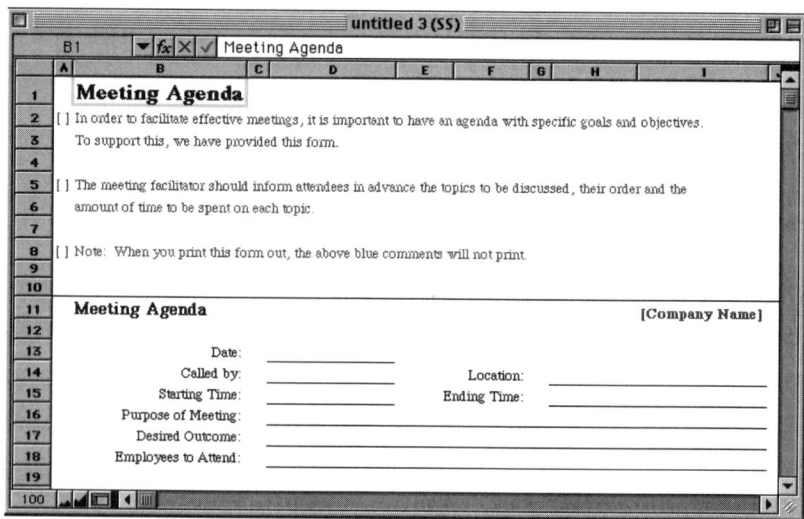

FIGURE 16-4. Meeting Agenda

Other Features for SOHO Users

There are other stationery templates you can use—certificates, announcements, press releases, etc. Not all of them are listed under Business Templates—they are not all business related.

On a rainy afternoon, explore the templates and assistants—you will find a treasure trove there. Also check out the Claris Web site (http://www.claris.com) and the other resources provided on the ClarisWorks Office CD-ROM: they change and provide a continuing stream of information.

Finally, keep an eye on Apple's Small Business Web site—http://www.smallbiz.apple.com. You do not need an Apple computer to appreciate this site with its tips from many sources and links to many others.

Keep Your Computer On

Today's computers and monitors usually come with energy-saving features built into them. You can usually specify that your monitor's screen will go dark after a certain period of inactivity and that your computer and its hard disk relax after other periods of time.

There are a number of reasons to keep your computer on. First of all, if you are using it to receive faxes and/or telephone calls, turning it off takes you out of communication with the world. Second, more and more applications allow you to defer processing. Backups, disk maintenance programs, and other software can run very happily overnight—leaving your computer ready for you to use it the next day.

Although prices of computers continue to fall, they are still expensive devices; using them overnight helps to spread that cost out.

Figure 16-5 shows the Mac OS Energy Saver control panel. (Similar control panels are available on other computers.)

310 • Chapter 16: Running the Small Office/Home Office with ClarisWorks

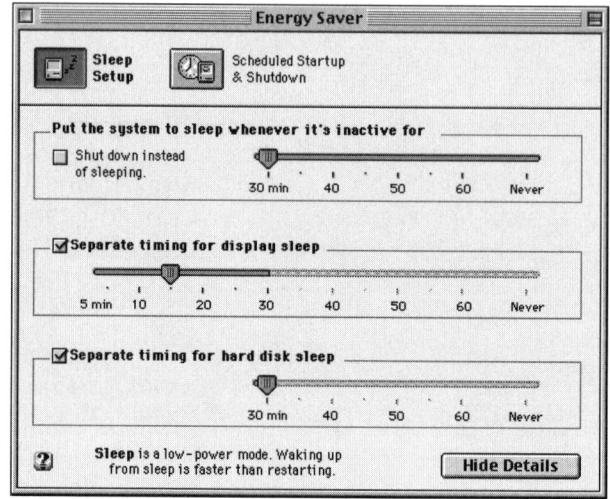

FIGURE 16-5. Energy Saver

Power

Particularly if your computer will be running unattended overnight, you need to make certain that its power supply is stable and good.

UPS (Uninterrupted Power Supply)

Starting at about a hundred dollars, there are UPS (uninterrupted power supply) devices that will help to protect your computer equipment from power outages. A UPS device provides a few outlets into which you plug your computer and other devices; should there be a power failure, it signals with some kind of alarm and provides a period of time—

often 10 minutes—of reserve power from batteries. This gives you time to shut down your equipment.

These devices provide many of the traditional features of power strips and surge suppressors in helping to make certain that the power they supply to your computer is good.

The prices of UPS devices quickly go up as new features are added. Among the additional features that you can pay for are:

- additional outlets and higher electrical capacity

- longer reserve power time

- more sophisticated alarms (some will automatically page you)

- automatic shutdown of computer equipment.

Prices rise steadily and can easily go into the thousands of dollars for devices that require licensed electricians to install. What matter for most SOHO people is that the low end of these devices is now increasingly affordable. You can get a respectable UPS device for about a hundred dollars; for five hundred dollars, you can be quite comfortable.

Power Strips and Surge Suppressors

If you do not invest in a UPS device, make certain that your computer equipment is connected to a good surge suppressor. A power strip is not a surge suppressor!

Surge suppressors today usually come with a guarantee that they will protect equipment valued up to something like $10,000 from damage. They typically cost $35 to $75 in the United States.

Power strips usually cost $15 or less; they come with no guarantee. (Of course, nothing prevents someone from selling you a $15 power strip as a $75 surge suppressor. This is one of the most critical components of your office: buy from a reputable dealer.)

Disk Maintenance

Once you have decided to keep your computer running at all times and have guaranteed a good power supply, turn your attention to your computer's disk drive(s).

Not many years ago, there was a magazine article with suggestions for people on how to manage a 1 MB hard disk. Today, 1 MB fits easily on a diskette—and multigigabyte disks are the rule.

An enormous amount of data fits on these disks, and corruption of such a disk is really unthinkable. Fortunately, hardware and software are more and more reliable, but you still should take precautions.

A disk diagnosis and repair utility program is essential for peace of mind. Most operating systems, computers, and third-party hard disks come with such software. If you choose to buy such products, $100 can buy a very useful and satisfactory program; note also that in this category specials are common. Odd though it may seem, if you purchase a disk maintenance program with a tax preparation program, you may get a good deal.

Backups and Archives

Prevention, though, is not enough. Disasters will happen. You must back up and archive your data. And you must test your backups.

The astute reader may note a difference in tone between this section and the rest of the book. In the rest of the book, it has been pointed out that there are many ways to use ClarisWorks, that there is usually no one right way to do anything, and that it is your data and your operation and you should do it the way you want to. Not in the case of backups and archives. If you do not follow these instructions, you run the risk of losing much if not all of your data. By special arrangement between Claris, Claris Press, and the author, a representative will be dispatched to your doorstep to say "I told you so." It will not be a nice scene.

Backups versus Archives

Backups are copies of your day-to-day data that are created on a regular basis (usually once a day). The purpose of a backup is to be able to restore your hard disk if there is a problem with it.

Archives are copies of data that are intended to be stored for a fairly long period. An archive is often created at the end of a project or at a specific time—the end of a month, for example.

Backups are often overwritten; archives are usually saved. The data on a backup is usually still present on your computer after the backup; the data on an archive is often removed from your computer after the archive. (The archive is the dead storage filing cabinet of the computer.)

Hardware

Backups and archives are usually created on removable media—diskettes, data cartridges, magneto-optical disks, or tape cassettes. These are all relatively low-speed devices that are fairly cheap and can be written and rewritten as needed. (Archives are often created on CD-ROMs, which have the advantage of being among the most permanent of media.)

The easiest way to manage your backups is to have a drive that is dedicated to tapes, MO disks, or whatever medium you use for archiving. Most such drives come with backup software which you can program to run in the dead of night. These products allow you to specify either that everything on a disk is to be backed up (an image copy) or that only the files that have changed since the last backup be backed up (an incremental backup).

Backup Strategy

A common backup strategy is to do an image copy once a week and incremental backups each night thereafter. (The image copy is often scheduled to run at the end of a week, so that it can run into the weekend if necessary.) If your backup device is large enough, this allows you to automate the entire process and to have to deal with it only once a week.

Each week, you change the tape or cartridge and start the process over again with another one. The previous week's data is then stored carefully—often off site.

This strategy allows for rotation of backup media (a good idea in case of failure there) as well as for off-site storage of the previous week's data. Variations on this strategy as well as other strategies can be devised in order to keep off-site copies of data more up to date, etc.

> *Remember that the point of backups is to protect your data; if the process of creating and maintaining backups distracts from your actual work, it is self-defeating.*

Key Points

Your backup strategy must be unobtrusive and effective: it is better to have a simple strategy that works than a complicated one that upsets everyone in the office. Furthermore, it is almost essential that the backup strategy work without human intervention. For this reason, make certain that the backup medium is large enough for the amount of data that you want to put on it. If you are planning on doing a full backup once a week and incremental backups on each subsequent day of the week, make certain that you have a backup device that is twice as big as you need.

And now, here is the really difficult part. Fire drills. At some point, you must take the backup of a disk in your hand, reformat that disk—destroying all its data, and then restore the data from the backup. Until you do it—and it works—you will not know if your backups are succeeding. You have to do this. It is quite traumatic if you have never done it before, but once you have done it you will be able to trust your backups—and that is the most valuable lesson of all.

Costs

Different backup devices have different prices. For a small/home office that is not involved in extensive multimedia or graphics, you can expect to buy a backup device for $300 to $800.

Networking

Within your office, your computers and printers are usually networked. You may have only one computer and one printer, but as your activities increase, you are likely to need the devices to be connected.

Some brands of computer are easier to network than others; some operating systems typically are more convenient to connect than others. Here are few—very few—issues in networking today. This section is not designed to make you a networking expert; rather it is designed to give you the briefest of overviews so that you can have a general idea of what is going on.

The most common way to network computers and printers within an office or home environment is by using Ethernet. On Mac OS, an earlier technology known as AppleTalk has been built into most computers for a decade. For IBM PCs and clones, networking has usually been an add-on; the token-ring architecture is common in that environment.

Ethernet, however, is becoming a standard for all environments. You can buy the components that you need from local computer stores or through the mail.

Transceivers

For each computer, you need networking capabilities and a transceiver. The networking capabilities are often built into a card that you put into your computer, a PCCIA removable card (particularly for laptops), or into other parts of your computer. The easiest way to get networking, of course, is to buy it as part of your computer.

From the Ethernet card (or its equivalent), cables go to a transceiver. This may be built into the computer (as it is with many Power Macintosh computers), or you may need to buy a transceiver to plug into your Ethernet card. (Expect to pay under $50 for a transceiver.)

Cabling

A cable plugs into the transceiver and then is connected to other computer or other parts of the network. Here you have two primary choices:

1. An RJ45 connector looks like a slightly wider modular telephone plug. It goes at the end of 10 Base-T cable. The other end is plugged into an Ethernet hub.

2. A BNC connector is the same kind of round plug with locking ring that plugs into the back of many television and cable boxes. It goes at the end of 10 Base-2 cable; the other end of that cable can be plugged either into an Ethernet hub or into another computer or printer.

Cable is rated by its capabilities; today you need Category 5 or better cable. If you are installing it inside walls or new construction or remodeling, you may need to consult an architect or electrician to find out about building codes. This, of course, is the best-looking way to manage cables.

Many people need to manage with cables behind desks and hidden in every way possible. Look in office supply stores and in mail order catalogs for data communications suppliers: ingenious devices to hide cables are on the market today.

Hubs

There are two basic network architectures in use today:

1. A daisy chain connects computers and other devices from one to the next. This requires the use of BNC connectors and 10 Base-2 cable.

2. A hub has a number of computers and other devices connected directly to it (in a star-shaped topology). This is most commonly done with RJ45 connectors and 10 Base-T cable. The cable runs are usually longer, but this usually provides a more stable environment; also the cable is cheaper and the total cost may be less than that of a daisy chain.

The two architectures are often combined: you can link hubs from one to the other (with 10 Base-2 cable and BNC connectors). This may form a backbone of a network—for example, running up the floors of a building. One or more hubs on each floor can manage the devices on those floors.

You can purchase hubs for six to eight devices for around $100; prices go up for additional devices. (Hubs require a small amount of power; they must be located near an outlet, but not necessarily near a computer.)

Routers

Routers let you share a modem or other telecommunications device over a LAN. Routers and hubs often interact. The entire area of routers, shared modems, and LAN-based Internet access is changing very rapidly.

Most recently, relatively low-cost routers have entered the market that allow you to share modems among several computers. For between $300 and $600, you should be able to buy such a device (called an analog router). You can plug several (usually up to three) modems into one side of it. On the other side, you can plug in several (usually up to four) computers; you can also plug another device into one of those connections, effectively increasing the number of connections for the modems.

Each modem requires its own phone line and its own Internet account; however, all of the computers can share the modems and the phone lines. This allows you to create a much more efficient environment than the basic one in which each computer has its own modem and phone line or even the more complicated one in which the computers on a LAN share a single modem and phone line.

If your Internet use is relatively light, you could start by connecting a single modem and letting several computers share it. For light Internet usage (the occasional e-mail, light Web browsing, etc.), this may be quite satisfactory.

As your needs increase, you have several ways to increase your capabilities:

- You can upgrade the modem to a faster speed.

- You can add additional modems (although each additional modem will require its own telephone line and Internet account).

- You can add more computers.

Many people find that this type of architecture is very attractive: a relatively modest initial cost allows you a number of upgrade routes. Until 1997, devices such as these were not available: the only way to share an Internet connection among computers on a LAN was to have a high-speed dedicated line connecting a high-speed modem to an Internet access provider. Depending on local telephone costs, it usually was more cost-effective to install three or four standard telephone lines than to install one of these high-speed lines. Now that dial-up lines can routinely support modems of up to 56 kbps, and with the advent of devices such as these, things have changed drastically.

Remember that you are not the only person trying to connect computers and a LAN to the Internet; yesterday's technologies and architectures were cost-effective for corporations and large organizations such as schools and hospitals. Along with the other people in the SOHO world, you are part of a very large marketplace, and the vendors are responding.

Laptops and PowerBooks

Many people have laptops or PowerBooks for use when they are on the road, at home, etc. Interestingly enough, many people make a critical mistake when they buy a laptop.

The argument goes, "I just need it for word processing—my main computer is on my desk. I don't need a fancy laptop."

In fact, your laptop should be your most powerful machine. Unlike your desktop computer—even with UPS attached—the laptop is designed to be used for hours at a time without power. Outfitted with a large hard disk and with a network connection to your desktop computer, the laptop can become a backup device, possibly even eliminating the need for removable media. Dragging off-site backup disks and tapes around is a big bore, but carrying your laptop to home and work may often be a chore that you would do anyway.

No matter what type of hardware or operating system you use, think very carefully before you economize on your laptop.

Summary

ClarisWorks fits very comfortably into the small/home office. The tips in this chapter should help to make your life there easier.

17

ClarisWorks for Kids— for Adults

ClarisWorks for Kids is an application designed to let kids learn about computers and use them for their own purposes. It is a version of ClarisWorks in which the standard interface has been replaced with a kids-oriented one.

This chapter provides an overview of ClarisWorks for Kids along with some tips on using ClarisWorks to prepare documents for ClarisWorks for Kids.

The Interface

The replacement of the standard ClarisWorks interface provides an interesting glimpse into how software is designed and developed. This is not just a peek behind the scenes: it gives you a look at what developers do and how they think.

One of the greatest frustrations for many software developers and designers is that consumers and end users are so accepting and uncritical of their efforts. Most software could be much better than it is, but since consumers rarely complain, companies are hard pressed to devote the resources to sophisticated software interface design. Claris and Apple have been outstanding examples of advanced user interface design.

The features and functionality of ClarisWorks are unchanged in ClarisWorks for Kids, although some of them are hidden. As a result, you can open ClarisWorks for Kids documents in ClarisWorks and edit them with all of the ClarisWorks features.

In short, the interface of ClarisWorks has been totally separated from the program's functionality. This is referred to as factoring the software, and it is a hallmark of modern software design. From a technical point of view, once the software has been factored into interface and functional parts, many new adventures are possible.

In particular, three avenues are open:

1. As with ClarisWorks for Kids, an entirely new interface can be created on top of the application's basic functionality. That interface can be a complete world in and of itself, with the graphics and jargon that are appropriate to its users. (Yes, kids use jargon: it may

not be computer gobbledygook, but it is just as incomprehensible to parents as the most obscure technobabble.)

2. The application's functionality can be accessed through scripting. You can use a tool such as AppleScript to automate processes within the application. With scripting, the entire interface is removed and replaced with scripted commands.

3. A combination of these two techniques is available with assistants (such as those that ship today with ClarisWorks). In the future, you can expect that Claris—and others—should be able to create new assistants that provide new interfaces and automated processing of various tasks.

The Kids Interface

As you can see in Figure 17-1, the graphics in ClarisWorks for Kids are different from those of the standard ClarisWorks product. They are bigger and brighter; the text is bigger, too—and many messages have been reworded.

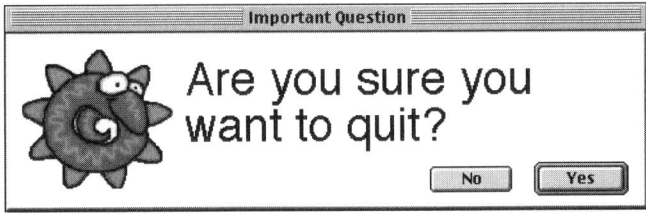

FIGURE 17-1. ClarisWorks for Kids Alert

The Scripting Interface

ClarisWorks and ClarisWorks for Kids provide the ability to write AppleScript commands to control the applications, although this feature is provided only on Mac OS. The scripting support in ClarisWorks 5.0 is much more extensive than that in ClarisWorks for Kids, but both provide significant support.

To see the sorts of commands that you can enter, use the Script Editor application (found in the Apple Events folder of the Apple Extras folder) to open the ClarisWorks dictionary. (Choose Open Dictionary from the File menu.) You will see the complete list of scripting commands to which ClarisWorks responds; a section of the scrolling window is shown in Figure 17-2.

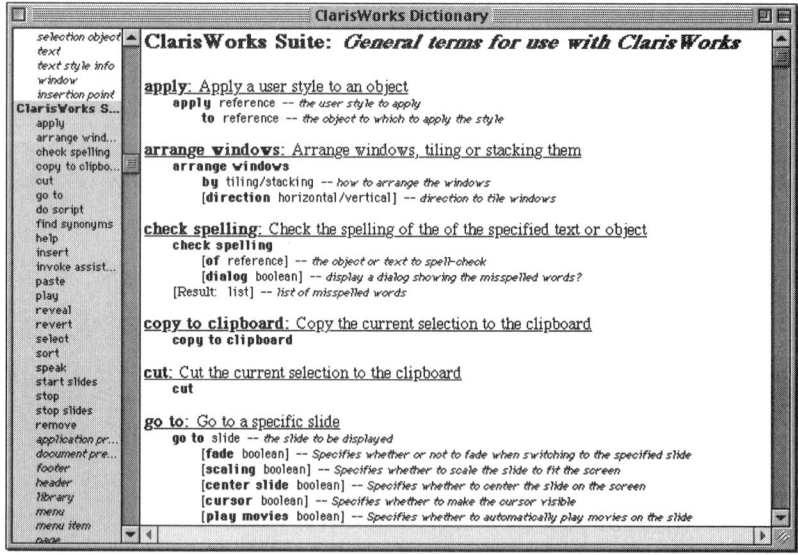

FIGURE 17-2. ClarisWorks AppleScript Commands

Documents, Files, and Folders

As you can see from Figure 17-3, not only are the graphics different, but also the navigation to open files is different. The four tabs let you select different folders in which files are stored. Each file is shown as a single-click button icon (such as Art Pad in the illustration).

The New Work folder contains ClarisWorks stationery files that let you create draw documents (Art Pad), spreadsheets (Graphing Pad), databases (List Pad), and word processing documents (Writing Pad).

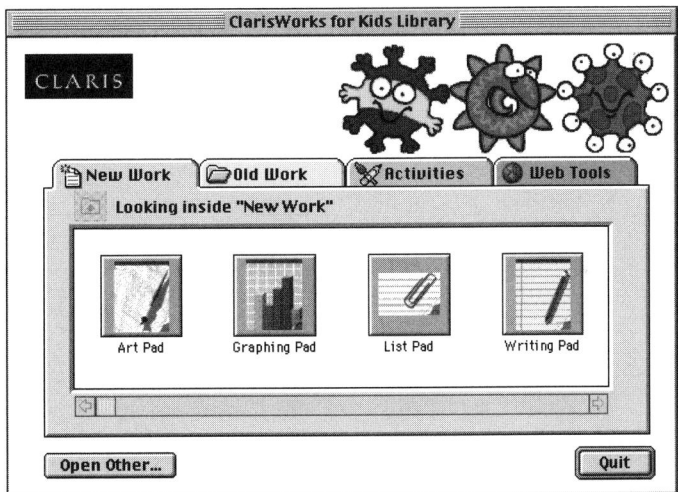

FIGURE 17-3. ClarisWorks for Kids

These tabs correspond to folders in the ClarisWorks for Kids folder, which is shown in Figure 17-4.

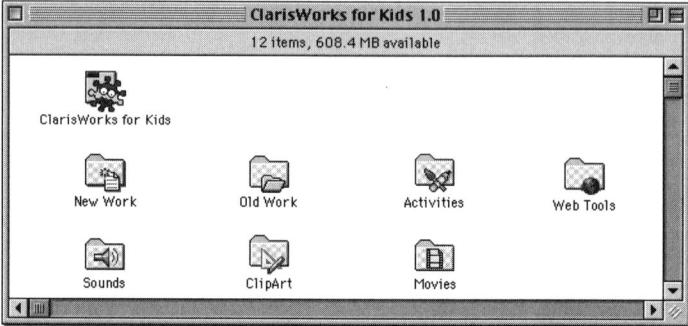

FIGURE 17-4. ClarisWorks for Kids Finder Window

In addition to the documents that ship with ClarisWorks for Kids, you can create ClarisWorks documents and save them as stationery in the ClarisWorks for Kids format; if you place them in one of the subfolders of the New Work folder, their buttons will show up in this window.

Figure 17-5 shows the ClarisWorks Save As dialog; the ClarisWorks for Kids format is selected, as is the option to save the file as stationery. (Note that this dialog is opened with the Save As... command, not the Save command.)

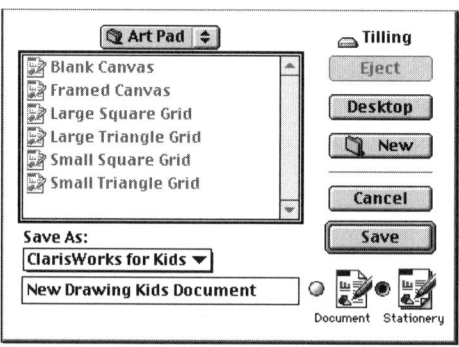

FIGURE 17-5. Save As Dialog

Although this simpler interface for opening files is provided in ClarisWorks for Kids, you or the kids can still use the standard file opening dialog to open a file. If you click the Open Other... button in the lower left of the window shown in Figure 17-3, a standard file opening dialog is shown as in Figure 17-6.

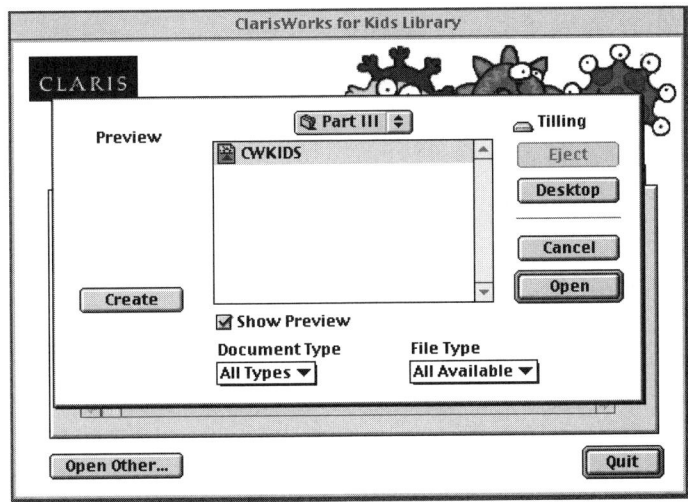

FIGURE 17-6. ClarisWorks for Kids Standard File Opening Dialog

Menus

The ClarisWorks for Kids menus are similar to the ClarisWorks menus; however, they are a little shorter, a little simpler, and they have graphical elements in them as shown in Figure 17-7.

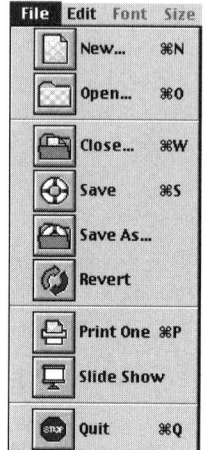  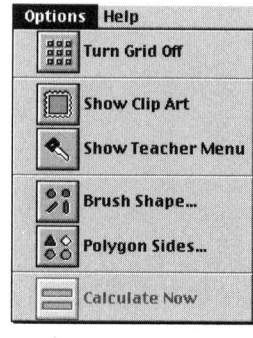

FIGURE 17-7. ClarisWorks for Kids Menus

A traditional menu is available from the Options menu with the Show Teacher Menu command; you need to enter a password to get to the Teacher menu, so kids cannot change the settings shown in Figure 17-8.

FIGURE 17-8. ClarisWorks for Kids Teacher Menu

Note that this menu is the only one that rearranges ClarisWorks commands—in the other cases, commands either are where they are in ClarisWorks or they do not exist in ClarisWorks for Kids.

Creating and Modifying Documents with ClarisWorks

You can use ClarisWorks to create and modify ClarisWorks for Kids documents. Here is an example.

The Things to Do ClarisWorks for Kids document in shown in Figure 17-9.

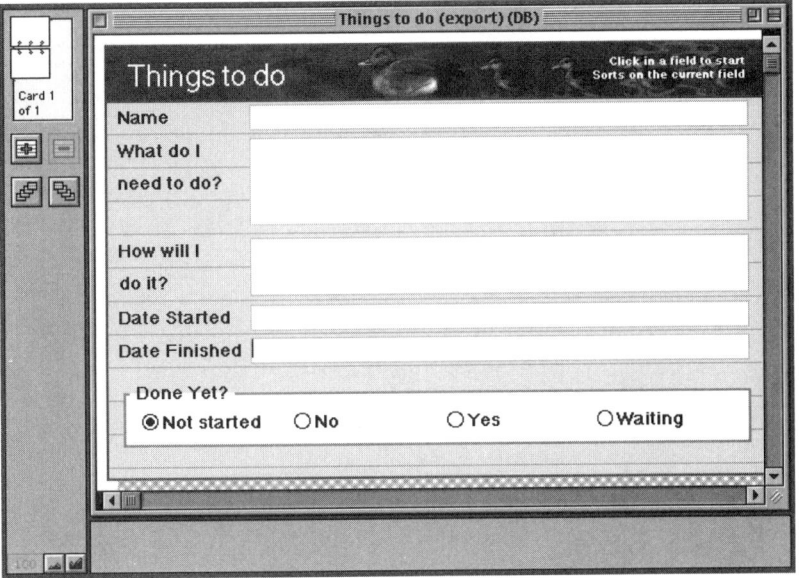

FIGURE 17-9. Things to Do

In the tools palette at the left of the window you can see the kids' interface: simpler and larger images for the basic operations. If you open the same document with ClarisWorks, you see the standard database document window shown in Figure 17-10.

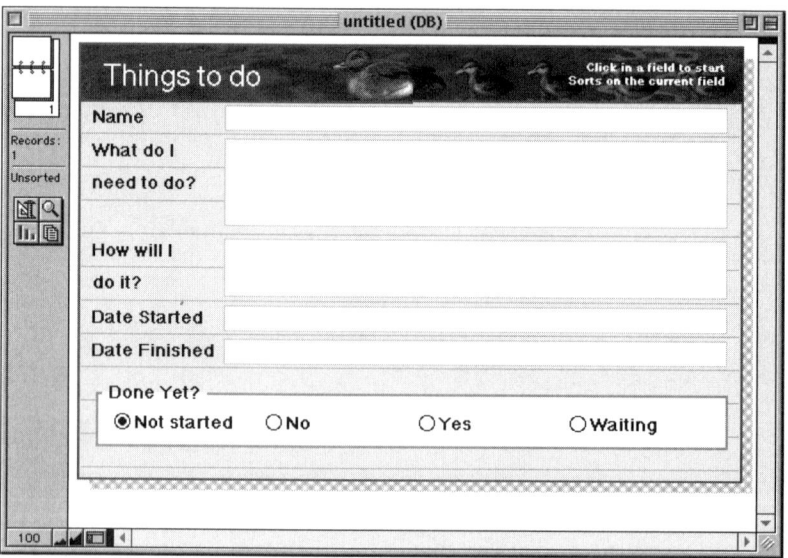

FIGURE 17-10. ClarisWorks Things to Do (ClarisWorks)

One of the simplifications of ClarisWorks for Kids is that there is no layout mode for database documents: you cannot add fields, redesign the layout, or do any of the things you normally do to modify a database. However, when you open the database document in ClarisWorks, those tools are available to you, and you can modify the layout as shown in Figure 17-11. Here a field has been renamed ("Date Begun" instead of "Date Started"), and a new field has been added ("Who" with the label "Who should do it?").

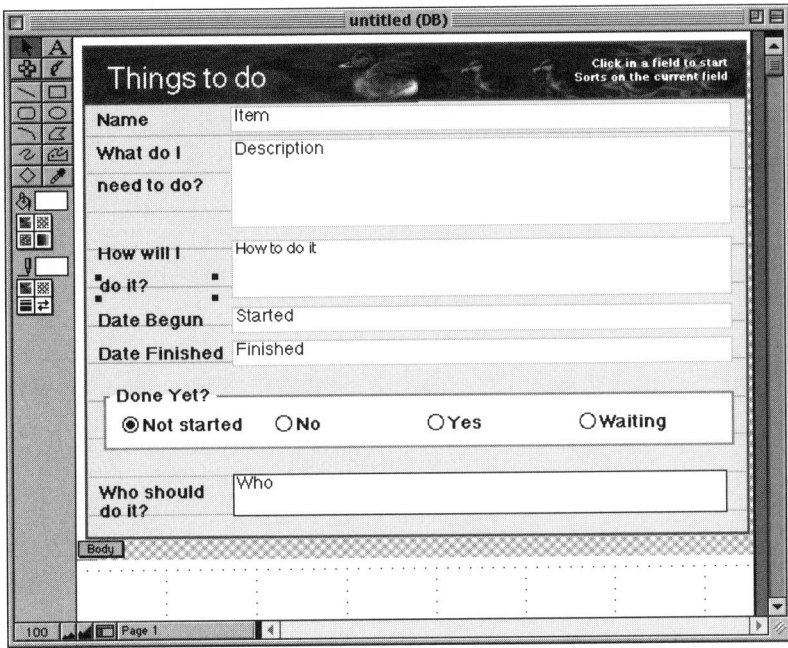

FIGURE 17-11. Things to Do in ClarisWorks

Save the file in ClarisWorks for Kids format (using the Save As… dialog shown in Figure 17-5); you do not have to save it as stationery unless you want it to appear in the New Work window.

When you reopen the file in ClarisWorks for Kids (Figure 17-12), the changes to the layout are in place, and the kids can work with the database. (Be careful, though, that you save the file while it is in Browse mode; if you save the file while it is in Layout mode—that is, while the drawing and field editing tools are available—ClarisWorks for Kids will open it as a draw document rather than as a database.)

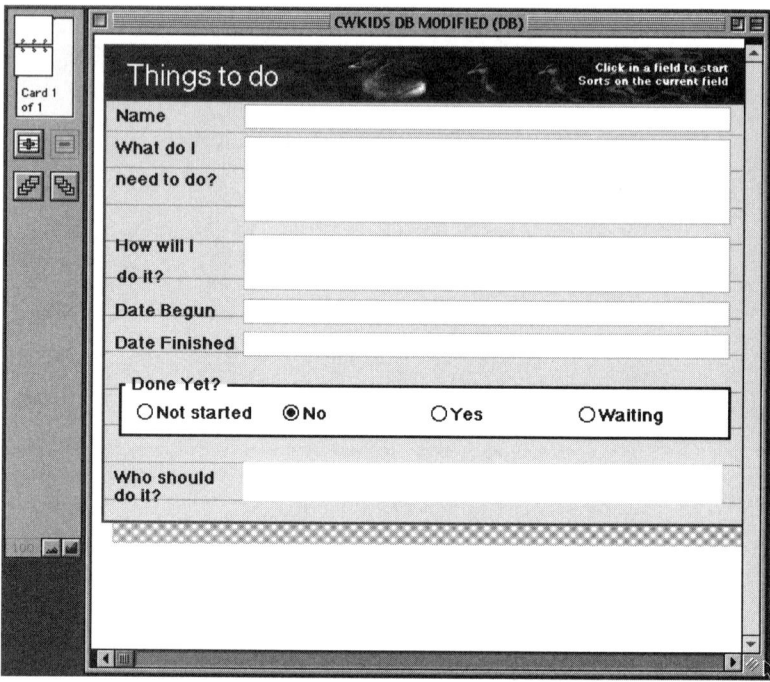

FIGURE 17-12. Things to Do Back in ClarisWorks for Kids

Summary

The documentation that comes with ClarisWorks for Kids is great for adults and children. The software is an excellent example of how a common set of functionality (ClarisWorks) can be presented in different ways with different interfaces. (You can build on this structure by devising scripting interfaces to ClarisWorks yourself.)

To no one's great surprise, Claris has provided an elegant kids-oriented interface that is fun to use: it is hard to imagine how kids would not enjoy using it. (The clip art that ships with ClarisWorks for Kids has more images of spiders and sounds of squishes and splats than most adults would normally think of.)

Since the underlying software is in fact ClarisWorks, kids can graduate from ClarisWorks for Kids and take their documents with them. By the same token, if there is one little thing that they cannot do in ClarisWorks for Kids, you—or they—can modify the documents in ClarisWorks and then save them back as ClarisWorks for Kids documents so that the work and play can continue.

This ability to move easily from one interface to another is very important (technically it is called scalability). Documents can move in both directions, and, like bicycle training wheels, the kids' interface can be jettisoned when necessary.

What's in ClarisWorks Office

Like most software today, ClarisWorks is distributed on a CD-ROM. (You can get diskettes instead if you must, but the CD-ROM is smaller and more reliable than diskettes.) Although different versions of the product exist, there is always a Begin Here! file and often files containing late-breaking news and revisions. Take a moment to read these files.

ClarisWorks Office provides much more than just Claris-Works 5.0. In addition to ClarisWorks 5.0, here are some of the items you will find on the CD-ROM. (The actual contents may vary.)

JIAN BusinessBasics

JIAN BusinessBasics are tools and templates for a wide variety of uses (mostly business). These are installed as part of the standard ClarisWorks installation. You can also install them separately.

There is a discussion of JIAN BusinessBasics in "Running the Small Office/Home Office with ClarisWorks" on page 301.

Documentation

The ClarisWorks manual is available on the CD-ROM; you can print out additional copies as needed. You can also search through it electronically.

Claris Home Page Lite

If you want to create your own Web pages, you can use ClarisWorks itself (see "Posting the Newsletter on the Web" on page 259) or you can use a separate application such as Claris Home Page. The full version of Claris Home Page provides all the professional Web authoring tools that you need; Claris Home Page Lite provides more tools than you have in ClarisWorks but fewer than in the full product. Take your pick.

Internet Access

In this folder you will find software that help you access the Internet and configure your computer appropriately. Read the Read Me files (and refer to "Making Documents Communicate—Integrating the Internet" on page 121 to help you find your way through the terminology). Depending on the version of ClarisWorks Office that you have (and the country in which it is distributed) you will find different products as well as offers for Internet access.

If your computer already has Internet software installed on it and you are happy with it, you don't need to change it. *ClarisWorks is designed to work with whatever Internet software you have on your computer—you don't need a specific browser or communications program.* If you don't have Internet software, these tools and installers can make the process of getting onto the Internet very simple.

Software to browse the World Wide Web changes very rapidly; new versions of Netscape Navigator and Microsoft Internet Explorer are released frequently and can be downloaded from the Internet. The latest versions on the Internet are likely to be more recent than the versions on the CD-ROM—but often the improvements and revisions matter only to the cognoscenti.

In general, it is a good idea to do the simplest possible Internet installation in order to make certain that all the pieces work together (modem, communications software, Internet account, passwords, etc.). Once you know that everything is working, you can upgrade individual components as you see fit.

Other Items

Finally, you will find a number of interesting and useful other folders including

- Information about support and training from Claris.

- C•WUG—Information about the ClarisWorks User Group.

- An assortment of trial software from Claris.

Index

.cwk files 262
.html 142
.html files 262
.pdf files 274, 278
.ps files 278
10 Base-2 cable 317, 318
10 Base-T cable 317

A

About Printing Labels layout 241
Acrobat Distiller 277
Address List assistant 242
Address List Assistant window 244

Adobe
    Acrobat Distiller 277
America Online 127
Anarchie 278
anchors (in HTML documents) 146
Apple Events 326
Apple Internet Connection Kit. 135
Apple Video Player 93–95
AppleScript 325, 326
application layer 60
Archie 278
archives. *See* backups
Art Pad 327
assistants 28–31, 212–214, 325
    Address List 242

Claris Registration 154
Newsletter 212
Presentation 286
Table 28
automatic hyphenation 157
Avery labels 240

B

backgrounds
   for HTML documents 148
backups and archives 313, 314
BNC connectors 317, 318
Book Mark dialog 112
book marks 107
   in HTML documents 146
Browse mode. *See* databases
browser 55
Business Templates 303
Business Tools Index 304
Button Bar 33–37
   creating and editing 36
   creating buttons 34

C

cable
   dubbing 88, 90
cable (for connecting to the Internet) 130
cabling
   10 Base-T 317
   10-Base-2 317
   BNC connector. *See* BNC connector
   Category 5 317
   for networks 317
   RJ45 connector. *See* RJ45 connector
   twisted pair. *See* twisted pair
calculations
   in databases 246
Claris Registration assistant 154
Claris Registration document 155

ClarisWorks
   assistants 28–31
   Button Bar 33–37
   drag-and-drop 31–32
   equation editing 45
   integrating browsers with 137–138
   libraries 37–41
   stylesheets 41–44
ClarisWorks for Kids 323
   Teacher menu 330
   Things to Do document 331
ClarisWorks for Kids stationery
   Art Pad 327
   Graphing Pad 327
   List Pad 327
   Writing Pad 327
ClarisWorks links 270
client side image maps. *See* image maps
composite documents 22
CompuServe 127
Contact Database stationery 238
continuation indicator 228
convergence 84
creating PostScript files 274
   Mac OS 277
Cyberdog 278

D

daisy chain 318
databases 170–190
   Browse mode 179
   calculations 246
   creating 172
   defining fields in 173
   entering and editing data 179–180
   fields
      adding 246
      automatic editing 249
      breaking down 246
      Define Fields window 247
      defining 173, 246

　　　　formulas 185
　　　　Record Info type 247
　　　　Summary type 185
　　　　unique keys 249
　finding data 189–190
　Layout menu 175
　Layout mode 175
　layouts 173, 236
　　　　modifying 174–179
　　　　sub-summaries 180–186
　mailing list 234
　names and addresses 234
　Search Popup 239
　sorting 187–188
　Tools
　　　　Layout Popup 240
　Tools strip 239
Define Fields window (for databases) 247
Department Newsletter stationery 260
digital media 84
digitizing cards 87, 89–90
　cables and connectors 89
digitizing software 88, 90
digitizing video 92
disk utilities 312
document links 107
　creating 113
domain names 132–134
　virtual 133–134
dot matrix printers 71
drag-and-drop 31–32
Draw documents
　Tool palette 169
　with embedded spreadsheets 167
dubbing cables 88, 90
Dye sublimation printers 71

E

Edit Master Page (presentations) 288

Editing a Style window 216
Energy Saver control panel (Mac OS) 309
energy saving features 309
equation editing 45
Ethernet 316
Ethernet hub 317

F

Fetch 278
fields (in databases). *See* databases
file suffixes
　.cwk 262
　.html 142, 262
　.pd 278
　.pdf 274
File Transfer Protocol 60
find. *See* databases
firewalls 63
footers. *See* headers
Format menu 159
Format Section window 266
forms 75
　preprinted 302
Frame Links command 227
frame relay 130
frames
　in Draw documents 167
　spreadsheets 167
FTP 60, 109, 278

G

GIF 147
graphics
　creating for image maps 197
Graphing Pad 327

H

headers
    for Web pages 146
headers and footers 158
    compared to spreadsheet titles 163
home office. *See* SOHO
home pages 55, 58
HTML. *See also* stylesheets
    backgrounds for 148
    modifying for client side image maps 203
    tables in 148
HTML Export (Advanced) window 151
HTML Export (Basic) window 149
HTML files 259
HTML filters 259
http (Hypertext Transfer Protocol) 56, 109
hybrid documents 167
hypertext 104

I

ID numbers (in databases) 250
image libraries 291
image maps 194–204
    client side 194
        creating in ClarisWorks 197–204
    creating graphics for 197
    locating hot spots in 199
    server side 195, 196
index.html 58
ink jet printers 71
interactive media 21
Internet
    background 122–126
    connecting to 127–132
        cable modems 130
        frame relay 130
        ISDN 129
        ISPs 129
        online services 127
        persistent connections 131
    creating your own Web site 134
    domain names 132–134
    getting to from ClarisWorks 137–138
    IP addresses 132
        static 132
    static IP addresses 132
    virtual domain names 133–134
Internet service providers. *See* ISPs
InterNIC 53
intranet 63
IP address 132
    static 132
ISDN 129
ISPs 129–132, 278

J

JIAN Business Basics 306
JIAN. *See* Business Templates
JPEG 147

K

keys. *See* databases

L

labels 75, 234
    Avery 240
Laser printers 70
law office 302
Layout Popup 240
layouts 236. *See also* databases
libraries 37–41
    creating 39
    images 291
    putting objects into 39
    using objects from 39

link indicator (in word processing documents) 227
linking
    continuation indicator 228
    Frame Links command 227
    link indicator 227
    text frames 226–230
links
    Book Mark dialog 112
    book marks 107
    creating 111
    creating a document link 113
    creating and managing 106–117
    creating URL links 114
    designing 117–119
    document links 107
    in HTML 146
    Links palette 106
    Links Palette Special menu 117
    managing 116–117
    New Document Link dialog 113
    New URL Link dialog 115
    URL links 107
List Pad 327
lists
    in HTML 147
Local Area Networks (LANs) 61

M

Mac OS 8 135
Mail Merge
    menu 252
    windoid 253
mail merge 250–256
mailing lists 233
    Avery labels 240
    labels 234
margin control
    in word processing documents 160
Meeting Agenda (business template document) 307

meta-data 236
Monitors & Sound control panel 97
multithreaded communications 50

N

network hubs 318
networking 316
New Document Link dialog 113
New URL Link dialog 115
New Work folder 327
Newsletter assistant 212
    Tips and Hints 213
Newsletter stationery 211
Newsletter Tips and Hints (in Newsletter assistant) 213

O

online services 127–128
Options menu
    Slide Show 284
outlining
    in word processing documents 160
overhead transparencies 282
    output to 81

P

packets 50
pages (Web) 55, 58
paper 75–79
    history 13
    limits of 21
    preprinted forms, labels, and papers 75
    weight 76
Paragraph Formatting window 217
PCCIA cards 317
PDF files. *See* .pdf files

persistent connections 131
personal computers
    costs of 17
physical layer 60
posting files on the Web 278
PostScript files 277
    creating (Windows) 277
    creating (Mac OS) 274
power strips 311
preprinted forms 302
Presentation assistant 286
presentations
    Edit Master Page 288
    formats 282
    master page 288
    paper-based 283
    stationery for 290
    templates 287
print spooling 73
printers 70–74
    dot matrix printers 71
    dye sublimation printers 71
    ink jet printers 71
    laser printers 70
    local (non-networked) 72
    networking 72
    print spooling 73
    thermal wax printers 71
printing
    history 13
    large-format 81
    T-shirts 81
protocols 48
publish and subscribe 217–226
publishing 219–220

Q

QuickDraw 3D 24, 101
QuickTime 84, 99–102
    hardware abstraction 101
    time-dependent media 100

QuickTime extension 87
QuickTime Media Layer 101
QuickTime movies
    creating 87–99
QuickTime VR 25, 101

R

RCA plugs 89
record info fields 247
RJ45 connector 317, 318
routers 318

S

schemes 56, 109
scripting 325, 326
Search Popup 239
server side image maps. *See* image maps
Show Teacher Menu 330
sites 55
Slide Show Options window 285
Slide Show window 284
slide shows 282, 284
slides
    output to 79
Small Business Web site 309
SOHO (small office/home office) 302
Sort dialog 166
sorting
    databases 187–188
    spreadsheets 166
spreadsheet frames 167
spreadsheet titles 163
    compared to headers and footers 163
spreadsheets 19, 162–170
    as HTML tables 148
    formatting for presentation 164
    inside Draw documents 167
    Sort dialog 166
    sorting 166

stationery 211–212, 305
    Contact Database 238
    Department Newsletter 260
    Newsletter 211
    Presentation 290
styles. *See* stylesheets
stylesheets 41–44, 214–217
    creating and modifying styles 41
    Editing a Style window 216
    HTML 142. *See also* HTML
        headers 146
        links 146
        lists 147
    HTML Normal Text style 145
    Paragraph Formatting window 217
    Stylesheets window 215
    window 215
subscribing 221–226
surge suppressors 311
S-video 89

T

Table assistant 28
tables
    in HTML 148
TCP/IP 125
TCP/IP connection 51
Teacher menu 330
telecommuting 301
telnet 109
text frames
    linking 226–230
Thermal wax printers 71
Things to Do (ClarisWorks for Kids document) 331
titles
    creating 163
Tool palette 169
transceivers 316
transparencies
    output to 81

overhead 282
T-shirts
    printing to 81
twisted-pair 61

U

uninterrupted power supply. *See* UPS
UPS (Uninterrupted Power Supply) 310
URL links 107
    creating 114
URLs 108–109
    schemes 109

V

VCR 87, 94
video 84
    benefits of in documents 85
    cables and connectors 88
    digitizing process 92
    disadvantages of in documents 86
    RCA 89
    recording media 92
    sources 88
    S-video 89
    tapes and cartridges 92
virtual domain names 133–134

W

Web
    creating your own site 134
Web site
    saving files for 262
Wide Area Network (WAN) 62
word processing 156–161
    automatic hyphenation 157
    margin control 160

outlining 160
Writing Pad 327
Writing Tools
　　Automatic Hyphenation 157

www.claris.com 309
www.philmontmill.com 140
www.smallbiz.apple.com 309

SHARE IT, MANAGE IT, PUBLISH IT ON THE WEB.
FILEMAKER PRO LETS YOU DO IT ALL.

Create a working database and your whole operation runs more smoothly. Do it with FileMaker® Pro software for Windows or Mac®OS, and the entire process is a breeze. That's because FileMaker Pro provides solutions to the tasks that you're using other applications for now. With a multitude of complete solutions included,* such as expense reports, inventory systems and personnel forms, all you have to do is add data. Or you can also develop your own solutions. Create sales reports, real estate and property listings, price lists, or any other documents you need. Any way you slice it, FileMaker Pro is ready to go right out of the box.

With features like these, FileMaker Pro is ready to help you do it all:
- Built-in word processing makes for easy text handling
- Mail merge capabilities let you breeze through mailings
- Because it's relational, a change in one database will automatically be reflected in other databases containing the same fields. (Say good-bye to doubling up your data entry.)

Need to share your information with co-workers or customers? FileMaker Pro lets your users access its databases over the Internet.** In fact, FileMaker Pro has recently become a leading solution for database publishing on the Internet via TCP/IP and its built-in templates. You can use FileMaker Pro as a search engine for web sites; or manage inventory, customer lists and other database applications across corporate intranets. So not only is FileMaker Pro one of the easiest ways to manage and share your data, it's also one of the best ways to get it online.

FOR MORE INFORMATION OR TO ORDER FILEMAKER PRO, VISIT US AT WWW.CLARIS.COM.

Simply powerful software.™

© 1997 Claris Corporation. All Rights Reserved. Claris, FileMaker and Simply powerful software are registered trademarks of Claris Corporation. Mac is a registered trademark of Apple Computer, Inc. All other trademarks are property of their respective owners. *Available on CD only. **An account with an Internet Service Provider is required.

The Internet represents an entire world of opportunity. All you have to do is utilize it. That's why we integrate powerful Internet technology into Claris® software that allows you to easily take advantage of what's available. Successful Internet access solutions are integrated in our email management, web publishing, web page creation and personal organization software programs. Because let's face it, the Internet is the most advanced informational tool on the planet. It only makes sense to have software that helps you use it to your advantage.

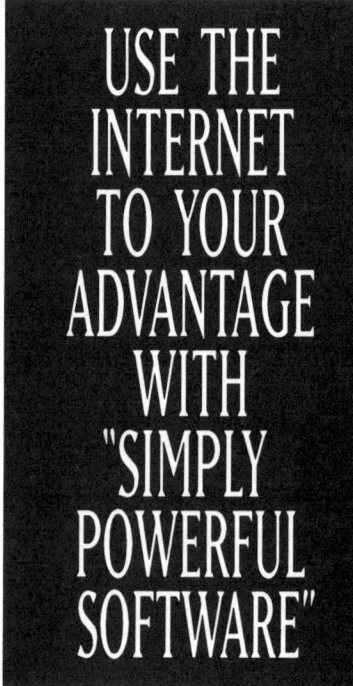

CLARIS HOME PAGE
Windows 95, Windows NT and Mac® OS

Whether it's your cyberspace calling card or just a virtual home, having a web page is becoming a must. That's why Claris Home Page™ software makes it incredibly easy to create dynamic web pages without the need for technical expertise. (It generates code transparently, so you don't need to know HTML.) With Claris Home Page you can use tables, frames, forms and multimedia to make your web site come alive. And you can easily post web pages to servers without having to use separate FTP software*. It's the cross-platform authoring tool for everyone.

FILEMAKER PRO
Windows 3.1, Windows 95, Windows NT and Mac OS

Data, data everywhere. Even on the Internet. That is, if you use FileMaker® Pro software: the award-winning relational database and a leading solution for database publishing on the web. With FileMaker Pro software's Internet talents, you can easily get your information online via TCP/IP with built-in templates, use it as a search engine for your web site, or manage inventory, customer lists and other database applications across your corporate intranet*. In short, it's the database for true webheads. (Or anyone else who happens to appreciate efficiency.)

CLARIS EM@ILER
Mac OS

Completely forgotten how to lick a stamp? You're not alone. Seems like everyone's relying on email these days. And that can be confusing with all the servers and addresses and hullabaloo. But never fear, because Claris Em@iler™ software sets it all straight. No matter how many different Internet or online services you rely on for your email, whether you use it at the office, at home, or on the road, Claris Em@iler offers powerful email management solutions for Mac OS based systems. Stamps?! Who needs 'em?

CLARIS ORGANIZER
Mac OS

You've got your dataminders, memofinders and myriad other leather-bound personal "saviors." But do any of them allow you to link with the Internet? Hardly. Enter Claris Organizer® software: the power-packed, life-simplifying information manager that features a built-in ability to quickly link to email and web sites*. With Claris Organizer you can launch Claris Em@iler or Netscape Navigator™ with a single click, create contact lists with hot links to email addresses and web sites.

**FOR MORE INFORMATION ON ALL CLARIS PRODUCTS, VISIT OUR WEB SITE AT WWW.CLARIS.COM.
FOR MORE INFORMATION ON OTHER BOOKS FROM CLARIS PRESS, VISIT WWW.CLARIS.COM/CLARISPRESS.**

Simply powerful software™.

© 1997 Claris Corporation. All Rights Reserved. Claris, Claris Organizer and FileMaker are registered trademarks and Claris Em@iler, Home Page and Simply powerful software are trademarks of Claris Corporation. Mac is a registered trademark of Apple Computer, Inc. Netscape Navigator is a trademark of Netscape Communication Corporation. All other trademarks are the property of their respective owners. *Requires account with an Internet Service Provider.